PARENTING ACROSS THE DIVIDE
A Trauma-Informed Co-Parenting Workbook

by
Nahomie Julien, LCSW, CADC II, CAMS II, CDVS II

NJI Publishing
Lawrenceville, Georgia

For information, inquiries, or permissions:
NJI Publishing
Lawrenceville, Georgia, USA
www.NJIPublishing.com
permissions@njipublishing.com

ISBN (Print): 979-8-9998751-2-9

Cover design: NJI Creative Studio
Interior design: NJI Publishing

Printed in the United States of America

Disclaimer & Professional Use

Professional & Legal Disclaimer

This workbook, *Parenting Across the Divide—A Trauma-Informed Co-Parenting Workbook*, is intended solely for **educational, reflective, and supportive purposes**.

- **Not a Substitute for Professional Services:** The information, tools, and exercises provided are not intended to be a substitute for the diagnosis, assessment, or treatment of any medical, psychological, legal, or financial condition. Readers should seek the advice of a licensed professional (including a licensed therapist, clinical social worker, attorney, or financial advisor) for any clinical or legal concerns.
- **No Therapeutic Relationship:** Use of this workbook does not establish a therapist-client or attorney-client relationship between the author (N. Julien) or NJI Publishing and the reader.
- **Inherent Risks:** The topics addressed in this workbook—including trauma, conflict, and emotional regulation—may be triggering or distressing. The reader assumes all risks associated with their application of the tools and exercises. If you are experiencing an immediate crisis or emergency, please contact 911 or your local crisis hotline.
- **Legal Documentation:** While this workbook contains tools designed for objective legal documentation (e.g., the Court-Safe Documentation Log), the use of these tools does not guarantee any specific legal outcome. All documentation should be reviewed and approved by a qualified attorney familiar with your jurisdiction.

Professional Licensing & Use

The author and publisher are committed to ensuring this workbook is accessible for clinical use while protecting intellectual property.

- **Individual & Clinical Use:** This workbook may be purchased and used by **licensed clinicians, therapists, social workers, and custody professionals** for individual client sessions or therapeutic groups, provided a separate copy is purchased for each client receiving the material.
- **Reproduction of Worksheets:** The **worksheets and tools** sections in the latter half of this book may be reproduced **for personal or single-client use only** by the purchaser of this material. They may not be reproduced for commercial resale or widespread distribution.
- **Prohibited Use:** No portion of this workbook (including text, chapters, original models, or the **Table of Contents**) may be reproduced, distributed, adapted, taught, or used in professional training or workshops without the explicit prior written consent of NJI Publishing

•

Dedication

To the **children**—whose stability, peace, and well-being are the sole purpose of this work.

And to the **courageous parents** who choose to lead with regulation, who prioritize steadiness over the struggle for control, and who commit to healing so their child can finally be free.

May you find your ground, may you reclaim your voice, and may this resource be a balm on your journey

Acknowledgments

To the families and clients who trusted me with their stories—your honesty shaped this book.
To my colleagues and mentors who hold the line for trauma-informed care, your rigor keeps the work real.
To my communities of color, queer kin, and fellow artists of healing—you remind me that resilience has rhythm.
And to everyone who knows that healing is not a luxury—it's a right.
Thank you for teaching mwhat restoration truly looks like.

"You don't have to call it perfect for it to be real."
—N J

Table of Contents

Disclaimer & Professional Use iii

Professional & Legal Disclaimer iii

Professional Licensing & Use iii

Preface xix

How to Use This Workbook xxi

For Individual Readers xxi

For Clinicians, Facilitators, and Coaches xxii

Introduction xxiii

Purpose and Clinical Orientation xxiii

Structure and Progression xxiv

How to Engage with the Material xxv

Language and Inclusivity xxv

The Clinical Rationale xxvi

Expected Outcomes xxvi

In Closing xxvii

Part I: Your Steadiness Foundation 1

1 3

The Ground You're Standing On 3

Introduction—The Child in the Middle 3

Your Unacknowledged Foundation: Trauma and Stress.............4

Why Traditional Advice Falls Short 5

Your Trauma-Informed Lens—Shifting Your Focus 6

The Hidden Impact on Kids 7

The Emotional Landscape of Co-Parenting 8

For Therapists & Facilitators 8

For Self-Guided Parents 9

Your Path Forward—Your Power of Repair..............9

2 11

Where Are You Now? 11

Introduction—Checking Your Internal GPS 11

A Moment of Orientation—Embracing Your Raw Reality 11

Reading Your Reflections—Not a Score, a Signal 14

Understanding Co-Parenting Styles—Choosing Your Track 15

• Honesty Fatigue—The Cost of Clarity 17

Critical Modifications for Safety and Trauma 21

Reflection & Progress Marker..............22

3 23

Your Body's Language—Mapping Your Nervous System 23

Introduction—Your Engine, Your Alarm System..............23

The Window of Tolerance—Your Green Zone 24

Three Zones of Survival—Mapping Your Extremes 25

Mapping Your Personal Zones..............27

When Your Alarm is Too Sensitive—The Trauma Lens 33

Closing Thoughts 34

PART II: Regulation—Your Internal Leader..............37

4 39

Your Regulation Toolkit—Simple Skills for Steading Your System 39

Introduction—The Skill of Self-Steadiness 39

Your Core Regulation Tools—The Big Three 40

Building Your Personalized Toolkit 42

Zone-Specific Strategy Guides—Your Targeted Kits 44

Closing Thoughts 45

5 47

Your Regulated Response—Real-Time Skills for Your Nervous System 47

Introduction—The Hijack Sequence 47

Decoding Your Dysregulation Pattern 48

Your Three-Stage Regulation Protocol 52

Parenting While Activated & Your Power of Repair 54

Building Your Personal Rescue Plan 55

Integration—Your Pattern-Interrupt Practice 58

Closing Thoughts 60

Part III: Your Strategic Communication in Practice 61

6 63

Your Parenting Values & Intentions 63

Introduction—The Compass You Lead With: Your Anchor in the Storm .. 63

Uncovering Your Parenting Blueprints 65

Your Core Values Discovery and Definition 67

Your Values Under Pressure: Your Conflict Test 69

Defining and Living Your Parenting Vision 71

Integrating Insight and Moving Forward 75

Closing Thoughts 79

7 81

Your Regulated Communication 81

Vignette—The Email That Reopened the Wound 81

The Regulation-Communication Bridge 82

The Core Principles of Trauma-Informed Communication 84

Mastering the Art of the Boundary 87

Applying Boundaries in Real, High-Conflict Scenarios................90

The Three Contexts of Regulated Communication................95

Closing Thoughts 99

8 103

Your Regulated Communication & Your Boundaries................103

Introduction—Turning Your Intention into Interaction................103

Regulate, Recalibrate, and Respond (Your Three-Step Filter) 106

Your Ground Rules for Respectful Communication................108

Scripts & Starters—Communication by Intention................110

Parallel Parenting—When Distance Restores Peace 113

Child-Centered Communication and Repair................116

Reflection & Progress Marker—Anchoring Your Peace................117

Closing Thoughts 119

9 121

Creating Consistency Across Your Child's Homes 121

Introduction—The Steady Beat Beneath Two Rhythms 121

Why Consistency Matters—The Science of Predictability................123

Your Emotional Predictability................124

Where Structural Consistency Matters Most 127

Transition Planning—Keeping the Edges Soft 130

Reflection and Commitment—The Consistency Compass 132

Closing Thoughts 134

PART IV: Child-Centered Protection................135

10 137

Repair and Resilience: Healing Your Child in the Middle................137

Introduction—You as Your Child's Buffer 137

Your Core Task—Modeling Recovery, Not Perfection................138

Your Power of Repair—The Antidote to Rupture................139

Your Three-Part Trauma-Informed Apology Framework................140

Your Child's Regulation Toolkit: Skills for Stress 142

Protecting Your Child from Loyalty Conflict................................ 146

Fostering Resilience: Your Long-Term View 149

Closing Thoughts... 152

11 153

Understanding & Supporting Your Child.. 153

Introduction—Returning to the Heart of Co-Parenting 153

Decoding Behavior—The Feeling Beneath the Action............... 155

Understanding Your Child's Developmental Needs by Stage 157

Empathy Mapping—Seeing Your Child's Life Through Their Eyes 159

Co-Regulation, Sensory Tools, and Scripts................................. 162

Your Final Commitment—From Pressure to Presence 164

Closing Thoughts 165

12 167

What to Do When it's Hard (Conflict, Control & Distance) 167

Introduction—When Peace Isn't Possible (Yet)......................... 167

Identifying Your Dynamic: High Conflict vs. Control................... 169

Parallel Parenting—Your Strategic Distance 171

Documentation Without Obsession 173

Protecting Your Child from Emotional Fallout 175

Your Grief Release and Long-Term Steadiness 177

Closing Thoughts... 179

13 181

Parenting with a Toxic Co-Parent... 181

Introduction—When Love is Used as a Weapon......................... 181

Recognizing Coercive Dynamics (Clarity Over Diagnosis)........ 183

Your Digital Safety and Disengagement Strategies 185

Protecting Your Child from the Fallout 188

Reclaiming Your Energy and Identity 191

Closing Thoughts 193

14 195

High-Stakes Co-Parenting Logistics: Public Events, Holidays, and Crisis
Management 195

Introduction—Your Protocol Is Your Peace 195

Managing Shared Public Events 196

Your Holiday Exchanges and Travel Protocol 198

Your Child's Medical and Crisis Management 200

Child-Centered Logistics—Preparation and Repair 203

Your Final Action & Integration 207

Closing Thoughts 207

15 209

Introducing Your New Partner & Blended Family Transitions 209

Introduction—Love After the Storm 209

Readiness Assessment—Pacing for Protection 210

Preparing Your Ecosystem—Your Partner and Child 214

Managing the Aftershock—Your Child's Emotional Responses 217

Navigating Your Ex-Partner Dynamic (Protection, Not Permission) 219

Blending or Co-Existing—The Art of Slow Integration 221

Your Final Safety Measures 223

Closing Thoughts 225

PART V: Integration and Sustainability 227

16 229

Protecting Your Child Against Manipulation 229

Introduction—When Love Gets Twisted 229

A Child's Internal Impact—Rewiring for Safety 230

Teaching Your Child Inner Clarity—Using Questions as Bridges 233

Your Protection Strategy—Neutrality and Documentation 236

Your Final Guardrails—Digital and Relational Boundaries 239

Closing Thoughts 241

17 243

Financial & Power Dynamics in Co-Parenting 243

Introduction—When Money Stops Being Neutral 243

Recognizing Economic Abuse and Financial Power Plays 245

Responding to Financial Bait (Your Dignity Script) 248

Talking to Your Child About Money Without Shame 251

Your Financial Dignity and Emotional Wealth 254

Closing Thoughts 256

18 257

Your Spiritual & Cultural Anchors in Co-Parenting 257

Introduction—Returning to Your Roots 257

What Counts as Spiritual or Cultural Anchors 258

Navigating Belief Differences Between Your Child's Homes 259

Practices that Ground and Heal (Your Safety Rhythm) 262

Intergenerational Healing and Belonging 265

Including Your Child—Without Pressure 266

Spiritual Safety Check 267

Closing Thoughts 269

19 271

Looking Ahead—Your Next Turn in the Road 271

Introduction—Your Journey Continues 271

Your Progress Inventory—What Your Growth Looks Like Now 272

Planning for Your Transitions: Stay Rooted in Your Response 274

Reclaiming Your Identity and Healing Path 277

Your Integration Ritual—Releasing and Carrying Forward 279

Closing Thoughts 281

20 283

Your Master Toolkit—Tools, Trackers and Resources 283

Introduction—Your Healing in Quiet Patterns 283

Your Master Toolbox Index (24 Tools) 284

Your Daily/Instant Tools 289

Your Weekly Practice Tools 307

Your As-Needed Documentation Tools 328

Your Planning & Vision Tools 369

Navigating Your Master Toolkit to Practice Calm 393

21 397

Your Master Toolkit System in Action 397

Introduction—Integration and Execution 397

Your Toolkit Philosophy—Fact Over Feeling 397

Your Core Workflow—The Four-Phase Loop 398

Your Integration Drills—Practice Makes Permanent 401

Strategic Application—Working with Professionals 404

Conclusion—Your Sustained Mastery and Legacy 406

References & Further Reading 409

About the Author 413

Permissions & Licensing 414

Preface

Co-parenting after separation is one of the most complex and under-supported transitions a family can experience. It profoundly challenges not only logistics and communication but also the **nervous system**, attachment patterns, and one's sense of self as a parent. Even the most well-intentioned individuals can find themselves reacting from stress rather than responding from steadiness.

This workbook was developed to meet that reality. It combines principles from **trauma-informed care**, attachment theory, and family-systems psychology with practical exercises for emotional regulation and communication. Its aim is to help parents and professionals understand co-parenting not merely as a legal or logistical task, but as a deep **relational and physiological process** that requires awareness, structure, and compassion.

Across two decades of clinical work in trauma recovery, family therapy, and behavioral health, I have observed how unresolved emotional activation undermines co-parenting efforts far more than any court order or parenting plan. Families do not fall apart because they lack information; they struggle because their nervous systems remain locked in survival mode. Trauma-informed co-parenting begins with recognizing this truth: **regulation is leadership.**

Each section is designed to engage both the mind and body. Readers will find reflective prompts, regulation tools, and structured activities that intentionally build the capacity for **awareness before action**. The exercises are adaptable for use in individual therapy, family sessions, or self-guided reflection. Clinicians can confidently integrate them as psychoeducational interventions to complement existing therapeutic frameworks.

The material is intentionally trauma-responsive and **culturally inclusive**. It acknowledges that family systems are diverse and that parenting occurs within broader social, cultural, and systemic contexts. The language and tools invite flexibility, honoring each parent's unique history, values, and community reality.

This is not a workbook that asks for perfection or harmony. It asks for **presence**—the ability to pause, to notice, to regulate, and to return to the work of parenting with integrity and care. Co-parenting is not simply about managing another adult; it is about modeling safety and adaptability for the child at the center.

My hope is that these pages serve as both a guide and a grounding space—a professional resource that helps parents, clinicians, and communities understand that **healing and structure can coexist**. The work of steadiness is clinical, emotional, and spiritual. It is also learnable.

May this workbook help you and those you serve create systems of parenting where safety, accountability, and compassion are no longer in conflict, but in collaboration.

—Nahomie Julien, LCSW, CADC II, CAMS II, CDVS II

How to Use This Workbook

This workbook isn't meant to be rushed or mastered.

It's meant to be lived with—slowly, gently, and honestly.

Inside, you'll find reflection prompts, core grounding tools, and exercises designed to meet you exactly where you are. Some days, that might mean writing out entire pages. Other days, it might mean simply pausing, taking a single breath, and walking away. Both count. This is not homework; it's heart work.

For Individual Readers

Begin with Self-Awareness.

Before you start, pause and notice what you're bringing into this space—your hopes, your fatigue, your fears, your faith. You don't have to fix anything first. Just notice.

Move Through Each Section Slowly.

Healing is not linear, and neither is this workbook. You can go in order, skip ahead, or return to sections that call you back. The goal is integration, not perfection.

Embrace the Mess.

Write in the margins, underline, or use a separate notebook. These pages are for your truth, not performance. Your handwriting, doodles, and pauses are all part of the process.

Check In With Your Body.

If a prompt feels heavy or overwhelming, stop. Take a walk, stretch, breathe, or reach out for professional support. Remember the non-negotiable rule: Regulation before reflection. Always.

Return Often.

Each chapter was built to be revisited. As you grow, the same questions will meet you differently, revealing new insights.

This Is Your Healing Companion.

It's not a checklist. Not a test. A companion—one that holds space for your humanity while helping you build a core of steadiness, boundaries, and grace.

For Clinicians, Facilitators, and Coaches

This workbook is an excellent resource for trauma-informed reflection, whether used as structured in-session material or as homework between appointments. Encourage clients to move at their own pace, respect their activation limits, and choose the tools that align best with their unique nervous systems.

When utilizing this text in group settings, begin each session with a grounding practice and end with a structured debrief to ensure emotional closure is safely contained.

Over Time

Return to this book across seasons of your co-parenting journey. The exercises and reflections were designed to grow with you—to feel different as you do.

Take your time.
Your pace is right on time

Introduction

Parenting after separation, especially in the context of trauma or chronic conflict, requires a different skill set than parenting within an intact family system. It demands not only logistical organization and communication management, but emotional endurance, nervous system regulation, and a working understanding of relational safety. Traditional co-parenting resources often focus on behavioral strategies—communication rules, scheduling tools, or legal guidance—without addressing the physiological and psychological mechanisms that drive both conflict and recovery.

Purpose and Clinical Orientation

Parenting Across the Divide—A Trauma-Informed Co-Parenting Workbook was created to bridge that gap. It approaches co-parenting as a biopsychosocial process, integrating concepts from trauma-informed care, attachment theory, polyvagal theory, and family-systems psychology into a structured, reflective, and practical format.

This workbook was developed for three primary audiences:

1. Parents and caregivers navigating separation, high-conflict co-parenting, or parallel parenting dynamics.
2. Clinicians and facilitators seeking psychoeducational tools to complement individual therapy or group work.
3. Agencies and educators building trauma-informed parenting programs or family wellness curricula.

Its clinical orientation is grounded in trauma-responsive practice, which assumes that stress and dysregulation—not simply disagreement or personality differences—often underlie persistent co-parenting conflict. A trauma-informed approach to parenting across households prioritizes:

- Safety: Establishing predictable structure and emotional regulation as the foundation for all communication and decision-making.
- Trustworthiness and Transparency: Using clear, consistent boundaries to reduce ambiguity and anxiety for everyone in the family system.
- Empowerment and Agency: Strengthening each parent's sense of personal agency while fostering problem-solving that centers the child's well-being.
- Cultural and Contextual Humility: Recognizing that family dynamics are profoundly shaped by culture, race, identity, socioeconomic conditions, and systemic inequities.

These principles serve as the clinical backbone of the material and guide the reader's journey throughout each section.

Structure and Progression

The workbook is intentionally organized to follow a developmental sequence, mirroring the process of therapeutic stabilization and integration. Each chapter builds upon the last, balancing psychoeducation with experiential application.

- Part I: Your Steadiness Foundation (Chapters 1–3) introduces the trauma-informed lens, self-assessment, and essential nervous-system education. Readers begin by mapping personal triggers and understanding the core mechanics of regulation.
- Part II: Regulation: Your Internal Leader (Chapters 4–5) focuses on the core physiological skill set. These chapters provide evidence-based, real-time regulation techniques and simple skills designed to support immediate internal stabilization in moments of stress.
- Part III: Strategic Communication in Practice (Chapters 6–9) explores how to translate internal regulation into external structure. This section starts with defining parenting values and then applies that compass to communication frameworks, boundary setting, and conflict-management strategies.
- Part IV: Child-Centered Protection (Chapters 10–15) examines the developmental needs of children, the impact of inconsistency, and tools for supporting the

child's nervous system. It includes essential strategies for repairing relational rupture and navigating high-conflict dynamics.

- Part V: Integration and Sustainability (Chapters 16–21) concludes with self-compassion, long-term maintenance tools, and systemic integration. Readers are guided to create a master toolkit and a plan for ongoing emotional steadiness.

How to Engage with the Material

Readers are encouraged to move through the workbook at their own pace, following the order that best matches their needs. Each chapter includes a consistent structure:

- Educational Content—Clear, concise explanations of theory and context.
- Clinical Applications—Step-by-step frameworks and behavioral skills.
- Reflective Prompts—Guided journaling and cognitive integration exercises.
- Practice Activities and Tools—Worksheets, checklists, and regulation strategies for real-world use.
- Therapist Integration Notes—Suggestions for clinical or group facilitation.

For individual parents, the workbook serves as both a structured guide and a personal mirror. The goal is not perfection or cooperation at all costs; the goal is coherence—a nervous system and a parenting rhythm that feel safe enough to respond rather than react.

Language and Inclusivity

The language throughout this workbook intentionally avoids gendered assumptions, heteronormative frameworks, and moral hierarchies. It recognizes that families take many forms—biological, adoptive, blended, chosen, or foster—and that parenting can occur within complex cultural and relational realities. Trauma-informed care also demands awareness of intersectionality: how race, culture, faith, identity, and systemic barriers affect parenting access and emotional safety.

Each chapter invites readers to adapt the tools to their context. Reflection prompts and examples are inclusive by design, acknowledging that healing, like parenting, is deeply personal and culturally shaped.

The Clinical Rationale

Unresolved trauma and chronic stress narrow a parent's Window of Tolerance, limiting their capacity for empathy, patience, and executive function during high-stakes interactions. Research from neuroscience and attachment theory consistently demonstrates that self-regulation is the foundation of healthy co-regulation—and that children's emotional security is directly influenced by the predictability and regulation of their caregivers.

Therefore, the core aim of this workbook is capacity-building: expanding a parent's ability to stay regulated, connected, and aligned with their values even under pressure. Regulation precedes resolution. Emotional stability becomes the intervention.

Expected Outcomes

While every parent's experience will vary, consistent engagement with the material should yield measurable outcomes, such as:

- Increased awareness of trauma responses and activation patterns.
- Improved emotional and physiological regulation.
- Strengthened boundary clarity and communication consistency.
- Reduced escalation and reactive behaviors.
- Enhanced empathy toward self, child, and co-parent.
- Reframed understanding of conflict as information, not identity.
- Greater confidence in parenting independently or collaboratively.

This workbook is not a guarantee of harmony, but it is a framework for healing-centered leadership—the kind that transforms not only how you co-parent, but how you live within yourself.

In Closing

Parenting Across the Divide was designed to hold both rigor and compassion: to feel clinical enough for a therapist's office, and humane enough for a parent's kitchen table. It does not promise simplicity. It promises steadiness—the kind that grows when awareness meets practice.

You are invited to approach these pages as both professional guidance and personal refuge. The goal is not to erase difference, but to cultivate safety within it. Healing work of this kind is never wasted; it becomes the soil where new systems of care can take root.

—Nahomie Julien, LCSW, CADC II, CAMS II, CDVS II

Part I: Your Steadiness Foundation

Seeing What's True Before You Try to Fix It

"Awareness isn't about fixing what's wrong. It's about turning toward what's true—the body, the breath, the moment—and choosing to stay."

NJ

1

The Ground You're Standing On

Introduction—The Child in the Middle

"I'm tired of being in the middle."

He wasn't even ten. His sneakers dangled from the couch, tapping a rhythm that betrayed how much he'd learned to hold inside. Across the room, two adults sat stiffly—each convinced they were the reasonable one, each pleading to be heard. Their voices never shouted, yet the tension in the air was so heavy you could almost see it. The child flinched at every sigh and shift of weight, subtly preparing his body for conflict that might erupt— or for the quiet, suffocating anxiety that would inevitably follow.

When I asked what he meant, he said quietly, "Dad says one thing, Mom says another. I don't know who to believe. I just don't want to make anybody mad."

That single sentence contains an impossible choice. It's the moment a child's internal loyalty system fractures. For them, it's never about preference—it's about survival. They learn quickly that the safest path is to disappear or to become a chameleon, mirroring the emotional state of whichever parent they're with.

In that moment, I realized how easily adults mistake their own explanations for safety. Children don't need every story—they need peace.

That moment became the heartbeat of this book—because behind every custody order, every text exchange, every exhausted therapy session, there is usually a child trying to survive the crossfire of adult pain. That chronic uncertainty quietly teaches the developing brain that love is conditional and the world is unpredictable. The consequences reach far beyond childhood, shaping a child's stress tolerance, emotional regulation, and capacity for intimacy.

Reflection—The Courage of Noticing

Pause for a moment. If you've ever looked at your child and thought, *they deserve better than this*, you are already doing the hardest part—noticing.

What emotion does that realization trigger in you (guilt, pain, commitment, anger)? How does your body feel when you hold that thought?

_____

_____

_____

_____

That self-aware moment of pain isn't failure; it's courage. And it's the fuel for change.

Your Unacknowledged Foundation: Trauma and Stress

This workbook grew out of years spent in therapy rooms, living rooms, and court-mandated sessions. It's built around a simple truth:

Co-parenting after rupture isn't just logistics: it's nervous system work.

It's the process of learning how to breathe again when love, loss, and obligation collide in a pressure cooker.

These pages weave trauma science, practical tools, and lived compassion. They're designed for parents who want to protect their children from emotional fallout but aren't sure how—and for therapists and facilitators walking alongside them.

Here, "trauma" isn't limited to catastrophic events like abuse or natural disasters. It includes the cumulative impact of emotional stress: the constant low-grade fear, chronic relational uncertainty, and the internal bracing for the next conflict that becomes wired into the body and family system. This is the invisible trauma of the divide.

The body keeps score of every tense hand-off, every anxious email wait, every silent treatment.

Your pain and your struggle are valid. Understanding them is the only way to help your child.

This workbook won't tell you what to feel. It will invite you to notice what you already know, and to practice steadiness when everything in you wants to react.

This isn't a manual for perfection. It's a map for presence.

Why Traditional Advice Falls Short

"Just communicate better."

"Don't bad-mouth your ex."

"Keep it about the kids."

Those phrases are well-intentioned but meaningless when your nervous system believes it's in danger. Traditional advice assumes logic leads the way—that if you think right, you'll behave right.

But trauma doesn't speak logic; it speaks survival.

That advice may work for amicable separations where trust remains high. It collapses completely in the face of betrayal or deep emotional injury.

Consider Sarah, a parent reading a curt email from her ex-husband about a school matter. The message is technically compliant but dripping with contempt. The logical part of her brain says, *Just respond with the facts*. But her body spikes with heat; her jaw tightens; her mind races. She spends two hours drafting and redrafting a single line, terrified that one misplaced word could be weaponized in court. Even after she sends it, she's shaking.

Traditional frameworks offer no explanation for that shaking. They suggest she simply "manage her emotions."

This workbook offers a different truth: the shaking isn't weakness. It's her body's protective alarm system going off. That heat is the fight response. The paralysis is freeze.

This work will help you recognize those reactions and slow them down. You're not just dealing with an email—you're dealing with the physiological echoes of threat.

Learning to signal safety to your body—*"I'm safe enough, right now"*—isn't avoidance. It's regulation.

Regulation is leadership in the language of the body, and it's the most powerful message of safety you can send your child.

Your Trauma-Informed Lens—Shifting Your Focus

Being trauma-informed means changing the question from *"What's wrong with you?"* to *"What happened to you—or to us?"*

It means curiosity over control. It assumes that even harmful behavior has a backstory rooted in fear, pain, or protection. Understanding that doesn't excuse harm—it explains function. And that knowledge creates room for change.

The Four Core Principles

1. Safety First: Nothing matters—no schedule, no court order, no parenting plan—until emotional and physical safety are re-established. Your brain can't connect when it's in threat mode. Regulation always comes first.

2. Awareness Before Advice: We practice *feeling and noticing* before *fixing*. That pause is where wisdom enters.

3. Choice Over Control: You can't control the other parent's behavior, but you can always control your own tone, boundary, and next breath. That's your circle of influence.

4. Compassion as Accountability: Firm boundaries can coexist with empathy. Compassion sees the wound; accountability maintains the line. When you enforce limits calmly, they hold longer and teach more.

Reflection—Checking Your Current State

Pause here and check in:

1. When reading the four principles, was your breathing:

   □ Tighter and shallower? □ Softer and easier?

2. Which of the four principles above created the most sense of *resistance* or *tension* for you? Why?

The Hidden Impact on Kids

Children experience conflict in their bodies first.

They are hypervigilant sensors, reading the energy in the room before they can name it. Tight shoulders. Held breath. Laughter that's a little too loud. It's not "sensitivity." It's survival.

When the air between adults is thick with resentment or silence, a child's body releases cortisol and adrenaline—chemicals meant for short bursts of danger, not daily life. Over time, that chronic stress rewires their developing brain.

The Long-Term Costs

- Impaired Executive Function: Constant stress disrupts the prefrontal cortex, affecting focus, emotional control, and learning.
- Internalized Stress (Coping Roles): Kids develop coping roles to manage the adults:
  - The Peacekeeper sacrifices themselves to manage adult emotions, often growing into anxious or perfectionistic adults.
  - The Withdrawer shuts down, disconnecting to stay safe, later struggling with trust or intimacy.
  - The Attention-Seeker acts out, redirecting adult conflict toward themselves, trading chaos for connection.
- Compromised Immunity: A body perpetually on alert diverts energy from the immune system. Headaches, stomach aches, or fatigue often tell the story.
- Distorted Relational Wiring: When love and tension intertwine, love begins to feel like tension. Later, they may equate intensity with intimacy.

This is why your steadiness is not optional—it's a clinical intervention.

The antidote isn't guilt. It's intentional repair and consistent presence. When even one parent commits to calm, a child's nervous system begins to learn what safety feels like.

Your steadiness becomes their stability.

The Emotional Landscape of Co-Parenting

Co-parenting after rupture is emotional triage. Healing is rarely dramatic; it's measured in breaths and small non-reactions.

You will feel guilt, anger, resentment, grief, shame, or numbness—sometimes all in one day. None of these emotions make you a bad parent. In trauma-informed practice, emotions are messengers, not enemies.

Decoding the Messengers

- Anger often hides grief or powerlessness. It mobilizes to protect.
- Guilt says, "I want to repair." Shame says, "I am unworthy." Learn to answer guilt with repair and silence shame with compassion.
- Resentment signals overextension. It's a cue to rest or reset boundaries.
- Numbness isn't apathy—it's exhaustion. It means your system needs restoration.

Awareness creates choice. When you can ask, *What are you trying to tell me?* you shift from reacting to responding.

For Therapists & Facilitators

This workbook invites reflection, not compliance. The goal isn't perfect answers—it's embodied awareness.

Encourage clients to translate concepts into personal language (*"my Green Zone," "my reset mode"*) and to notice how they engage with each prompt. Avoidance, rushing, or intellectualizing are diagnostic data points.

Sample debrief prompts:

- Which ground rule feels hardest to honor right now?
- What sensations arise when you slow down to answer a question in the workbook?

- What changed between your first and last line in this exercise?

Regulation and reflection are inseparable—one deepens the other.

For Self-Guided Parents

If you're doing this work alone, know this: healing doesn't require two cooperative adults. One regulated parent changes the emotional climate.

Solo parenting through trauma recovery demands self-compassion and self-resourcefulness. Silence doesn't have to mean isolation.

Your steadiness is enough to start rewriting your child's nervous system story.

Your Path Forward—Your Power of Repair

Every pause before reaction is a rewiring. Every moment you take a breath instead of replying in anger is a small act of repair.

- Repair to your child: *"I'm sorry I raised my voice. That was my frustration, not yours."*
- Repair to yourself: *"I reacted, but I noticed. I can choose differently next time."*

Your child doesn't need perfection—they need proof that safety can return after rupture. You can be that proof.

When I think of that boy on the couch, I remember his quiet relief when the room finally calmed—when both parents simply paused. Nothing miraculous happened; they just stopped long enough for him to breathe.

That's where healing begins: one moment of calm that ripples outward.

You don't have to call it perfect for it to be real. You just have to start where you are.

2

Where Are You Now?

Introduction—Checking Your Internal GPS

You can't chart a meaningful path forward without knowing where you stand. This chapter invites you to pause, reflect, and orient—to see your co-parenting reality clearly, without judgment or shame. Whether you're navigating a cooperative partnership or a high-conflict separation, understanding your current landscape helps you choose the tools that actually work for you.

Think of this as your internal GPS check. Maybe your dynamic is stable, maybe it's stormy, maybe it changes by the week. All of that is valid. The goal here is honesty, not perfection.

You'll begin with a self-check to map your current climate, explore three common co-parenting styles, and choose a "track" that fits your experience right now. You don't need to fit neatly into one label; this is about awareness, not identity.

You don't have to have it figured out before you begin. You just have to be willing to see what's true.

A Moment of Orientation—Embracing Your Raw Reality

When parents first sit down to reflect, the urge to fix or justify often drowns out clarity. Imagine one parent, Amira, sitting in her car outside her child's school after another tense

11

exchange. She pulls out this workbook, exhales, and admits: *"I don't even know where to start."*

That moment—uncomfortable, real, and raw—is where awareness begins. Like Amira, you don't need to solve everything; you only need to notice where you are.

This chapter meets you right there. You're not being graded. You're being invited to locate yourself—to gather data on the ground you stand on before you start laying a new track.

Activity 2.1: Self-Check—Mapping Your Current Climate

Purpose
To take an honest, detailed snapshot of your current co-parenting dynamic.

Instructions
Rate each statement **1–5** (1 = Not at all True, 2 = Occasionally True, 3 = Sometimes True, 4 = Often True, 5 = Very True). Use the checkboxes to mark your score.

Statement	1	2	3	4	5
Communication—We communicate in a respectful way.					
Communication is timely and clear.					
Logistics—We have a consistent, reliable parenting schedule.					
We make basic parenting decisions together effectively.					
Emotional Safety—I feel emotionally safe interacting with my co-parent.					
Conflict, when it happens, is manageable and short-lived.					
System Support—I feel supported (or at least not undermined) as a parent.					
Our child experiences stability and calm between homes.					
Our child is not caught in the middle of adult conflict.					
Self-Regulation—I feel calm before, during, and after contact with my co-parent.					

Total Score: _____

Keep this number to compare with future self-checks later in the workbook.

Reflection Prompts

- **The Honesty Gap:**

    What was the single hardest statement to rate truthfully?

    _____

    _____

    Why did you feel pressure to rate it higher or lower than the reality?

    _____

    _____

- **The Urgency Factor:**

    Which areas feel most urgent to improve—and which are "good enough" for now? (We're aiming for sustainability, not immediate perfection.)

    _____

    _____

- **The Stuck Point:**

    Where do you feel "stuck," even if the numerical rating is high?

    _____

    _____

    _____

- **The Physical Cost:**

  When you think about the lowest-rated items, where do you feel the tension in your body?

  _____

  _____

This isn't a performance review; it's a flashlight to see what's true.

Reading Your Reflections—Not a Score, a Signal

This self-check isn't about judgment or diagnosis. It's a mirror, not a measuring stick. There's no "right" score—only patterns that show what your nervous system can currently sustain.

Interpreting Your Patterns (The Clarity Matrix)

- **High Scores (4–5 Average): The Cooperative Cluster**
  - Shared planning and respectful communication are realistic. Focus on refining trust and maintaining clear, functional micro-boundaries.
- **Mid-Range Scores (2–3 Average): The Mixed Cluster**
  - You're balancing hope and fatigue. Use discernment and self-care to manage the in-between. Cooperation may be conditional or intermittent.
- **Low Scores (1–2 Average): The Parallel Cluster**
  - Limited, structured contact is often safest. Stability, not symmetry or connection, is the most important goal right now.

Clinician Note
Invite clients to note which statements were hardest to rate. These often reveal unspoken pain points and openings for repair that are masked by surface-level agreement or compliance.

Emotional Weather Patterns (Expanding the Forecast)

Like the sky, your co-parenting climate shifts. Calm mornings can turn stormy by evening. This variability doesn't mean failure; it means humanity. When you expect storms, you pack an umbrella. Emotional preparedness works the same way: forecasting helps you plan rather than panic.

Forecasting your emotional weather helps you prepare—not predict.

Understanding Co-Parenting Styles—Choosing Your Track

Co-parenting isn't one-size-fits-all. Many parents move between these styles depending on the situation. The goal isn't hierarchy—it's **regulation and stability**.

Track	Definition	Trauma-Informed Goal	Success Indicator
The Cooperative Track	Frequent, flexible, and respectful communication. *Reality: "We don't always agree, but we make it work."*	Maintain safety while staying relationally open.	Low-stress transitions; child feels secure with both parents.
The Hybrid Track	Collaboration in some areas, distance in others. *Reality: "We're not friends, but we've found a rhythm."*	Discern where cooperation serves you versus where boundaries protect you.	Conflict stays contained; no spill-over to the child.
The Parallel Track	Minimal contact; independent routines; used for high-conflict or unsafe dynamics. *Reality: "It's not warm, but it's stable—and that's enough."*	Protect nervous-system safety; prioritize stability over connection.	Reduced personal anxiety with reduced contact.

Activity 2.2: Identifying Your Track and Its Purpose

Purpose
To understand why your current style exists and what it protects.

Instructions

15

Please write below, dedicating as much space as you need for these four prompts.

1. **Underline your current track:** Cooperative/Hybrid/Parallel

2. If Hybrid or Parallel, explain how that choice **protects** you and your child.

3. Name the **"Fantasy Track"** you wish you were on, and the belief that fuels that wish (e.g., *"If we were cooperative, the child would be fine"*).

4. Define **one practical boundary** you need to put in place right now to maintain your chosen track.

Honesty Fatigue—The Cost of Clarity

Self-awareness uses emotional muscles rarely exercised. When you feel, *"I can't keep doing this,"* it's time to rest, not quit. Fatigue means you're near a breakthrough—your nervous system just needs recovery.

Activity 2.3: Naming Your Relationship Honestly

Purpose
To describe your co-parenting reality without filters or self-censorship.

Instructions
Write freely for two pages—or speak aloud if that feels safer. Focus on honesty and context.

- The hardest part of co-parenting right now is…

- I feel most uncertain about…

- One thing I wish my co-parent understood is…

- Something I'm proud of in how I've parented is…

- A word or phrase that captures our dynamic is…

- What I don't say out loud is…

- **The Unspoken Fear:** What's the worst outcome you worry about, and one small thing you can do to prepare or reduce that fear? (Continue writing on the next page as needed.)

Reflection—Tracing Your Journey

This isn't about blame; it's about context. Notice patterns, growth, or pain you hadn't named before.

- How has co-parenting changed over time?

- What have I learned the hard way—and which tool would've helped then?

- How has this affected my relationship with my child?

- How has it changed how I see myself—as a parent or person?

- What part of this story needs to end?

- What still deserves to come with me?

Awareness doesn't demand change, it just asks you to stop pretending you're lost.

Critical Modifications for Safety and Trauma

Activity 2.4: If You're in Conflict or Trauma

Purpose
To modify for safety and pacing. If reading feels overwhelming, pause. You're not behind; you're being careful.

- **Pacing:** Skip ahead to Chapter 4 or 5 (regulation & high-conflict core tools).
- **Content:** Use two-sentence reflections instead of long paragraphs.
- **Focus:** Focus only on your immediate emotional and physical safety.
- **Choice:** All exercises in this book are optional.
- **Support:** Reach out for local professional support if needed.

Activity 2.5: Grounding Reminder (Your Immediate Reset)

Purpose
To regulate when emotions rise. Use this as an in-the-moment anchor.

1. **Feet First**—Press both feet firmly to the ground and notice the weight.
2. **Sensory Anchor**—Name five things you can see, four things you can touch (or feel on your skin), and three things you can hear.
3. **Breath**—Slow your breath: Inhale for 4 counts, Exhale for 6 counts. Repeat.
4. **Affirmation**—Silently state: *I am here. I am doing enough. I can stop anytime.*

If sight isn't grounding, use texture or sound instead. If you begin to dissociate, pause and come back later. Healing honors pacing, not pressure.

Reflection & Progress Marker

Activity 2.6: Documenting Your Starting Point

Purpose
To record where you began—your truth, not your test.

- **Date** _____
- **Current Track:** Cooperative/Hybrid/Parallel (Circle one)
- **Key Insight to Remember from Chapter 2:**

"This is where I began. I didn't have to be ready—I just had to be real."

3

Your Body's Language—Mapping Your Nervous System

Introduction—Your Engine, Your Alarm System

In Chapter 2, we recognized that co-parenting after rupture is not a battle of logistics; it's **nervous-system work**. When you find yourself shaking after a short text exchange or going numb during an argument, those are not signs of failure—they're signs of **survival**.

This chapter moves from the symptom (the fight, the fear) to the source (the wiring). We'll demystify the system that runs you, giving you the language and awareness to identify your physiological state and reclaim choice.

You are not broken. Your highly efficient survival system is simply stuck on high alert.

The Autonomic Nervous System (ANS): Your Engine and Your Alarm

The Autonomic Nervous System (ANS) is the body's automatic control center. It governs your heart rate, breathing, digestion, and stress responses—operating continuously beneath conscious awareness. Think of it as both an **engine** and an **alarm**, guiding your body between movement and stillness, safety and survival.

The ANS functions through two complementary systems that ideally work in balance:

1. **The Accelerator—Sympathetic Nervous System**
   This is your **mobilization system**—it energizes the body to respond to real or perceived threats. When activated, it increases heart rate, sharpens focus, and redirects energy toward **fight or flight**. It is the system of protection and performance, preparing you to act, defend, or escape.

2. **The Brake—Parasympathetic Nervous System**
   This is your **restoration system**—it allows the body to slow down, restore, and heal. When active, it lowers heart rate, deepens breathing, and brings you into the state of **rest and digest**. This is where calm returns, and connection and clear thinking become possible.

Healthy regulation doesn't mean staying calm all the time. It means having **flexibility**— the ability to move between the Accelerator and the Brake as needed, and to return to balance once the stress has passed. This rhythm between activation and restoration is the biological foundation of resilience.

The Window of Tolerance—Your Green Zone

Your **Window of Tolerance (WOT)** is the body's natural range of balance, the state in which your **Accelerator (Sympathetic System)** and **Brake (Parasympathetic System)** work together in rhythmic partnership. Inside this window, your body feels safe enough for your brain's higher functions—reasoning, empathy, communication, and creativity— to come online.

In this zone, your **prefrontal cortex** (the part of your brain that allows you to think clearly, plan, and connect) is in charge; while your survival centers (the amygdala and limbic system) are regulated and responsive, rather than reactive. You are calm but alert, engaged but steady.

The Green Zone isn't about being relaxed all the time—it's about staying **regulated enough** to respond wisely when life gets loud. In co-parenting, that means your nervous system can tolerate frustration, uncertainty, and difference without collapsing into shutdown or exploding into reactivity.

The Gold Standard of Parenting

When you are operating inside your Green Zone, you can:

- **Access patience and perspective** even when your child or co-parent is triggered.
- **Regulate your tone, volume, and body language**, keeping your presence steady.
- **Pause before reacting**, allowing space between emotion and action.
- **Choose curiosity over control**, asking, *"What's happening here?"* instead of *"What's wrong with them?"*
- **Hold firm boundaries with warmth**, offering stability rather than punishment.
- **Model regulation in real time**, showing your child what repair looks like after rupture.

This zone represents the **optimal range of human functioning**—where self-awareness and compassion can coexist with accountability and structure.

What Happens When You Leave the Window

The goal of regulation isn't to avoid leaving your Green Zone. Life, stress, and relationships will always pull you out. The real work is recognizing *when* it happens and learning how to return.

When you are pushed **above** your Window (Hyper-Arousal), your body shifts into **activation**—you might feel agitated, anxious, defensive, or on edge.
When you drop **below** it (Hypo-Arousal), your body moves into **shutdown**—you may feel numb, disconnected, or paralyzed.

Returning to your Green Zone requires awareness, compassion, and practice. It means catching the early cues—tightness in your chest, quickening breath, a sudden heaviness—and using your **regulation tools** before the reaction takes over.

Staying within or returning to your Window of Tolerance is not about perfection; it's about developing **flexibility**—the ability to recover quickly, restore calm, and reconnect with your values even after activation.

Three Zones of Survival—Mapping Your Extremes

Your body's reactions are not overreactions; they're protective reflexes. Each surge of emotion is your nervous system's attempt to ensure safety, even when the threat is no longer present. Every intense feeling is the nervous system's way of saying, *"I'm trying to keep you alive."*

Zone 1: Hyper-Arousal (Your Accelerator is Stuck)

The sympathetic system surges—energy floods the body to confront or escape threat.

State	Physical Experience	Emotional/Cognitive Experience	Co-Parenting Example
Fight (Rage/Anger)	Jaw clenching, racing heart, heat in face or hands.	Black-and-white thinking, defensiveness, explosive anger.	Snapping during exchanges, sending reactive, accusatory texts.
Flight (Anxiety/Fear)	Restlessness, tight chest, shallow breath, tense muscles.	Catastrophizing, frantic planning, micromanaging, over-control.	Rewriting emails for hours, obsessing over schedules, avoiding contact.

Body's Message: *Act now!* This burns energy fast and leaves exhaustion and guilt.

Zone 2: Hypo-Arousal (Your Brake is Slammed)

After prolonged stress, the system collapses to conserve energy (often due to overwhelming threat).

State	Physical Experience	Emotional/Cognitive Experience	Co-Parenting Example
Freeze (Stuck/Paralysis)	Heavy limbs, blank stare, slowed pulse, holding breath.	Brain fog, indecision, disconnection, inability to speak.	Ignoring messages, missing deadlines, inability to make a simple decision.

State	Physical Experience	Emotional/Cognitive Experience	Co-Parenting Example
Faint or Flop (Collapse/Numbness)	Exhaustion, dissociation, cold body, sense of hopelessness.	Apathy, depression, emotional numbness.	Isolating from support, checking out emotionally when the child is present.

Body's Message: *I can't cope; shut down.*

Mapping Your Personal Zones

Awareness precedes regulation.

Before you can steady your body, you have to learn how to *read* it. Regulation begins with recognition—the ability to notice your body's early warning signs before your emotions take over. This section helps you identify your personal physiological cues of stress so you can intervene sooner and more effectively.

When your body begins to leave your Window of Tolerance, it sends signals—small, subtle shifts that say, *"Something doesn't feel safe."*
Your goal in this section is to build a personalized **Stress Profile Map** so you can spot those shifts early and choose a skill to restore balance.

Activity 3.1: My Co-Parenting Stress Profile (Hyper & Hypo Maps)

Goal

Translate vague stress into concrete, actionable information.
This reflection turns your body's sensations into data you can understand, track, and work with. Over time, you'll begin to notice patterns that tell you when your nervous system is moving into fight, flight, or freeze.

Set aside two full pages for this exercise. It's meant to be written slowly and revisited often.

Hyper-Arousal Map—Your Accelerator Warning

This is what happens when your nervous system shifts into **high alert** mode. You may feel a surge of energy, pressure, or urgency. These are signs your "Accelerator" is being pressed—the body preparing to fight, fix, or flee.

Physical Signs

Where do you feel the first signs of fight or flight in your body? Describe the sensations in detail (e.g., *stomach tightens, breath becomes shallow, shoulders tense, jaw clenches, heat rises in chest or hands*).

Thought Patterns

What thoughts race through your mind when you're in this state? (e.g., *"I have to fix this now," "They're doing this on purpose," "I can't let this happen again."*)

Emotional Cues

How do you feel emotionally in these moments? (e.g., *angry, impatient, anxious, defensive, overwhelmed.*)

Behavioral Clues

What do you *do* when you're here? (e.g., *send long texts, over-explain, raise your voice, pace, micromanage, or argue.*)

Hypo-Arousal Map—Your Brake Warning

This is what happens when your system **shuts down** after prolonged stress. Your "Brake" slams to protect you from overwhelm, leaving you drained or disconnected.

Hyper-Arousal Map—Your Accelerator Warning

Physical Signs (Where do you feel Fight/Flight? e.g., *stomach tightens, breath shallow, shoulders tense*)

Thought Traps (What thoughts accompany this state? e.g., *"This will never end," "I must fix it now," "I can't believe they did that."*)

_____

_____

_____

Hypo-Arousal Map—Your Brake Warning

Physical Signs (Where do you feel Freeze/Numbness? e.g., *voice flat, hands tingle, body feels heavy*)

_____

_____

_____

Thought Traps (What thoughts accompany this state? e.g., *"What's the point?" "I can't deal with this," "I give up."*)

_____

_____

_____

The Warning Line—Your Earliest Cue

What is the very first, subtle signal you notice before a reaction builds (e.g., a specific shoulder clench, a quick inhale, a moment of dryness in your throat)? **Mark it with a star (★)** and practice pausing there.

31

My Earliest Cue (★):

_____

_____

Activity 3.2: De-Personalizing Your Trigger (The Smoke-Detector Analogy)

When triggered, the body believes danger is _now_. Use this exercise to separate the current irritation from the old injury.

1. **Scenario:** Describe a recent trigger factually (who, what, when).

_____

_____

_____

_____

2. **Body's Feeling:** Name the sensation (heat, tightness, numbness, tremor).

_____

_____

_____

_____

3. **Past Blueprint:** Ask, "When have I felt this overwhelming sensation before?" (Focus on the physical echo, often a relational injury from the past).

_____

_____

_____

4. **Smoke-Detector Analogy:** Is this toast or fire? What old danger does your body think is back?

5. **New Narrative (The Pause):** Write a statement to ground yourself in the present reality. (e.g., *"I'm reacting to the past, but I'm safe now and can pause."*)

When Your Alarm is Too Sensitive—The Trauma Lens

The Over-Sensitive Smoke Detector

A nervous system shaped by past **fires**—chronic stress, betrayal, or danger—can become **over-trained to detect threats**. When this happens, it begins to sound alarms for things that are not actually dangerous, such as a tense text message or an uncomfortable silence. You're not overreacting; you're *responding to history.*

Imagine two homes:

- **The No-Fire Home:** The smoke detector rings only for real, immediate danger.
- **Your System:** The alarm goes off for the smell of toast—memories, tones, or gestures that *feel* like danger, even when the present moment is safe.

Your body is doing its best to protect you with the data it has. The goal is not to silence the alarm entirely, but to **recalibrate** it—to help your nervous system distinguish between *then* and *now*, *fire* and *toast*.

Goal

Recalibrate the alarm so it rings only when necessary—not silence it completely. Healing doesn't mean becoming unbothered; it means becoming accurate.

The Cycle of Co-Reactivity

When two nervous systems are both in threat mode, they enter a **loop of mutual activation**—each person's survival state triggers the other's. In co-parenting, this often shows up as a predictable escalation pattern.

Conflict Triangle Example

1. **Parent A (Hyper/Fight)**—reacts with a sharp tone or immediate defensiveness.
2. **Parent B (Hypo/Freeze)**—withdraws, goes silent, or shuts down.
3. **Parent A** interprets silence as rejection or control, which **escalates** the anger.
4. **Parent B** retreats further, confirming Parent A's fear of disconnection.
5. The cycle continues, each nervous system reinforcing the other's alarm.

Interruption Point
Before responding, **locate your zone**.

Pause and ask: *"Is my body in fight, flight, or freeze right now?"*
If so, take one regulating breath and delay your response. A regulated pause breaks the chain of co-reactivity.

Clinician Note
Mapping each parent's activation pattern (Hyper, Hypo, or Green Zone) in session can externalize conflict—replacing blame with shared understanding. This helps clients name, track, and regulate their nervous systems in real time, reframing the conflict as a *body-based pattern*, not a character flaw.

Closing Thoughts

Regulation is your way out. The nervous system is **adaptable**. Regulation is not a personality trait—it's a *trainable skill*.

You've now learned to map your internal zones, recognize your body's signals, and name your physiological states without judgment. Awareness is the first act of regulation—it transforms chaos into clarity.

The shift from shame to skill begins here.
You're no longer asking, *"Why am I so angry?"*
You're learning to ask, *"My body just spiked into Hyper-Arousal—what can I do to recover?"*

That question changes everything. It moves you from reacting to relating—from self-blame to self-leadership.

The final concept in this chapter is **vagal tone**—the strength and flexibility of your parasympathetic "brake."
When your vagal tone is strong, your system can return to baseline more quickly after stress. It's the biological measure of resilience: how fast you come back to calm after activation.

Regulation isn't the absence of storms—it's the ability to return to stillness after they pass.

In the next chapter, you'll begin **building your Regulation Toolkit**—a practical, step-by-step guide for strengthening your Brake, calming your Accelerator, and widening your Window of Tolerance. This is where awareness becomes application—where science meets practice, and where the work of healing becomes visible in your everyday parenting.

Activity 3.3: Quick Recap: Foundations of Awareness

Concept	Key Takeaway	Workbook Application
Autonomic Nervous System	Two forces—Accelerator (Go) and Brake (Slow)—govern your state.	Notice which system dominates before you respond.
Survival Zones	Hyper = overdrive (Fight/Flight); Hypo = shut-down (Freeze/Collapse).	Map physical and mental cues for each zone.
Triggers	Triggers are over-sensitive alarms stemming from past pain or rupture.	Practice separating past pain from present facts.
Goal	Flexibility and repair (returning to the WOT) outweigh perfection.	Catch your **Warning Line** (★) and pause before action.

PART II: Regulation—Your Internal Leader

Calm Is the Most Powerful Form of Leadership

"Regulation isn't the absence of emotion; it's the wisdom to pause before your body makes the choice for you."

NJ

4

Your Regulation Toolkit—Simple Skills for Steading Your System

Introduction—The Skill of Self-Steadiness

In Chapter 3, you built your personal map, identifying the signs of your Hyper-Arousal (Accelerator) and Hypo-Arousal (Brake Slam) zones. You know the exact moment your **Smoke Detector** is triggered. That awareness is a massive victory, but knowledge alone won't calm a racing heart.

Regulation is a physical skill, not a mindset.

Think of it like learning to drive a stick shift. At first, you stall, you lurch, and you grind the gears. It's frustrating. But with consistent, small practices, the movements become automatic, transferring the action from the thinking brain to muscle memory. That's the goal here: to build a new muscle—the muscle of **self-steadiness**.

Your Regulation is Your Repair

Every time you choose a regulating action over a reactive one, you are sending two powerful messages:

1. **To Your Nervous System:** *"The threat is not critical right now. You can rest."* This slowly increases the flexibility of your system.

2. **To Your Child:** *"The world is predictable because my parent is predictable."* This is the foundation of their sense of security.

The goal is to find skills that are subtle, immediate, and effective. A co-parenting trigger rarely allows for a 30-minute meditation; the skill must be deployable in **five seconds or less**.

Matching Your Zone

The most critical principle of regulation is **specificity**. We use different tools for different zones:

- **For Hyper-Arousal (Too Much Energy):** We need tools that **ground and slow down** the Accelerator.
- **For Hypo-Arousal (Too Little Energy):** We need tools that **activate and mobilize** the frozen system.

What calms one zone can overwhelm the other. Trying to "breathe deeply" when you're already shut down (Hypo-Arousal) can feel suffocating. We must first know the zone, then choose the tool.

Your Core Regulation Tools—The Big Three

These are the most reliable, science-backed tools for immediate zone shifts, and they are designed for maximum accessibility.

Core Regulation Tool 1: Breathwork (Target: Hyper-Arousal)

Principle: When anxious or angry, the inhale is naturally dominant, fueling the Accelerator. To engage the **Brake**, we must focus on a **longer exhale**. This sends a direct, biological signal of safety to the brain via the vagus nerve.

1. **The 4–6 Breathing Anchor (The Foundational Skill)**
   - **Action:** Inhale slowly through your nose for a count of four seconds. Exhale slowly through your mouth for a count of six seconds.
   - **Co-Parenting Application:** Do this three times while reading a stressful email. The long exhale literally pushes the stress out.
2. **The Straw Breath (The Subtle Skill)**
   - **Action:** Inhale normally, then exhale slowly through pursed lips, as if blowing gently through a small straw.

- Co-Parenting Application: This is silent and can be done while sitting across the table during a high-tension exchange or while holding the phone before replying to a text. It forces the long exhale without anyone noticing.

Core Regulation Tool 2: Grounding (Target: Hyper-Arousal & Hypo-Arousal)

Principle: The overactive mind (Hyper) and the disconnected body (Hypo) both lose track of the present moment. Grounding uses sensory input to anchor the system back to the "**here and now**," reminding the brain, *"I am safe, and it is today, not yesterday."*

1. **The Foot Anchor (The Immediate Skill)**
   - **Action:** Press both feet firmly into the floor. Notice the pressure under your shoes or socks. Wiggle your toes. Feel the texture of the floor.
   - **Co-Parenting Application:** Use this during hand-offs or when stuck in court. It reconnects the dissociated body and gives the mind a single, simple, neutral task.

2. **The 5-4-3-2-1 Technique (The Distraction Skill)**
   - **Action:** Silently name: **5** things you see, **4** things you touch/feel (e.g., the chair, your clothes), **3** things you hear, **2** things you smell, and **1** thing you taste.
   - **Co-Parenting Application:** This is highly effective when thoughts are racing (Hyper-Arousal). It forces the attention outward, interrupting the anxious feedback loop.

Core Regulation Tool 3: Movement (Target: Hypo-Arousal)

Principle: When the system is **frozen**, the body needs to complete the survival cycle—to release the frozen adrenaline. Gentle, intentional movement is required to awaken the body from freeze and signal the Brake to ease up.

1. **The Shake-Out (The Release Skill)**
   - **Action:** Set a 60-second timer and gently shake your hands, arms, and legs. Roll your shoulders and gently shake your jaw.
   - **Co-Parenting Application:** Do this privately after an exchange where you felt silenced or numb. It literally shakes off the stored activation.

2. **The Cross-Body Tap (The Re-Activation Skill)**

- ○ **Action:** Gently tap your left hand to your right knee, then your right hand to your left knee. Repeat for 30 seconds.
- ○ **Co-Parenting Application:** This bilateral stimulation helps connect the two hemispheres of the brain, a process that can be disrupted during Freeze. It subtly re-engages the thinking brain and mobilizes the body.

Building Your Personalized Toolkit

Activity 4.1: Your Three-Column Regulation Plan

Goal

To translate your awareness into an accessible, ready-to-use map for every future trigger.

Column 1: My Warning Line (First Sign)	Column 2: My Zone (Hyper or Hypo?)	Column 3: My Go-To Tool (Skill to Deploy)
Example: Tightness in stomach/throat.	*Example: Hyper-Arousal (Fight/Flight)*	*Example: 4–6 Breathing Anchor (3 rounds)*
Your Sign 1:		
Your Sign 2:		
Your Sign 3:		
Your Sign 4:		

Commitment Cue

Circle the one tool you will use every day this week, regardless of stress level, to reinforce the muscle.

Activity 4.2: Scenario-Based Skill Deployment (Reflection)

Goal
To simulate using the tools before a real crisis occurs. Dedicate ample space to walking through these scenarios.

1. **The Hostile Text:** You receive a lengthy, critical text from your co-parent accusing you of neglecting your duties.

   o **Identify Zone/Sign:** What is your first physical reaction?

   o **Skill Deployment:** What two tools will you use before you type a single word?

   o **The Response:** Write out the first sentence of your response after using the tools. (It must be regulated, brief, and factual.)

   o **The Delay:** How long is your mandatory delay before sending?

2. **The Silent Freeze:** You need to work on a financial document related to the divorce, but every time you open the folder, you feel heavy, numb, and overwhelmed, leading to procrastination.

   o **Identify Zone/Sign:** What are your hypo-arousal signs (e.g., brain fog, heavy limbs)?

   o **Skill Deployment:** What movement or sensory activation tool will you use first?

   o **The Smallest Step:** What is the single, easiest step you will commit to (e.g., "I will open the folder and read the date on one document only")?

3. **The Exchange Chaos:** You are ten minutes away from the child exchange, and your stress level is spiking (Hyper-Arousal).

   o **Identify Zone/Sign:** What is the physical sign of your rising anxiety?

- **Skill Deployment (In the car):** What silent breath or grounding tool will you deploy right now?

- **The Boundary:** How will you use your regulated state to keep the exchange brief and neutral, even if provoked?

Zone-Specific Strategy Guides—Your Targeted Kits

The key to successful regulation is having a tool customized for the specific energy you are experiencing.

Activity 4.3: Hyper-Arousal Emergency Kit

When you feel frantic, hot, or explosive, your vagus nerve needs a dramatic sensory interrupt to tell the brain, *"The emergency is over."*

Tool	Action	Why it Works (Client-Friendly Science)
Temperature Shock	Splashing very cold water on your face, especially your cheeks and forehead, or holding an ice cube.	This activates the **Diving Reflex**, causing an immediate drop in heart rate. It's a rapid, biological reset button.
The Pause and Delay	Before hitting "send," enforce a mandatory **30-minute waiting period** for any heated communication. Write the reactive text, but save it as a draft.	Gives your **Prefrontal Cortex** (thinking brain) time to come back online. The intensity of your reaction peaks and subsides during the delay.
Physical Redirect	Rapidly and intensely changing focus: doing 20 jumping jacks, or forcefully organizing a bookshelf for 5 minutes.	Releases the excess adrenaline and cortisol that your body mobilized for the "fight" it didn't have, completing the stress cycle.

Activity 4.4: Hypo-Arousal Activation Kit

When you feel paralyzed, heavy, numb, or dissociated, your system needs a gentle, safe nudge back into life.

Tool	Action	Why it Works (Client-Friendly Science)
Sensory Activation	Using strong, stimulating inputs: a very bright light, a strong sour candy, or sniffing peppermint oil or a lemon slice.	Forces the system back to the present moment. The intensity of the flavor/scent cuts through the brain fog of **dissociation**.
The Smallest Step	When paralyzed by overwhelm, do one tiny, immediate task that is unrelated to the stress (e.g., put one dish in the dishwasher, throw away one piece of paper).	Movement creates momentum. This small action breaks the grip of the freeze response and signals to your body that safe, intentional action is possible.
Physical Warmth	Wrapping yourself tightly in a blanket, wearing tight clothing (like compression socks), or holding a hot mug.	Gentle, constant pressure (called **proprioceptive input**) can be calming and help re-anchor the body's boundaries when feeling disconnected.

Closing Thoughts

Aim For Consistency, Not Perfection.

You now have the map and the toolkit. The rest is practice.

Remember, the goal is not to be a perfectly steady parent—no one is. The goal is to dramatically shorten the time you spend outside your Window of Tolerance. If you slip up, if you yell, if you freeze:

1. **Repair to Yourself:** Recognize the slip, use a tool, and forgive the reaction. Your resilience is defined by your ability to return to steady.

2. **Repair to Your Child:** Model accountability. *"I'm sorry I raised my voice. My body felt frustrated, and that was my feeling to manage. I'm taking a breath now, and I'm okay."*

Every time you choose a tool, you are strengthening your **vagal tone**, increasing your system's flexibility, and building your child's innate resilience.

Now that you have the internal skills of regulation, the next step is applying them to the external challenges of communication and boundary setting.

You now possess the essential, science-backed tools for quickly steering your nervous system back into your Window of Tolerance. These tools are effective, but they are designed for immediate, controlled deployment. The real challenge begins when a co-parenting text, a missed hand-off, or a holiday schedule hijacks your body before you can think.

Chapter 5 takes these fundamental skills and integrates them into a powerful defense system. We will dive deep into identifying your specific patterns—fight, flight, or freeze—and build a **Personal Rescue Plan** for meeting those high-stakes moments with practiced choice instead of reflexive chaos.

5

Your Regulated Response—Real-Time Skills for Your Nervous System

Introduction—The Hijack Sequence

You've built your foundation: awareness of your nervous system (Chapter 3) and your Core Regulation Tools (Chapter 4). This chapter is the critical link that translates those tools into real-time survival.

Co-parenting is often a state of chronic, low-grade stress. When a co-parenting trigger hits—a hostile text, a late hand off, a financial demand—your body can be **hijacked** before your thinking brain, the prefrontal cortex, can intervene. This is a survival instinct, not a flaw.

Regulation isn't calm; regulation is choice.

This chapter equips you with the advanced skills to interrupt that hijack sequence:

- Identify your personal default pattern (Fight, Flight, Freeze).
- Use self-compassion to manage the shame that follows a lapse.
- Build a practical, automated **Rescue Plan** for moments of crisis.

Vignette—The Text That Hijacked the Morning (Analysis)

When Sam received the late text, their body reacted with **Activation** (heart racing, jaw tight). This activation bypassed the thinking brain and led to **Displacement** (snapping at the child).

Your task: Learn to insert a **30-second pause** between the Activation and the Response. That pause is the space where regulation lives.

Decoding Your Dysregulation Pattern

Dysregulation is your body doing its job—predicting and preparing for threats. Understanding your default pattern is the first step toward changing it.

The Three Core Survival Patterns

Pattern	Co-Parenting Manifestation	Nervous-System Purpose	Physical/Emotional Signs
Fight	Arguing, proving, sending long emotional texts, replaying arguments, passive-aggression.	Mobilizing against threat (*Belief: If I fight, I win/survive.*)	Tight jaw, loud voice, racing heart, heat, overwhelming urge to **do something**.
Flight	Overworking, frantic scrolling/cleaning, avoiding calls/texts, compulsive "fixing."	Escaping danger (*Belief: If I run/stay busy, the threat can't catch me.*)	Shallow breath, restless legs, difficulty sitting still, urgency, constant distraction.
Freeze/Fawn	Zoning out, perfectionism, over-apologizing,	Appeasement/Numbing (*Belief: If I disappear or comply, I won't be hurt.*)	Foggy mind, heavy chest, numbness, lack of appetite, coldness.

Pattern	Co-Parenting Manifestation	Nervous-System Purpose	Physical/Emotional Signs
	immediately giving in to avoid conflict.		

Activity 5.1: Deep Dive—Trauma-Informed Pattern Mapping

(Separating the present moment's inconvenience from the past pain it echoes.)

Purpose
To identify how current co-parenting triggers awaken old, unprocessed emotional patterns. This exercise helps you separate the *present event* from the *past echo* it activates in your nervous system, allowing you to interrupt automatic reactions and re-regulate before responding.

When to Use
- After a strong emotional or physiological reaction (fight, flight, freeze, or fawn).
- During reflection when you notice recurring themes in conflict.
- In therapy or coaching sessions to uncover deeper emotional patterns beneath surface reactions.

Instructions for Use *(The Mapping Process)*
Complete this exercise when you are calm or in a "Green Zone" (regulated state), reflecting on a recent "Yellow" or "Red" event (activated or dysregulated state).

1) **Identify the Trigger**

- In the first column, write a brief, factual description of what occurred.
- Keep it objective—no interpretation or blame.

Example: "Co-parent was late for pickup." "Didn't respond to my message about the school form."

2) **Define Your Default Response Pattern**

- In the second column, identify how your body and emotions reacted.
- Choose one of these trauma-response patterns:
  - **Fight:** anger, defensiveness, control, verbal or written attack.

- Flight: anxiety, pacing, avoidance, overworking, over-explaining.
- Freeze: numbness, silence, brain fog, disconnection, fatigue.
- Fawn: appeasing, apologizing, minimizing your needs to avoid conflict.

3) Uncover the Echo (Deeper Fear/Old Story)

- In the third column, explore what past experience this reaction resembles.
- Ask: "What does my body believe is happening?"

Examples: "I'm being rejected again." "If I don't fix this, I'll lose love." "Conflict means danger."

4) Pinpoint the Core Belief

- After completing the table, reflect:
  - *What belief about myself hurts most when I'm triggered?*
  - *Examples:* "I'm not good enough." "I'm always to blame." "My needs don't matter."

Trauma-Informed Pattern Mapping Worksheet

Current Co-Parenting Trigger *(Factual Event)*	My Default Response Pattern *(Fight/Flight/Freeze/Fawn)*	The Deeper Fear/Old Story It Echoes
Example: Feeling ignored (unanswered message)	Example: Freeze	Example: "My needs don't matter."
Example: Loss of control (plans change without input)	Example: Fight	Example: "If I don't control things, I'll be abandoned."
Example: Milestone/Holiday stress	Example: Flight	Example: "Joy isn't safe—good things end in chaos."
My Top Trigger:	My Default Pattern:	Echoed Story:
My Second Trigger:	My Default Pattern:	Echoed Story:
My Third Trigger:	My Default Pattern:	Echoed Story:

Reflection—Your Core Wound

Prompt
What belief about yourself is the most painful when you are triggered? *(e.g., "I am not respected." "I am always alone." "I am disposable.")*

Follow-Up Reflection

- How has this belief shown up in your co-parenting relationship?

- How does your body signal it before your mind even notices?

- What truth can begin to replace it? *(Example: "I can't control others, but I can protect my peace.")*

Clinician Note
This activity externalizes blame and builds narrative safety. Encourage clients to track patterns over multiple events—consistent echoes often point to a central wound

(abandonment, betrayal, invisibility). Pair with grounding or breathwork before reflection to reduce emotional flooding.

Your Three-Stage Regulation Protocol

Vignette—Bracing for Impact

Jamie opened the parenting app already bracing for impact. One unread message. The moment she saw her co-parent's name, her chest tightened and her breath caught.
Her body had already decided: *fight first, breathe later.*
That moment—the 10-second surge of heat, tension, and tunnel vision—is what this protocol is built for.

You can't eliminate those spikes, but you can retrain your body to meet them differently.

Your regulation plan works best when it's divided into clear, repeatable phases.
Each stage meets the nervous system where it actually is—**before, during, and after activation**—so you can move from reaction to recovery without losing control.

Your regulation plan must be segmented to work effectively. By dividing the process into three clear stages, you give your nervous system **specific, achievable goals** for different moments of stress.
Each stage supports a different nervous system state—before, during, and after activation—helping you return to steadiness faster.

Stage 1: Before Contact (Proactive Grounding)

Goal
Ground your system to expand your Window of Tolerance.
This proactive step acts as a **buffer** against predictable triggers.

Tool Highlight

Use the **Foot Anchor** (see Core Regulation Tool 2 in Chapter 4) for 60 seconds every time you open the parenting app, prepare for a hand-off, or anticipate a challenging exchange.

Press your feet into the floor. Feel the support beneath you. Stability starts here.

Intention Setting
Before engaging, pause and ask:

"What is my highest intention right now—clarity or control?"

If the answer is control, wait.
Clarity serves connection. Control feeds reactivity.

Stage 2: During Activation (Containment and Pause)

Goal
Interrupt the emotional hijack sequence with a **physical and cognitive pause**. The aim here is not to solve the problem—it's to prevent escalation.

Tool Highlight
Use the **30-Second Pattern-Interrupt** whenever you feel the spike—the moment your pulse quickens, your breath shortens, or your body tenses.

Say internally or aloud: "This is not an emergency. I need to pause."

Tactile Anchor
Keep a small smooth stone, coin, or piece of fabric in your pocket. Touching it pulls your awareness back to the present moment and away from the threat narrative.

Your mind remembers danger, but your body can learn safety.

Mantra
"I don't have to match their energy."

Repeat this phrase until the physical spike begins to settle.

Stage 3: After Conflict (Release and Reset)

Goal

Safely discharge trapped stress energy (adrenaline, cortisol) from the nervous system and complete the body's stress cycle.

Vocal Release (The Vagus Hum/Sigh)

Hum a low, steady sound or sigh deeply with the sound *"Haaaaaah"* for 5 seconds.
This activates the vagus nerve, signaling to the brain: *"The threat has passed."*

Physical Release

Do a **Shake-Out**—gently shake your hands, arms, or legs for 60 seconds, or stomp your feet privately 10 times.
Movement restores flow where the freeze response locks tension.

Important Guardrail

All discharge must be **private, safe, and non-intimidating**—no slamming doors or raising your voice near others. Regulation is leadership, not performance.

Parenting While Activated & Your Power of Repair

You will have moments when you are activated in front of your child.
Your success lies not in **perfection**, but in **recovery and honesty**.

The Slow-Down Strategy (When You Can't Walk Away)

Use this protocol to minimize harm when you must remain present with your child while activated.

1. **Stop**
   Drop what you are doing. Step back.

   (Put down your phone, the keys, or the argument.)

2. **Foot Anchor**
   Plant both feet flat on the ground (see Chapter 4) and take two slow breaths.

3. **Speak Softly**
   Lower the **volume and speed** of your voice by half.
   A slower voice slows the heart.

4. **Use Simple Phrases**
   Say:

   > *"I'm having a big feeling, but it's not your fault. I need two minutes."*

5. **Repair Later:**
   This is the most critical step. Never let a lapse go unaddressed.
   When both you and your child are calm, model accountability.

   > *"I was frustrated earlier and used a loud voice. That was my mistake. I'm sorry. I'll work on keeping my voice calm next time." (See Chapter 10 for detailed repair practices.)*

The Compassionate Reframe (Post-Lapse)

When you snap, the shame voice says: *"You failed. All this work was for nothing."*

Replace it with the **Regulated Voice (Self-Compassion):**

"I'm a human under chronic stress who had a lapse. That lapse is proof I'm tired, not proof I'm broken. What is the kindest step I can take to repair?"

Why it Matters
Reframing *is* regulation.
It stops the shame spiral before it hijacks your body again.
You are not erasing accountability—you are **leading yourself through repair** with compassion instead of punishment.

Building Your Personal Rescue Plan

A **Rescue Plan** is your automatic protocol for when you are deeply dysregulated—in full "Red Zone" shutdown or overwhelm. It removes the need to think when the rational brain goes offline.

Goal
To have a **printed, visible plan** that immediately directs you toward safety, steadiness, and support.

Why it Works

You're building **procedural memory**—training your body to default to healing habits instead of panic or shutdown.

Your Personal Rescue Plan Should Include:

1. Your Grounding Tool

Your go-to 60-second reset: (e.g., regulation techniques highlighted in Chapter 4, like the Foot Anchor, 4–6 Breathing Anchor, and Temperature Shock via a cold water splash, etc.).

2. Your Scripted Phrase

A pre-written thought interrupter: (e.g., *"I'm not in danger—this is discomfort."*)

3. Your Boundary Reminder

Protective limits that preserve your peace:

"No texting after 8 PM."
"Delay replies for 24 hours."

4. Your Contact Support

One trusted friend, coach, or professional you can text: *"I'm spiraling. Can you check in with me?"*

5. Your Safe Space

A physical anchor space (the car, patio, or your bed) where you can reset without judgment.

Activity 5.2: My Personal Rescue Plan—Print and Keep Visible

Purpose

To create a simple, automated rescue protocol for moments when your system is hijacked.
This plan is not about perfection; it's about *having a map when your mind goes blank.*
Think of it as your emergency manual—the boundary you set for yourself when stress takes over.

Instructions for Use

1. Complete this worksheet when you are calm and regulated.
2. Post it somewhere visible (your phone, fridge, office wall, or journal).
3. Use it anytime you notice early signs of overwhelm—racing heart, foggy thinking, or emotional flooding.
4. Follow each step **in order**, even if it feels mechanical. The goal is to re-engage your body's safety systems through repetition, not willpower.

Step 1: My Top 3 Immediate Tools

Which physical tools or grounding actions help me most when I feel flooded or reactive?
(e.g., Foot Anchor, 4–6 Breathing Anchor, cold water splash)

Step 2: My Steady Phrase

What short, steady phrase can I repeat when my thoughts spiral?
(e.g., "I'm safe right now." or "This is discomfort, not danger.")

Step 3: My Safe Person

Who can I text or call for 3 minutes—someone calm, non-judgmental, and grounding?
(Name | Phone | Preferred contact method)

Step 4: My Safe Place

Where can I go when I need to decompress or step away for a moment?
(e.g., the car, backyard, office, porch)

Step 5: My Closure Ritual

How will I close the loop after a crisis—to signal to my body that it's over?
(e.g., 5-minute journal, breath prayer, stretching, brief walk)

Your 10-Minute Rescue Protocol

Crisis Step	Protocol	Location/Time Commitment
Activation	Use one of your Top 3 Tools + repeat your Steady Phrase.	1 minute
If Flooding Continues	Move to your Safe Place and continue grounding until you can breathe steadily.	5 minutes minimum
When Done	Contact your Safe Person + perform your Closure Ritual.	10 minutes

Pro Tip
Keep this plan *printed* and within reach—emotional regulation relies on visibility, not memory.

Clinician Note
Clients using a visible, step-based plan re-engage their prefrontal cortex faster after stress. The goal is repetition, not reliance—the plan trains procedural safety.

Integration—Your Pattern-Interrupt Practice

The goal of this chapter is to build a stronger **Pause Muscle**—your ability to delay reaction long enough for your nervous system to choose steadiness over survival.

Each time you interrupt an old reaction pattern, you teach your body that safety can exist *even in tension.*

That's how repair becomes a reflex—one pause at a time.

Activity 5.3: Pattern-Interrupt Experiment

Purpose

To strengthen your pause muscle and retrain your system's instinct to react.
This experiment helps both parents and clinicians measure progress by tracking small shifts in timing, awareness, and restraint.

Instructions for Use

1. **Identify one difficult habit or reactive behavior.**
   (Example: Checking the parenting app immediately upon waking, texting back too quickly, or rereading messages when anxious.)
2. **Delay the behavior by 60 seconds** for the next 7 days.
   The delay teaches your nervous system that discomfort is tolerable and control isn't urgent.
3. **During the 60 seconds, u**se a micro-regulation strategy such as:
   o 5 slow breaths
   o Naming your sensations ("heat in my chest," "tightness in my shoulders")
   o Orienting to the present (look around, name 3 neutral objects)

Clinician Insight

Encourage clients to record physiological cues rather than emotional labels.
The goal isn't to suppress the urge—it's to observe the body's activation curve and practice staying with it.

7-Day Tracking Table

Day	Habit Delayed?	Felt Easier/Harder?	Outcome Shift *(Did I say/do less?)*
Day 1	☐ Yes/☐ No		
Day 2	☐ Yes/☐ No		
Day 3	☐ Yes/☐ No		

Day	Habit Delayed?	Felt Easier/Harder?	Outcome Shift *(Did I say/do less?)*
Day 4	☐ Yes/☐ No		
Day 5	☐ Yes/☐ No		
Day 6	☐ Yes/☐ No		
Day 7	☐ Yes/☐ No		

Reflection Prompts

What did these seven minutes of pausing teach you about your emotional rhythm?
How did holding the moment—instead of reacting—shift the tone or outcome of your interactions?

"You're not learning to avoid reaction; you're learning to lead it."

Closing Thoughts

Every return to awareness is progress.
Every pause is power.

You've learned how to pause the storm.
Now it's time to decide what guides you once the calm returns.
Regulation gives you choice—but it's your values that give those choices direction.

In the next chapter, you'll uncover the compass behind your parenting: the beliefs, hopes, and principles that shape how you lead, respond, and repair. Because steadiness isn't just about slowing down—it's about knowing *what you're slowing down for.*

Part III: Your Strategic Communication in Practice

Boundaries Create Breathing Room for Connection

"Boundaries are not walls; they're rhythms of respect. They teach others how to approach your peace."

NJ

6

Your Parenting Values & Intentions

Introduction—The Compass You Lead With: Your Anchor in the Storm

After successfully building your foundation (Chapters 1–3) and mastering the core tools for stabilization (Chapters 4–5), you now understand the *how* of regulation.
Now, we turn to the *why*—the purpose and principle behind your calm.

Why do you pause before hitting send?
Why do you choose the grounded response instead of the defensive one, even when provoked?

The answer is your **values and intentions.**
When co-parenting feels unpredictable or volatile, your values become your internal compass—the quiet laws that orient you toward steadiness. They govern how you show up for your child and for yourself, even when the environment around you is unstable.

Values are not abstract ideals. They are the daily, observable actions that turn your integrity into practice. They transform you from a reactor into a leader—one whose stability becomes a model of safety.

This chapter will help you:

- Clarify what matters most to you as a parent and as an individual.

- Define how you choose to parent *through* conflict, not *because* of conflict.
- Build a vision rooted in steadiness rather than circumstance.

You'll explore your deepest beliefs, identify the values that anchor you, and translate those values into visible, felt behaviors your child can trust.

The Bridge from Regulation to Intention

Regulation gives you access to choice; intention gives that choice direction.
When your body is calm, your mind becomes capable of conscious leadership.

In this space of steadiness, your prefrontal cortex—the brain's moral and reasoning center—comes back online.
This is where the shift happens: from reflex to responsibility, from protection to purpose.

Here, you can ask yourself:
"What kind of parent do I want to be right now?"

This is the work of integration—aligning physiological calm with moral clarity.

Before you continue, pause.
Take three slow breaths.
Unclench your jaw.
Remind yourself:
"I am not reacting. I am responding. I am leading with intention."

Vignette—Reclaiming the Compass

During one session, a father named Malik sat in quiet frustration.

"I don't even recognize myself anymore," he said. "I swore I'd never yell at my kids like my dad did… but last night, I did."

His confession wasn't about anger—it was about grief. He was mourning the distance between the father he intended to be and the one his nervous system became under stress.
His values—*Patience* and *Respect*—had been hijacked by survival.

64

But instead of collapsing into shame, Malik began to repair. The next morning, he taped a small note to his dashboard that read:

Pause. Lead with patience.

Every time he saw that note, he was reminded that growth isn't linear—it's cyclical. He wasn't striving for perfection; he was practicing return.

That's the essence of values work: the continual act of finding your way back to your compass after losing your bearings.
Because your success as a parent is not measured by how rarely you falter—it's measured by how quickly and honestly you return to what matters most.

Uncovering Your Parenting Blueprints

Before you can align with your values, you must uncover the unconscious blueprints that shape them. These are the internalized beliefs about love, discipline, safety, and worth that live beneath your parenting behaviors.
Some of these blueprints are inherited through family or culture; others are built from survival—formed in response to stress, loss, or trauma.

We often repeat the parenting patterns that once regulated us—or that we wish someone had used with us. Understanding these internalized beliefs allows you to decide what to **preserve**, what to **release**, and what to **rebuild**.

Deep Dive—Examining Your Inherited Beliefs (Journaling Assignment)

Purpose
To consciously explore the unconscious patterns that influence how you parent today.

Each question invites reflection—not judgment. Take your time and respond honestly.

1. **Your Inherited Image**
   When you picture *"good parenting,"* what comes to mind?
   Describe the image vividly. Then identify where it came from—your parents, a teacher, a cultural ideal, or media portrayals.*Example: "Good parents always stay calm." Source: My grandmother, who never raised her voice."*

2. **Your Parental Legacy**
   Growing up, what did affection, correction, or love look like in your home?
   Describe the unspoken lessons you absorbed about emotional expression,
   discipline, or approval *Example: "I learned that love had to be earned by being helpful."*

3. **Your Transformation**
   How are you intentionally choosing to parent differently?
   Reflect on one pattern you are consciously rewriting. *Example: "I validate emotions
   before correcting behavior. My child learns that feelings are safe."*

4. **Your Preservation**
   What do you want to carry forward?
   Name the traditions, habits, or qualities that still align with your values of safety,
   consistency, or connection. *Example: "Family dinners—they created stability and
   belonging."*

5. **Your Release**

   Which core belief are you ready to question or let go of? *Example: "Children should never question adults." New Belief: "Respect includes curiosity and voice."*

You don't need perfect answers—only awareness of the script you've been following. Awareness is the doorway to choice.

Your Core Values Discovery and Definition

Activity 6.1: Core Values Discovery Activity

Purpose

To identify the guiding qualities that anchor your parenting—the traits and principles that hold steady even when emotions, circumstances, or co-parenting dynamics shift.

Your values are the heartbeat of intentional parenting. They give direction when everything else feels uncertain.

Step 1: Identify Your Anchors

Circle or highlight the 5–7 values that resonate most deeply with you. Add your own if needed.

As you read through the list, notice which words make you exhale—those are often the values your body already trusts.

Value Group	Values to Consider
Relational	Respect, Empathy, Honesty, Trust, Kindness, Emotional Awareness
Character	Responsibility, Accountability, Integrity, Generosity, Courage
Systemic	Safety, Stability, Structure, Consistency, Advocacy
Flexibility	Patience, Humor, Curiosity, Adaptability, Self-Control
Growth	Self-Expression, Creativity, Education, Joy, Resilience

Step 2: Define Your Top Three

Now, narrow your focus to three values that are *non-negotiable* in your parenting legacy. These are the qualities you want your child to associate with you—not in theory, but in how they feel in your presence.

For each value, complete the reflection below.

Value Chosen	How I Practice This Value Daily (Micro-Action)	Why it Matters to My Child's Security	What I Hope My Child Learns
Example: Patience	"I take 4–6 breaths before replying to a frustrating question."	"It teaches them that their presence isn't an inconvenience."	"That calm is possible, even when things are hard."
Value 1:			
Value 2:			
Value 3:			

Reflection Prompt
As you complete this, remember—values are not ideals to perform. They are practices to return to.
Every micro-action, every moment of awareness, is a quiet act of leadership.

Clinician Insight

Encourage clients to focus on values that create *safety and flexibility*, rather than perfection. When in conflict, values like *calm*, *curiosity*, and *consistency* reduce activation and model self-regulation for children.

Remember: Even good values can collide.
The work is not choosing the "right" one—it's choosing the one that serves *safety and connection* right now.

Your Values Under Pressure: Your Conflict Test

Your values are clearest when you are calm—and most tested when you are not.
When your nervous system shifts into survival mode, logic and empathy temporarily go offline.
In those moments, your behavior is driven by physiology, not philosophy.

The greatest gap often exists between the value you *hold* and the action you *take* when triggered.
This is not hypocrisy—it's a nervous system in distress.
The work of regulation is learning how to return to your values faster after rupture.

Your Values Under Hyper-Arousal (Fight/Flight)

When anger, fear, or urgency takes over, your system surges into **Hyper-Arousal**—a physiological state designed to protect you from threat.
Unfortunately, it also blocks your access to patience, reasoning, and compassion.

Example: The Value—Respect
You value treating your co-parent and child with dignity, even when emotions run high.

Then an email arrives—full of accusations and personal attacks. Your pulse races, your jaw tightens, and your chest burns. The instinct to defend yourself floods in.

In that state, **the reactive action** might be to fire off a sharp reply that mirrors their tone—a short-term discharge that feels like control, but erodes trust and reinforces conflict.

The **regulated action** looks different.
You apply the **Pause and Delay** method (see Chapter 4)—stepping away before responding, breathing until your heart rate lowers, then drafting a reply that addresses

only the logistics.
You lead with respect, not reaction—modeling emotional maturity for your child, even when respect feels undeserved.

This isn't compliance; it's containment. You are choosing to protect your peace, not their ego.

Your Values Under Hypo-Arousal (Freeze/Avoidance)

Sometimes, the opposite happens—your system shuts down.
In **Hypo-Arousal**, energy collapses inward. You freeze, withdraw, or feel detached. This is not laziness; it's a physiological shutdown designed to protect you from overwhelm.

Example: The Value—Responsibility
You pride yourself on reliability—following through on commitments, especially for your child's well-being.

But when the summer schedule conversation looms, you feel dread so heavy it's paralyzing. The logistics blur together. Instead of responding, you shut down and avoid the task altogether.

That **reactive action**—postponing or ignoring—protects you in the short term, but it also creates confusion for your child and chaos for the system you're trying to stabilize.

A **regulated action** begins with movement. You engage Core Regulation Tool 3 (see Chapter 4)—e.g., shaking your hands, or even walking for two minutes to restore your momentum.
Then, you take **The Smallest Step**—opening your calendar, sending one neutral message, or completing one single task.

The goal is not perfection—it's motion.
Each micro-action honors your value of responsibility, even when full energy hasn't returned.

Clinician Note
When a parent acts against their values, it is rarely moral failure—it is nervous system overload.
Reactivity reflects physiological dysregulation, not a lack of care.
Guide clients to re-engage their core regulatory tools before discussing behavioral change or repair.

Reflection Prompts

Think of one recent conflict. Which value did you lose contact with in that moment—and how can you reconnect with it faster next time?

Defining and Living Your Parenting Vision

Values are roots.
Your **parenting vision** is how those roots express themselves in everyday life.
It's the internal compass that reminds you who you are when conflict, fatigue, or fear pull you off course.

When practiced, your vision becomes the throughline—the way your child experiences your steadiness, even when life feels unpredictable.

Activity 6.2: The Legacy Exercise—Defining Your Vision

Purpose
To connect your values to their long-term, observable impact—the legacy your child will carry forward from your parenting.

This is not about perfection. It's about direction. Each response plants a seed for the kind of relationship and emotional inheritance you want your child to grow up with.

1. **Your Future Reflection**

Imagine your child at **age 25**, describing you to someone who asks, *"What kind of parent did you have?"*

What three values do you hope they name—and how would they describe how you lived them? *Example: "They modeled courage by leaving an unsafe situation."*
Example: "They were always accountable and made things right when they were wrong."

Use this reflection to clarify what *lasting imprint* you want to leave—not just in your child's memory, but in their nervous system.

2. Your Modeling Plan

Values without modeling remain theories.
Think about the daily, tangible actions that allow your child to witness your values in motion. *Example: "I want to model how to admit a mistake," or "how to prioritize self-care even when things are chaotic."*

List the specific behaviors that will embody your chosen values.
The small, repeated actions—not the grand moments—will define your legacy.

3. Your Core Message

Complete the sentence: "I want to raise a child who knows…"

What is the single most important belief about themselves you want them to internalize?
Is it that they are safe? Capable? Worthy of repair? Loved without condition?

When your child encounters life's inevitable difficulties, this message will be the voice they hear in your tone—the anchor they return to when they lose their own footing.

Write Your Personal Parenting Vision (1–3 Sentences)

Use this space to combine your reflections into a clear statement.

Example: "My parenting is grounded in calm, honesty, and connection. I model repair and accountability so my child learns that love and truth can coexist."

Your vision doesn't need to be perfect—only practiced.
Every day you return to it, you are shaping your child's sense of safety, resilience, and belonging.

Activity 6.3: Micro-Moments of Modeling

Parents often overestimate the power of their lectures and underestimate the quiet strength of their modeling.
Children don't learn calm from being told to calm down—they learn it by *feeling* your nervous system settle in real time.

Every small, consistent behavior you model becomes an emotional cue:
"This is what safety feels like."
"This is how repair happens."

Micro-moments of modeling are not about perfection—they're about repetition. Each one builds trust in your child's body, teaching them that stability is possible even in moments of stress.

Micro-Moments in Practice

Value	Behavior You Model (Micro-Moment)	Immediate Impact on the Child
Respect	You pause and let your child finish speaking before responding—even when you disagree.	They feel heard and valued, learning that communication doesn't require control or interruption.
Accountability	You use your **Three-Part Apology** (see Chapter 10) right after a reactive moment—no delay, no justification.	They experience repair as safety. They learn that mistakes can be addressed without shame.
Stability	You maintain predictable bedtime and morning routines, even when co-parenting dynamics feel unstable.	Their bodies relax; they internalize that predictability can exist even when adults disagree.
Patience	You visibly use your **4–6 Breathing Anchor** before responding to defiance or frustration.	They learn that emotions can be regulated—that heat can cool without harm.
Compassion	You acknowledge your child's emotions ("That was hard for you") before redirecting behavior.	They learn that empathy and limits can coexist; that love doesn't disappear during correction.

Reflection Prompts

Think of three moments this week where your actions taught calm, connection, or courage more powerfully than your words could.

What did your child learn about safety, repair, or resilience through watching you?

Clinician Note (for group or session use)
Micro-modeling exercises can help parents experiencing shame reconnect with efficacy. Each "small win" activates the parasympathetic nervous system, building a sense of competence and internal safety. Encourage clients to identify one recurring micro-action that strengthens trust.

Integrating Insight and Moving Forward

Activity 6.4: Vision vs. Reality—The Gap Analysis

Purpose
To identify where your current actions deviate from your values, so you can bridge the gap between your best intentions and your real-time behavior.

This exercise helps you turn awareness into alignment—not by striving for perfection, but by tracking patterns with compassion and clarity.

My Top Value

(Example: Patience)

My Action When Regulated—(e.g., "I pause and validate their feelings before responding.")

_____

_____

_____

My Action When Triggered—(e.g., "I sigh loudly and rush them.")

_____

_____

_____

My Gap Plan

Which regulation tool from Chapter 4 will I use the next time I feel this gap? (e.g., the 4–6 Breathing Anchor or Pause and Delay.).

_____

_____

My Second Value

(Example: Honesty)

_____

_____

My Action When Regulated—(e.g., "I give factual, age-appropriate answers about the divorce.")

_____

_____

_____

My Action When Triggered—(e.g., "I vent frustration about my co-parent to my child.")

My Gap Plan

What phrase or boundary can help me stay aligned next time?
(e.g., "I'll discuss this with another adult, not my child.")

My Third Value

(Example: Compassion)

My Action When Regulated—(e.g., "I check in with my child's emotions after conflict.")

My Action When Triggered—(e.g., "I focus only on their behavior, not their feelings.")

My Gap Plan

What reminder can help me reconnect to this value?
(e.g., "Soft first, structure second.")

Reflection—Honoring Your Work

"Awareness without action breeds guilt; awareness with intention builds integrity."

1. What did I learn about the difference between my *ideal self* and my *regulated self*?

2. Which value feels most alive for me right now—and why?

3. What is one *specific, micro-action* I will commit to practicing this week that demonstrates one of my core values?

Reflection & Progress Marker—Anchoring Your Values

(Complete at the end of this chapter or in session.)

Purpose
To track how you are integrating your values into real-life interactions—not through performance, but through presence.

Check-In	Reflection Prompt	Progress Notes
Day 1	Which value guided my actions today?	
Day 3	Did I notice a moment when I caught myself before reacting?	
Day 5	What helped me return to my value after a rupture?	
Day 7	Which value feels easier to live in my body now than a week ago?	

Clinician/Facilitator Note

Encourage clients to use this tool as a mirror rather than a measure. The aim is not to close the gap overnight, but to notice it sooner and respond differently. Each reflection strengthens emotional regulation and self-accountability.

Closing Thoughts

Awareness turns into change one small, intentional action at a time.
Every pause, repair, and realignment is evidence that you are parenting from integrity—not impulse.

Remember: Growth is not about being consistent—it's about being *committed.*

7

Your Regulated Communication

Vignette—The Email That Reopened the Wound

It started with a simple message:
"Please confirm if you're still planning to pick up on Sunday."

But by the third line, it wasn't simple anymore. The tone turned sharp, the accusations familiar.

Maya felt the flush of heat in her chest—that now-familiar warning of a nervous system hijack.

Her first instinct was to defend herself, to prove the story wrong. But for the first time, she paused.

She took one breath, then another.

Instead of writing back, she closed the screen.

That single act—not replying—was her nervous system choosing safety over control.

Later, when she finally did respond, her words were brief, factual, and calm. It wasn't perfect, but it was peaceful.

That was progress.

The Regulation-Communication Bridge

Regulated communication is the intersection of your body's steadiness and your values in action.
It's not about perfect phrasing—it's about physiological grounding.

When conflict rises, the body speaks first:

- The throat tightens.
- The heart races.
- The mind rehearses arguments.

If you respond while your body is still in defense mode, your message becomes protection, not connection.
Every text, every tone, every sigh carries the nervous system's fingerprint.

Regulated communication begins with recognizing this:
Your body sets the tone before your words ever do.

Your Nervous System's Role in Communication

When you are in your **Window of Tolerance**, your words can serve your values—clarity, respect, responsibility.
But when your system shifts into **fight, flight, or freeze**, those same words become weapons, walls, or silence.

State	What Happens in the Body	How It Sounds in Communication
Hyper-Arousal (Fight/Flight)	Increased heart rate, faster speech, heat, agitation	Rapid texts, long explanations, defensive tone, over-clarifying
Hypo-Arousal (Freeze/Avoidance)	Slowed speech, flat tone, emotional numbness	Delayed responses, detached or curt messages, ghosting or withdrawing
Regulated Zone (Green)	Calm alertness, balanced breath, open focus	Grounded tone, clear boundaries, factual and concise language

Regulation gives you access to language that doesn't leak panic, prove worth, or punish silence.
This is how communication becomes both boundary and bridge.

The Pause Before Replying

The pause is your most powerful communication tool—the nervous system's way of buying time for clarity to return.
In high-conflict co-parenting, silence is not avoidance; it's strategy.
Every pause signals *I am leading with regulation, not reaction.*

Practice

Before responding to any message that stirs you, use this 3-step grounding sequence:

1. **Breathe:** One full 4–6 Breathing Anchor cycle (inhale 4, exhale 6).
2. **Name it:** "I'm feeling activated—not unsafe."
3. **Wait:** Delay your reply by at least 20 minutes (or one nervous-system reset).

You're not waiting to be passive—you're waiting to be effective.

Communication as Co-Regulation

Every interaction—written or spoken—is a co-regulatory exchange.
When you steady your system, you are also shaping your child's sense of safety and your co-parent's threshold for conflict.

In trauma-informed communication, calm is not compliance—it's containment.
You regulate to protect your peace, not to earn approval.

Your goal is not to control the dialogue, but to control your contribution to it.

Clinical Insight

When working with clients on co-parenting communication, start with the body before the script.
Ground first, then language. Otherwise, the "regulated" message becomes a disguised trauma response—polite words wrapped around a threat signal.

Now that you understand how physiology and communication intertwine, we'll explore **how to set and hold boundaries** without aggression or guilt.
You'll learn to identify your triggers, choose your tone, and build language that protects peace without erasing truth.

Boundaries are not barriers—they are the architecture of mutual safety.

The Core Principles of Trauma-Informed Communication

Before we discuss scripts and strategies, we must first shift the mindset.
Traditional communication advice often prioritizes harmony—*"stay calm, don't argue, just compromise."*
But in trauma-informed co-parenting, harmony cannot exist without **safety**.

Our goal isn't to "get along." It's to communicate clearly enough to reduce confusion, escalation, and nervous system overload—for everyone involved.
In this framework, your priorities are simple and non-negotiable: **Clarity, Brevity, Neutrality, and Consistency.**

The Pause—Your Greatest Power

The single most powerful act in trauma-informed communication is the **Pause.**
A dysregulated nervous system craves control—it pushes you toward immediate reaction.
Your regulated self, however, knows that clarity lives in delay.

The 24-Hour Rule
For any non-emergency message, enforce a waiting period—even one hour helps.
The longer the delay, the lower your emotional intensity.

Draft and Delete
When emotions rise, write the unfiltered version first.

Let it hold your frustration, your proof, your story—then delete it the next day.
This honors the emotion without making it the message.

Action Cue
Each time you feel the pull to "just reply," replace the impulse with a core regulation tool (see Chapter 4).

Example: Take one minute of **Straw Breath**—inhale normally, exhale slowly through pursed lips.
By the time you finish, your brain will have shifted from reactivity to discernment.

Every pause is a nervous system intervention disguised as a communication skill.

The CBNC Framework—Clarity, Brevity, Neutrality, Consistency

This framework is the trauma-informed standard for all co-parenting communication, especially in high-conflict or emotionally charged exchanges.

Principle	Why it Matters (Trauma Lens)	Application in Practice
Clarity	Ambiguity invites confusion, argument, and control. Clear language lowers activation in both parties.	Use plain language. State only the fact and the action required. *("The appointment is at 3 PM. I'll confirm arrival by 2:45.")*
Brevity	Long messages are targets—easily skimmed, distorted, or weaponized.	Limit written communication to **three sentences max.** If more context is needed, change the medium (e.g., app note, meeting).
Neutrality	Emotionally charged or evaluative words trigger defense and escalate threat perception.	Focus on **who, what, when, where.** Remove "I feel," "You always," or "This is unfair." Replace judgment with fact.
Consistency	Predictability calms the nervous system. Each steady, patterned response reinforces emotional safety for you and your child.	Use the same regulated tone and boundary every time. *("I'll respond when the topic concerns parenting logistics.")*

Clinician/Facilitator Note

When teaching CBNC, start with body awareness before behavior change.
Parents often "sound calm" but type while in hyper-arousal. Encourage them to regulate before drafting any message.

CBNC is not a tone-policing strategy—it's a **nervous-system stabilizing tool** that protects long-term co-parenting functioning.

Reflection Prompts

Before moving on, pause here. Think of one recurring communication that drains you—a text, email, or in-person exchange.
Ask yourself:

1. Which CBNC principle would make the biggest difference if I applied it consistently?

2. What does my body do before I hit "send"?

3. How could I use my next pause as practice, not punishment?

Write one sentence applying the principle you chose.

Example: *"I will respond with facts only, not feelings, when I receive critical messages."*

That's not avoidance—it's alignment.

Now that you've established the nervous system foundation for communication, we can apply it to real scenarios.

The next section— *"Mastering the Art of the Boundary"*—will teach you how to translate CBNC into language that protects peace while maintaining respect.
Boundaries are not about withholding contact—they're about redefining the terms of connection.

Mastering the Art of the Boundary

A boundary is not a wall—it's a structure that defines where your responsibility ends and someone else's begins.
It's not about controlling the other parent; it's about protecting your **safety, energy, and integrity** when control is not possible.

Boundaries are an act of regulation.
They require calm enforcement because holding the line—especially when it's repeatedly tested—is physiologically stressful.

A regulated boundary says:

"I can stay steady without surrendering my peace."

Types of Boundaries—Protecting Your Space

Each boundary is a form of **emotional containment**—a way to give your nervous system predictability in an unpredictable environment.
When chosen with intention, boundaries become the structure through which calm can live.

Type of Boundary	Purpose	Example
Time Boundaries	Define *when* communication will happen so you're not constantly on alert.	"I only check co-parenting messages once per day at 6:00 PM."
Topic Boundaries	Define *what* you will and will not discuss to prevent emotional flooding.	"I will only discuss our child's schedule and medical needs. I will not discuss personal history or past conflicts."
Medium Boundaries	Define *how* communication occurs to reduce misinterpretation and emotional access.	"All schedule requests must be placed in the parenting app. I will not respond to text messages about this topic."

Clinical Insight

Time, Topic, and Medium boundaries help restore executive function.
Each one protects your prefrontal cortex—the part of your brain that enables reasoning, planning, and empathy—from being hijacked by reactive impulses.

Your Three-Step Boundary Script (Your Regulated Response)

Boundaries are most effective when practiced as a script—a predictable rhythm that calms both you and the system around you.
Think of this as your *communication muscle memory*.

When triggered, the goal is not to sound confident—it's to stay consistent.

Step	Action	Example Response	Why it Works
1. Acknowledge (Briefly)	Validate receipt of the message without agreeing to the content.	"Thank you for sharing your thoughts on the subject."	Demonstrates presence without submission. Prevents escalation by signaling engagement, not agreement.

Step	Action	Example Response	Why it Works
2. State the Boundary (Firmly)	Use "I will" statements to define your limits and your behavior, not theirs.	"I will only address factual questions regarding the exchange time."	Reclaims control over your own actions—the only domain you truly govern.
3. Disengage (Clearly)	State the closure point and exit the interaction calmly.	"If there are no factual questions, I will not be responding further to this thread."	Closes the loop. Prevents reactivity and ends circular conflict without emotional charge.

When practiced regularly, this script becomes your **emotional firewall**—a way to stay connected where necessary but detached where required.

Boundary Practice Tips

1. **Write It First:** Draft your most common boundary phrases before you need them. Under stress, your cognitive recall will fail; your written plan won't.
2. **Regulate Before Sending:** Use one grounding tool (e.g., Foot Anchor or 4–6 Breathing Anchor) before every boundary message. Calm delivery makes the boundary effective.
3. **Don't Over-Explain:** Each extra word weakens the boundary. Say less, mean more.
4. **Repeat Without Variation:** Predictability is your nervous system's best ally— and your co-parent's worst weapon loses its power against it.

Reflection Prompts—The Boundary You Fear Most

- Which boundary feels the most uncomfortable to hold right now—and why?

- Is your discomfort rooted in fear of their reaction or fear of disconnection?

- What would it look like to protect your energy, even if they never understand your limit?

Remember: The goal of a boundary is not agreement—it's **peace with yourself.**

Applying Boundaries in Real, High-Conflict Scenarios

In this section, you'll test these principles in motion.
Through real-world co-parenting scenarios, you'll learn to identify your triggers, apply your boundary script, and reinforce calm communication—even when provoked.

Boundaries are not about distance; they are about direction—toward safety, stability, and integrity.

Goal
To rehearse real-world co-parenting interactions in a safe, structured space using the **CBNC Principles** and the **Three-Step Boundary Script.**

This section transforms practice into prevention—allowing you to train your nervous system and language skills before the next conflict arises.

Each exercise simulates a specific nervous system state. Approach each scenario slowly. Pause, regulate, and notice your physical cues as you move through them.

Awareness is your first intervention; practice is your second.

Scenario 1: The Accusation (Hyper-Arousal Trigger)

Context
Your co-parent sends an email accusing you of *"confusing the child on purpose"* and calls you *"irresponsible."*
Your Warning Line (see Chapter 3) is a spike of heat and racing thoughts—classic hyper-arousal.

Regulation First
Stop. Do not respond yet.
Deploy one Regulation Toolkit strategy from Chapter 4 (e.g., the **Temperature Shock** or **4–6 Breathing Anchor** highlighted) for at least three minutes.
You are not avoiding the issue—you are preparing your nervous system for clarity.

Identify CBNC Failures
What are the emotional or baiting words in their message?

Which phrases pull at your need to defend, explain, or justify?

Circle or write them down. This isolates the trigger from the truth.

Draft Your Reactive Text (DO NOT SEND)
Write out exactly what your unfiltered, defensive response would sound like.
Let the emotion move through words on the page—not through your inbox.

Draft Your Regulated CBNC Reply (Final Draft)
Use the **Three-Step Boundary Script** below. Keep your tone factual and unhurried.

Step	Regulated Draft Response
1. Acknowledge	"I've received your email regarding the schedule."

Step	Regulated Draft Response
2. State Boundary	"The co-parenting app lists the exchange time as 5:00 PM. I'll adhere to that court-ordered time."
3. Disengage	"I will not respond to personal comments. Please document any scheduling concerns in the app."

Clinical Note

This response models regulation, not passivity.

The brevity and neutrality lower reactivity and close the loop—protecting your energy without amplifying the conflict.

Scenario 2: The Fishing Expedition (Topic Boundary Violation)

Context

Your co-parent calls asking for money but shifts the conversation to your new job and dating life.

Your Warning Line (Hypo-Arousal) shows up as tension in the jaw or a blank, frozen feeling—your system sensing intrusion.

Regulation First

Stay seated. Press both feet into the ground.

Use the **Foot Anchor** to reconnect your body to the present.

Your tone is part of your boundary—calm, measured, steady.

Identify Boundary Type

Which boundary is being crossed?

- Time (too long a call)?
- Topic (personal boundaries)?
- Medium (inappropriate platform)?

Deploy the Disengagement Script

Interrupt with clarity and compassion—firm, not sharp.

Practice aloud until your tone feels calm and grounded.

Script

"I need to interrupt you. I'll only discuss financial logistics. I'm not available to discuss my personal life. If the questions continue, I'll need to end the call."

Reflection Prompts

- What emotion rose first—irritation, fear, guilt, or shame?

- Which part of you felt obligated to keep talking?

- What does your body feel like when you successfully end the call on your terms?

Clinical Insight

The purpose of interruption is containment, not confrontation.
Every time you stop a violation early, you retrain your nervous system to associate boundaries with safety instead of guilt.

Scenario 3: The Freeze-Out (Hypo-Arousal Trigger)

Context

You've sent three factual emails about your child's upcoming medical appointment.
Your co-parent has not replied.
The silence pulls you into anxiety and self-doubt—a Hypo-Arousal state.

Regulation First

Your system is freezing—activate movement immediately.
Use the **Core Regulation Tool 3** (Shake-Out or Cross-Body Tap) for two minutes.
Reengage your body before you reengage communication.

Identify the Next Right Action

Ask: "What can I control right now?"
You cannot control their silence—only your clarity and documentation.

Final Documentation

Write one neutral, factual email that records your decision without emotion or urgency.

Script

"Since I haven't received a response regarding the appointment on [Date] at [Time], I've scheduled the visit and documented details in the co-parenting app. The post-visit summary is attached. I'll accept financial updates through the app."

(Do not include frustration, interpretation, or apology.)

Reflection Prompts

- What story does your mind tell you when they don't respond?

- How does that silence echo old fears of rejection or invisibility?

- How does it feel to reclaim your power by documenting instead of pleading?

Integration—Practicing for Real Life

Rehearse these scenarios out loud.

Your nervous system learns through repetition, not logic.

You're teaching your body to respond to conflict with **procedure over panic.**

Quick Reinforcement Prompts

- "Boundaries are not emotional weapons—they're emotional armor."
- "My calm response protects my child more than my perfect argument."
- "Clarity is compassion."

Now that you've practiced how to apply boundaries in simulated conflict, the next section explores **where** to use these tools—in emails, texts, parenting apps, and face-to-face exchanges.
Each platform requires a different balance of tone, timing, and boundary precision.

In trauma-informed communication, your platform is as important as your phrasing—structure protects safety.

The Three Contexts of Regulated Communication

Every communication medium carries a different emotional charge and level of exposure. An email can be re-read and weaponized; a text can be impulsive; an in-person hand-off can trigger body-level panic.

Your goal is not to communicate more—it's to communicate *strategically*.
Applying the **CBNC principles (Clarity, Brevity, Neutrality, Consistency)** within each medium allows you to stay regulated and documented at the same time.

Email and Text—The Permanent Record

Rule
Assume everything you write could be read aloud in court or to your child one day.
Let that awareness refine—not censor—your words.

Best Practice
Before replying, copy or screenshot the hostile message into a neutral space (Word, Notes, or your private log).
This simple separation breaks the emotional tether between their tone and your nervous system.

Read the message again only after regulation.
Ask:

- *What are the facts?*
- *What actually requires a response?*

Language Audit Exercise

List **five emotional or judgmental words** you will permanently remove from your co-parenting vocabulary. *(e.g., ridiculous, unbelievable, selfish, unfair, frankly.)*

_____

_____

_____

_____

Replace them with **fact-based descriptors** instead.

Example: "You're being unfair" becomes "That change is not reflected in our parenting plan."

_____

_____

_____

_____

Clinical Insight

Removing emotional language doesn't make you passive—it reclaims cognitive control. It allows your prefrontal cortex (thinking brain) to lead instead of your amygdala (alarm brain).

Co-Parenting Apps—The Buffer Zone

Rule

Use your app as the single source of truth.
It protects both parties from "he said/she said" confusion and reduces direct emotional exposure.

Best Practice

If you receive a text, DM, or social media message outside the app, do not engage emotionally.

Send one neutral redirect:

"I'll respond when this is placed in the co-parenting app."

Then stop.
No defense, no elaboration, no further contact.

This one-sentence boundary reinforces your **Medium Boundary** (the *how*) and retrains your system to view the app as your professional workspace—not an emotional arena.

Reflection Prompts

- How does it feel to redirect communication instead of reacting?

- What resistance or guilt surfaces when you enforce this limit?

- Which part of you still wants to "explain" before disengaging?

Pro Tip for Clinicians
Have clients draft and save their redirect message in Notes to remove hesitation during real-life moments.
Practice saying it aloud—calm tone, no apology.

In-Person Exchanges—The Minimalist Approach

Rule
Your only role during hand-offs or shared spaces is logistics, not emotional resolution. You are the pilot, not the passenger—your calm body sets the tone of safety for your child.

Best Practice
Before arrival, use the **Foot Anchor** (Core Regulation Tool 2 in Chapter 4): Press both feet firmly to the ground.
Remind yourself: *"I am safe enough to stay steady."*

Then, limit your words to three calm, rehearsed phrases:

Purpose	Example Phrase	Tone Cue
Fact-Based Statement	"They are here."	Neutral, simple delivery.
Neutral Closing	"Have a good week."	Polite, brief, monotone.
Boundary Redirect	"I'll address that by email."	Even tone, no edge.

Goal
To make the interaction so calm, brief, and procedural that the other parent's attempts to engage in conflict lose their fuel.
Predictability becomes your armor.

Reflection Prompts
- What physical cues (jaw clench, breath hold, posture) arise during in-person exchanges?

- Which phrase feels easiest to say calmly? Which feels hardest?

- How might your child's body respond when *your* tone stays steady?

Integration Reminder
Regulated communication isn't about being polite; it's about protecting your peace and preserving your credibility.
Tone and timing are trauma tools—not personality traits.
Each medium offers a chance to model self-governance, showing your child that calm is a form of strength, not surrender.

Closing Thoughts

Setting and maintaining a boundary is not an act of control—it is an act of care.
Each time you hold a line with steadiness, you are sending a message to your nervous system:

"I am safe enough to protect my peace."

Boundaries are how you reestablish agency after experiences of powerlessness.
They teach your body that safety is no longer dependent on the other person's behavior—it comes from your clarity and follow-through.

This work is not about *winning* a co-parenting battle.

It's about reclaiming the energy you've spent managing chaos, proving your point, or softening your truth.

Every clear, calm limit you hold restores a fragment of that energy to your well-being.

The Regulation Ripple

Consistency is the nervous system's love language.

Every time you use your **CBNC voice**—calm, brief, neutral, and consistent—you reinforce safety for everyone in the system.

- You teach the other parent how you will and will not engage.
- You teach your child that peace can exist even when people disagree.
- You teach your own body that protection does not require reactivity.

Your boundary is your child's invisible shield against adult chaos.

It's not the silence between you and your co-parent that heals; it's the steadiness you bring into that silence.

Reflection Prompts—Integration and Intention

- Which boundary has changed your energy the most since starting this chapter?

- What does your nervous system feel like when you hold a boundary successfully—calm, grounded, or proud?

- What is one boundary you will recommit to this week, not out of anger, but out of care for yourself and your child?

Take a deep breath.

That pause between reaction and response—that moment of self-leadership—is the practice.

It's where safety begins again.

Expanding Your Skills

Now that you've learned *where* and *how* to use the CBNC framework, Chapter 8 will expand your practice through **intentional scripts, boundary fatigue recovery, and parallel parenting strategies.**

You've also learned to speak from regulation, to lead with clarity, and to choose consistency over conflict.

In Chapter 8, we'll expand these skills into the relational space—exploring how to use your steadiness to guide your child through stress, transitions, and emotional recovery. You'll move from **regulation in theory** to **regulation in conversation**—the difference between silence and skill.

Boundaries were the practice. Now, we return to the heart of co-parenting: **connection through calm.**

8

Your Regulated Communication & Your Boundaries

Introduction—Turning Your Intention into Interaction

In the previous chapter, you practiced tactical defense: the **CBNC framework**, the **24-Hour Rule**, and firm boundary scripts. That chapter was your flight simulator for moments of crisis—the structured "stop" protocol for when emotions surge.

Now we shift from survival to sustainability.
With your nervous system regulated and your values clarified (see Chapter 6), this chapter focuses on **relational endurance**—the ability to communicate consistently from steadiness rather than reaction.

Every text, every silence, every exchange at the curb carries emotional weight.
Here, communication becomes the living expression of your regulation work.

The goal isn't simply to *avoid harm*—it's to actively *model health*.
You're no longer just stopping escalation; you're teaching your child, through language and tone, what safety sounds like.

You can't control the tone on the other end.
But you can control how much peace you bring to yours.

Your Bridge from Tactical Defense to Relational Presence

Focus	Chapter 7: Your Regulated Communication	Chapter 8: Your Regulated Communication & Your Boundaries
Core Skill	Crisis containment—the *Stop button*	Relational engagement—the *Go button*
Assumption	You are activated and need immediate guardrails.	You are regulated and ready for nuance.
Goal	Prevent escalation.	Model steadiness and repair.
Focus Tools	CBNC rules, boundary scripts, pause protocols	Value-based phrasing, child-centered language, reconnection skills

This progression mirrors nervous-system work: first stabilization, then expansion. You've learned to pause; now you learn to *proceed* with clarity.

Communication Realities—Recognizing Your Patterns

Co-parenting communication carries old residues: history, fear, and expectation. When stress is chronic, communication style becomes an *autonomic reflex*—a nervous-system behavior, not a conscious choice.
Most parents default to one of three unregulated patterns:

1. Over-Communicating (The Anxious/Fighting Pattern)

Long texts. Re-explaining. Emotional venting.
The underlying belief: *"If I clarify enough, they'll finally understand."*
Intent: To gain control or reassurance.
Impact: Escalation and fatigue.
Mantra—"I just need you to understand why this matters."

2. Under-Communicating (The Freezing/Fleeing Pattern)

Avoiding calls or texts. Delaying responses. Withholding updates.
The underlying belief: *"If I stay quiet, I can't be hurt."*
Intent: Self-protection.
Impact: Silence that creates confusion and anxiety.
Mantra—"If I don't engage, it can't hurt me."

3. Triangulating (The Deflecting/Unregulated Pattern)

Using the child as a messenger or emotional buffer.
The underlying belief: *"It's easier if someone else handles it."*
Intent: Efficiency or avoidance.
Impact: Emotional burden on the child; blurred roles.
Mantra—"Tell your mom I'll be late."

Activity 8.1: Deep Dive Self-Check—Your Communication Pattern & Goal

Purpose
To identify your default communication reflex and choose a new, regulated alternative. Complete this exercise when calm. Be honest—you're not grading yourself; you're mapping your nervous system in action.

Use this scale to rate how often each statement reflects your behavior during co-parenting communication. **Rating: 1—Rarely True, 2—Occasionally True, 3—Sometimes True, 4—Often True, 5—Very True**

Pattern Statement	1	2	3	4	5	My Goal Micro-Action
I send long, emotional texts.	☐	☐	☐	☐	☐	Goal: Use the CBNC 3-sentence rule.
I avoid responding when stressed.	☐	☐	☐	☐	☐	Goal: Commit to a 24-hour response time.
I ask my child to pass messages.	☐	☐	☐	☐	☐	Goal: Use the Redirect Script consistently.
I worry that every word will be used against me.	☐	☐	☐	☐	☐	Goal: Review the Child-Centered Prompts before sending.

Follow-Up Reflection
Based on your highest-rated pattern, what emotion or belief drives it?

- Over-communication is often fueled by fear of being misunderstood or judged.
- Under-communication often hides fear of conflict or hopelessness.
- Triangulation often stems from fear of direct confrontation or loss of control.

Reframe
These aren't personality flaws; they're adaptive survival responses.
Recognizing them lets you bring compassion to your own communication habits—and choose something steadier next time.

Once you've identified your communication reflex, you can begin retraining it.
The next section offers a **three-step process** to pause, reset, and respond from a centered state—the bridge between emotional awareness and practical skill.

Regulate, Recalibrate, and Respond (Your Three-Step Filter)

Before you engage in any co-parenting dialogue, your greatest responsibility is not the message itself—it's the *state of the messenger.*
Your nervous system is the first communicator in every exchange. Bringing a regulated body into a difficult interaction ensures that your words reflect your values (Chapter 6) rather than your reactivity.

Recognizing Your Escalation Cycles—Your Perpetual Spiral

Every high-conflict exchange follows the same physiological sequence—a pattern that can only be broken through awareness.
When you can name the stage you're in, you regain choice.

Stage	What Happens	How It Feels
Trigger (Activation)	The other parent's action or tone lands as a blow.	Sudden tension, heart rate spike, mental replay of past conflict.
Reaction (Flooding)	The body floods with adrenaline and defense.	Heat in the chest, urge to prove or fix, tunnel vision.
Escalation (The Spiral)	Words or texts leave before regulation returns.	Argument builds; logic goes offline; history enters the room.
Shut Down (The Crash)	The aftermath—fatigue, shame, silence.	Emotional exhaustion; withdrawal; self-doubt.
Repeat	The next contact begins with residual tension.	The cycle restarts faster each time.

Clinical Insight
Escalation isn't evidence of failure—it's evidence of activation.
Your body is trying to protect you from perceived danger.
Use that awareness as a cue to pause, not to judge.
The pause is the hinge that breaks the loop.

Your Three-Question Response Filter

The pause isn't passive.
It's the moment where reactivity transforms into leadership.
Once you've used a **Regulation Tool** from Chapter 4 (e.g., breathing, grounding, movement), pause and ask yourself these three questions before responding:

1. **What is my highest intention right now—clarity or control?**
   If the answer is control, wait.
   Control belongs to fear; clarity belongs to values.
2. **Does this message honor my most important parenting value?**
   If your core value is *Respect*, does your tone reflect it?
   If it's *Safety*, does this message de-escalate or inflame?
3. **Would I want my child to overhear this exact exchange?**
   This question activates your empathy and accountability faster than any external rule.

Mantra for Your Pause
"Pause is a full sentence."
Sometimes, it's the only one you need.

Reflection Prompts—Recalibration in Real Time

- Which stage of the Escalation Spiral feels most familiar to you?

- What's your physical "tell" that you're entering it?

- Which of the three filter questions stops you most effectively?

- What would change if you treated every co-parenting message as something your child would someday read?

Now that you've learned how to slow your internal response, the next section builds the external framework.

You'll explore **the Seven Guardrails**—clear, values-driven rules for communication that preserve dignity and emotional safety on both sides.

Your Ground Rules for Respectful Communication

Healthy co-parenting doesn't require constant conversation; it requires intentional communication anchored in values.

Respectful communication is not about being agreeable—it's about staying aligned with clarity, safety, and your child's emotional security. These ground rules are the guardrails that keep both you and your child within the lane of regulation.

Your Seven Guardrails (Your Value-Driven Checklist)

Think of these not as etiquette rules but as *nervous-system boundaries*—practices that keep you out of activation and anchored in steadiness.

Guardrail	What it Means	Why it Matters (Trauma Lens)
1. Keep it child-centered.	Every topic must ultimately connect to the child's safety, schedule, or developmental needs.	Focus shifts the nervous system from "defend" to "protect," grounding communication in purpose.
2. Be brief and factual.	Use concise, specific sentences; avoid extra commentary or justification.	Over-explaining is a symptom of anxiety. Brevity signals safety and confidence.

Guardrail	What it Means	Why it Matters (Trauma Lens)
3. Avoid inflammatory language.	Eliminate words that carry emotional charge ("always," "never," "ridiculous," "unfair").	Emotional words activate the other parent's limbic system—facts engage the thinking brain.
4. Time your replies thoughtfully.	Use the **24-Hour Rule** (Chapter 7) or pause until you feel physiologically calm.	Response timing is regulation in motion. Calm delivery equals clear delivery.
5. Never use your child as a messenger.	All communication must remain adult-to-adult, even when it's hard.	Protects the child from triangulation and emotional burden (Chapter 10).
6. Allow space for delayed responses.	Assume the other parent may not be regulated when you reach out.	Patience interrupts the urgency reflex and models emotional maturity.
7. Document only when necessary.	Record only factual, safety-relevant information.	Over-documentation keeps you mentally inside the conflict. Documentation should protect peace, not feed fear.

Each guardrail honors your values of *stability, respect, and safety*—values your child learns by watching you practice them, not by hearing you explain them.

Activity 8.2: Deep Dive—Analyzing Your Hardest Rules

Purpose
To uncover the emotional roots beneath communication habits.
When you understand *why* a rule feels difficult, you can begin to regulate around it.

1. Rule Violation
Which of the seven guardrails do you struggle with most often, and why?

- What emotion drives that difficulty—fear, urgency, guilt, or anger?
- Example: *Rule: Avoid inflammatory language. Fear: If I don't sound strong, I'll be ignored.*

2. Honest Justification

If you were explaining to a therapist why you break that rule, what would your most honest reason be?

- Example: *I answer too quickly because silence feels like losing control.*

---

3. Reframe & Mantra

Create a short, grounding phrase that represents your new intention (3–5 words).

- Examples:
    - *My urgency is not truth.*
    - *Calm is my authority.*
    - *Respect keeps me steady.*

This mantra becomes your anchor—a quick-access cue when you feel pulled toward reactivity.

Scripts & Starters—Communication by Intention

Once your values are defined, they must become *visible*—translated into the tone, pacing, and phrasing of your communication. Predictable, low-energy scripts protect your nervous system from escalation and model regulation for your child.
Every sentence becomes a mirror of your steadiness.

Scripts Organized by Your Intention

Each of the following scripts serves a specific *intention* rather than a reaction.
The more you practice these, the less energy each exchange will take.
They are concise, respectful, and aligned with trauma-informed communication principles.

Intention	Safe/Neutral Script Example	Value Modeled
Inform	"I need to confirm the schedule. Please reply by 6:00 PM today."	Clarity, Responsibility
Request	"There's a meeting on [date/time]. Let me know if you'll attend."	Inclusion, Efficiency
Redirect	"I will only respond when the tone is respectful. Please send a revised message."	Respect, Boundary
De-escalate	"I'm stepping away for now; I'll reply when I'm calm and able to focus on logistics."	Patience, Self-Control

Clinical Note

Predictable scripts recondition your nervous system to associate communication with *control and safety* rather than *chaos and threats*. Each use reinforces the physiological link between *pause and peace*.

Boundaries 101: Clarity Over Control

Boundaries are not about changing the other parent—they are about managing yourself with consistency and dignity.
A regulated boundary is a calm, clear statement of self-governance: *"This is what I will do to stay steady."*

Boundary Type	Definition	Example Statement
Topic Boundary	Defines what belongs in the conversation and what doesn't.	"I will only discuss parenting matters. I won't discuss your finances."
Time Boundary	Defines when you are emotionally and practically available.	"I check communication at 8:00 AM and 6:00 PM."
Emotional Boundary	Defines the tone and energy required for dialogue.	"If the conversation feels attacking, I'll pause and respond later."

Key Insight

Boundaries are not barriers—they are agreements with yourself about how to stay aligned with your values when pressure builds.

Activity 8.3: Boundaries in Action Worksheet—Managing Your Boundary Fatigue

Purpose
To translate abstract limits into observable action and to recognize that enforcing boundaries—especially with a dysregulated co-parent—takes emotional energy.

1. Identify the Boundary Needed

What recurring pattern drains or confuses you the most? Example: *"Repeated last-minute schedule changes."*

2. Define it Clearly

What will you *do* if that pattern repeats? Use positive, action-oriented language. *Example:* *"I will confirm the schedule once, and if no response comes, I'll proceed as planned."*

3. Hold it (Practice)

Write the exact, calm phrase you'll use to communicate the boundary. Then, say it out loud—steady voice, even pace. *Example: "I'll wait until 6:00 PM for confirmation. If I don't hear back, I'll assume we're proceeding with the plan."*

4. Managing Fatigue

Boundary enforcement drains energy, even when done calmly. Name one self-restoring act you'll commit to after holding your line. *Example: "Ten minutes of quiet walking" or "Texting a supportive friend who reminds me I'm doing the right thing."*

Clinical Reminder

Boundaries without follow-through invite chaos; boundaries enforced with calm repetition build trust. Clarity protects your nervous system—and your child learns emotional safety by watching you model it.

Parallel Parenting—When Distance Restores Peace

Some co-parenting dynamics are too charged for traditional collaboration. When communication becomes a repeated source of harm, the most compassionate choice is not more contact—it's less.
Parallel parenting is not a failure of co-parenting; it is a trauma-informed strategy that prioritizes *safety over sameness* and *peace over proximity*.

This model acknowledges that two healthy environments can exist separately. The goal is not to force cooperation—it's to protect stability.
When you reduce friction between homes, you restore predictability for your child's nervous system.

Why Parallel Parenting Works

The body does not distinguish between emotional chaos and physical threat.
Every hostile message, tense hand-off, or unpredictable interaction floods the nervous system with cortisol and adrenaline.
Parallel parenting removes those spikes by creating **consistent, structured boundaries**—predictable exchanges, written communication, and emotional neutrality.

Clinical Insight

When parents cease arguing, the child's body stops having to regulate two nervous systems at once. Their internal stress load decreases dramatically, leading to better sleep, fewer somatic complaints (headaches, stomachaches), and improved focus in school. Distance creates peace, not disconnection.

The Core Principles of Parallel Parenting

Principle	Practice	Why it Matters (Trauma Lens)
Communicate Only Logistics & Safety	Focus strictly on facts: schedules, health, school updates.	Keeps both parents in the prefrontal cortex (logic) and out of limbic activation (emotion).
Use Written Channels Only	Apps like OurFamilyWizard or TalkingParents; no texts or calls.	Written formats remove tone cues, lower emotional reactivity, and maintain a factual record.
Limit In-Person Contact	Use curbside or neutral exchanges with minimal dialogue.	Reduces exposure to verbal and nonverbal triggers.
Accept Silence as an Answer	If no response is required, consider the matter closed.	Breaks the cycle of reactivity by removing the need for validation.

Therapist Note
Parallel parenting transforms survival mode into structure. It teaches both the parent and the child that calm does not require consensus—it only requires consistency.

Activity 8.4: Your Parallel Parenting Plan—Maximizing Space

Purpose
To formalize a plan for minimal, structured contact that protects your nervous system and your child's peace.

1. Your Goal

Define your personal success marker for emotional steadiness.
Example: *"My anxiety level drops from an 8 to a 4 during transitions."*

This becomes your measure of peace, not the other parent's cooperation.

2. Your Exchange Protocol

Decide how hand-offs will occur in a way that minimizes exposure and conflict.
Example: *"We will use curbside drop-offs. The child walks from car to car. There will be zero parent-to-parent verbal contact."*

If third-party support is available (e.g., school staff, grandparent), include that structure as a stabilizing bridge.

3. Your Communication Protocol

Establish your official communication platform and the rules for use.
Example: *"All scheduling and updates will occur through the co-parenting app only. I will not respond to texts or personal emails."*

This boundary replaces verbal triggers with written clarity.

4. Your Acceptance Mantra

Every time your co-parent does something outside your control, repeat this personal anchor phrase: *"That is their house; this is mine. I can only control the peace inside my home."*

Acceptance is not surrender—it's strategy.
You're choosing to conserve energy for what truly matters: your child's emotional safety and your own calm.

Child-Centered Communication and Repair

The goal of regulated communication is not to win the argument—it's to model emotional health for your child.

When your words and tone remain steady, you become the calm mirror they need in a divided system. You show them that connection and accountability can coexist with difference.

Every boundary you hold, every pause you take, and every repair you initiate teaches your child this truth:

"Conflict doesn't destroy love; it invites repair."

Child-Centered Prompts (Focusing Forward)

When the history between you and your co-parent feels heavy, keep your focus forward—toward your child's stability, not the past.

The language you use is not just logistical; it's neurological. Each calm message signals safety to both your nervous system and your child's.

Prompt Type	Example	Value Modeled
Agreement	"To support [child] through this transition, I'd like to stick to the agreed-upon time."	Reliability, Predictability
Cooperation	"Can we agree on a plan to help them feel stable?"	Collaboration, Shared Focus
Shared Goal	"Even if we disagree, I know we both want what's best for them."	Mutual Care, Emotional Safety

Clinical Insight

These statements calm the body because they anchor attention in the present and reaffirm shared purpose. When you communicate as though the child is emotionally "in the room," your tone naturally becomes more protective and less reactive.

Conflict Repair—Reopening Dialogue

Repair is how respect breathes again after a rupture.
It is the process of *rebuilding connection without blame*—modeling emotional accountability for your child and emotional maturity for your co-parent.
Repair doesn't require agreement. It requires humility and a return to steadiness.

Repair Moment	Example Script	Modeled Skill
Repairing a Harsh Message	"I realize my last message sounded sharp. I needed to send it from a calmer place. Here is the factual update on the school form."	Accountability without shame
Repairing Silence	"I needed space before responding to ensure I was regulated. Here's where I am now on the logistics."	Emotional ownership and transparency
Repairing a Conversation	"Can we reset and return just to the main issue of the schedule?"	Resetting tone and focus
Receiving Repair	(No script needed) Simply meet the new, calmer tone without rehashing the past.	Acceptance and emotional restraint

Therapist Reflection
Repair is not weakness; it's regulation in action. It shows your child that accountability and love can occupy the same breath. When you model this, your child learns that safety isn't the absence of mistakes—it's the presence of return.

Reflection & Progress Marker—Anchoring Your Peace

Communication and boundaries are emotional labor.
Each message you regulate, each pause you choose, and each line you hold is an act of nervous system repair.
Before you move forward, pause to recognize the emotional strength it takes to communicate with clarity and calm in a system built on conflict.

This reflection is your grounding checkpoint—a moment to trace the signals your body sends, the tools that help you respond, and the commitments that keep you anchored in peace.

Activity 8.5: Your Triggers and Commitment Map

Purpose

To map the connection between your body's activation cues and your chosen regulation responses, reinforcing awareness through repetition and self-compassion.

Trigger	Body Signal (Chapter 3)	Core Regulation Tool (Chapter 4)	Action (Chapter 7 Script)
Criticism/Attack	Tight chest, rapid breath.	4–6 Breathing Anchor, Hand on Chest.	"I'll revisit this later when I'm regulated."
Silence/Avoidance	Shoulder tension, stomach clench.	Foot Anchor, Light Movement.	"Checking in tomorrow—noted."
Urgency Demand	Racing pulse, hot cheeks.	Pause & Delay.	"I'll respond by evening."

Personal Application

My Trigger
(What activates me the most right now—tone, silence, control?)

My Second Trigger
(Another pattern that consistently destabilizes me.)

Final Commitment Statement

"My personal mantra that supports my steady communication is:

Boundary Focus

"The one boundary I will absolutely hold this week is:

Closing Thoughts

Every message, silence, or limit you set can be an act of peace.
You are not just maintaining communication—you are rewriting the nervous system's relationship with safety, one calm exchange at a time.
Repeat your mantra until peace feels less like effort and more like home.

You've learned to steady your words, your tone, and your boundaries—skills that transform chaos into coherence.
Each pause, each rewritten message, and each regulated exchange has rebuilt safety one interaction at a time.

Now it's time to extend that steadiness beyond communication and into the daily rhythm of your child's world. Consistency—of tone, structure, and emotional presence—is the next form of regulation. It's what turns safety from a momentary feeling into a predictable environment.

In Chapter 9, you'll learn how to create that rhythm: how to make your home, your routines, and your responses a stable beat your child can rely on—no matter what storms surround them.

9

Creating Consistency Across Your Child's Homes

Introduction—The Steady Beat Beneath Two Rhythms

Co-parenting doesn't always mean parenting the same way—and that's okay.
This chapter isn't about perfect alignment between homes; it's about helping your child
feel safe, seen, and supported, no matter where they are.

Consistency is not uniformity. It's more than matching rules or routines. It's the
predictable rhythm of tone, presence, and follow-through that tells your child: *"You can
count on me."*
When a child's world shifts between households, they rely on that rhythm to find their
footing. Predictability gives children something to hold onto when their world shifts,
allowing their nervous system to relax and trust that safety exists even when
circumstances change.

Predictability is safety you can feel.

Your Bridge from Communication to Climate

In the previous chapters, you learned to manage the energy between adults—how to hold boundaries, regulate in the moment, and communicate from intention rather than reactivity.

This chapter shifts focus from the adult dynamic to the child's nervous system.

- **Chapter 7—Your Regulated Communication:** Focused on managing high-stakes interactions between adults. It helps with building safety through structure in high-stakes exchanges.

- **Chapter 8—Your Regulated Communication & Your Boundaries:** Focused on sustained, value-driven dialogue between adults. It helps with cultivating value-based interaction and relational steadiness.

- **Chapter 9—Creating Consistency Across Your Child's Homes:** Focuses on creating a stable, predictable environment for the child. It helps with translating that steadiness into the child's daily environment—the routines, rituals, and tone that make safety repeatable.

You've learned to manage the external storms; now you'll build the calm within your home—the steady climate that tells your child, "You can rest here."

Vignette—The Emotional Backpack

Eight-year-old **Jayden** double-checks his backpack every Thursday night.
He's not worried about forgetting his toothbrush—he's scanning for continuity.
The stuffed bear, the bedtime book, the blue hoodie—each object helps him carry a thread of sameness from Mom's place to Dad's house.

Children pack *objects*; parents pack *reassurance*.
Every predictable phrase, every calm transition, every consistent bedtime ritual tells your child:

"Even when the world around you shifts, my love and stability do not."

Your consistency is the invisible reassurance that travels with them.

Why Consistency Matters—The Science of Predictability

The human nervous system—your child's and your own—thrives on rhythm and repetition.
Predictable routines lower cortisol, regulate the stress response, and quietly communicate to the brain: *"The world is safe enough to connect, learn, and grow."*

When children can predict what's coming next—what time dinner happens, how a goodbye will sound, or which tone of voice greets them—they settle.
When those cues change suddenly or depend on which "version" of a parent or environment they encounter, the body moves from **connection** to **protection.**
That's when you see vigilance, anxiety, regression, or shutdown.

Consistency is not control. It's communication at the nervous-system level:

"You don't need to brace. You are safe to be yourself."

Neuroscience Snapshot—Consistency and the Amygdala

The amygdala—the brain's built-in alarm system—constantly scans for signs of threat or unpredictability.
When routines are stable and adult tones remain even, the alarm quiets.
This simple predictability allows the prefrontal cortex—the thinking, reasoning, and empathy center—to stay online.

Key Neurobiological Truths

- Predictable routines lower baseline cortisol (the body's primary stress hormone).

- The amygdala relaxes when sensory and relational cues stay consistent (same voice tone, same routine, same language).

- The prefrontal cortex stays engaged when surprise is replaced with structure—improving impulse control, learning, and empathy.

Clinical Summary
Consistency is the language the nervous system trusts.
Predictability tells the body: *"I don't have to brace anymore."*

What Children Need Most (by Stage)

Regardless of age, all children crave the same four safety ingredients: **Predictability, Consistency, Emotional Safety, and Clear Boundaries.**

Age	What They Need Most	Common Signs of Stress at Transition
Toddlers (1–3)	Repetition, sensory comfort, and a familiar caregiver presence.	Sleep disruptions, extreme clinginess, regression (potty training, speech).
School-Age (6–12)	Predictable rules, consistent expectations, and transition rituals between homes.	Comparison between households, testing limits, physical symptoms (stomachaches, headaches).
Teens (13+)	Emotional steadiness, clear boundaries, and connection without control.	Withdrawal, sarcasm, avoidance, or attempts to emotionally "parent" adults.

If your child's behavior changes dramatically after hand-offs, it's rarely rebellion—it's communication.

They may not have the words to say, *"I don't know what version of home I'm walking into."*

Your calm, consistent presence is the antidote.

Your Emotional Predictability

The most powerful consistency you offer is **emotional predictability**—knowing what version of you they will meet. Will you be calm or reactive? Present or distracted?

Your tone is the climate your child breathes.

Children may not remember every word you say, but they remember the *temperature* of your presence. The steadiness of your tone, the pacing of your breath, and the speed of your repair teach the body: *"This is what safe feels like."*

Clinical Insight

Children can tolerate frustration, sadness, or change when the *emotional climate* stays familiar. Predictability in tone is the bridge between moments of rupture and moments of repair.

How to Build Your Emotional Predictability in Real Time

Emotional consistency is not about perfection—it's about *pattern*. Your child doesn't need you to stay calm all the time; they need to trust that when things get tense, calm will return.

To build that trust, apply your **Regulation Toolkit** (Chapter 4) in daily, micro moments.

1. **Use Steady Phrases**
   During moments of stress, lean on simple, repetitive language.
   Say: "You're safe. I'm here. We'll figure this out together."
   These phrases regulate both nervous systems at once—yours and theirs.

2. **Repair Quickly (See Chapter 10)**
   If you lose your temper, apologize promptly and calmly.
   A short, honest repair—"That wasn't how I wanted to speak. I'm sorry."—restores safety faster than silence or justification.
   Aim to repair within the hour. The sooner your child sees safety restored, the sooner their body learns that conflict doesn't equal danger.

3. **Create Predictable Rituals**
   Begin and end interactions with consistent cues—your *signature of steadiness*.

   o   The same goodbye phrase.

   o   The same three-second hug.

   o   The same "You're home" greeting.
       These micro-rituals create rhythm. Rhythm builds security.

Activity 9.1: Deep Dive—Tone-Tracker Journal

Purpose

To gain awareness of your emotional baseline and identify the times you need extra regulation. For three days, track your tone during these three key transition moments:

Moment	Tone Rating (1–5, 5=Calm)	What Helped Me Stay Steady/Threw Me Off?	Child's Body Language Shift?
Morning Rush:			
Hand-off or Pickup:			
Bedtime:			

End-of-Day Reflections

- What version of me did my child get most today—rushed, reactive, or regulated?

- Which moment is calling for gentler structure, not more effort?

- What support or adjustment could make that steadiness easier tomorrow?

Integration Tip

The goal isn't to score yourself—it's to *see yourself.* Awareness turns emotional habit into emotional choice.

Where Structural Consistency Matters Most

While identical rules across homes aren't required, a predictable rhythm in your own home is vital.

Children don't need *sameness*—they need *stability.*

They need to know that certain anchors will hold no matter where they are, especially when the other environment feels unpredictable.

Your steadiness doesn't erase differences between homes—it gives your child the nervous-system rest they need to tolerate them.

Mapping Your Routines Side by Side (The Clarity Check)

The goal is not to compare parenting styles—it's to identify which differences create confusion or stress for your child, and which ones they can adapt to naturally.

Category	At My Home (The Rhythm I Control)	At Co-Parent's Home (As Known)	Stress Level on Child (1–5)
Sleep/Bedtime	8:30 PM story + lights out	Late bedtime, screens allowed	4
Meals	Family dinner at 6 PM	On-the-go or fast food often	3

Category	At My Home (The Rhythm I Control)	At Co-Parent's Home (As Known)	Stress Level on Child (1–5)
Discipline	Calm conversation + natural consequence	Unclear/inconsistent	5
Homework/Structure	After snack time, same workspace	Late evening/inconsistent	4
Transition Ritual	Hug + affirmation phrase	Quick car-to-car drop-off	4

Reflection Prompts

- Which differences score the highest (4–5) for your child's stress?

- What single, stabilizing routine can you reinforce in *your* home this week to counterbalance that stress?

- How can you communicate that routine as a source of safety rather than control?

Clinical Insight

Consistency in one home can buffer inconsistency in the other.
The goal isn't synchronization—it's nervous-system regulation through reliable cues.

The Tiered-Consistency Framework (Accepting the Reality Track)

Consistency looks different depending on the level of cooperation in your co-parenting dynamic.
This framework helps you focus your energy where it counts—within your sphere of control.

Track	Description	Consistency Focus (Your Home)
Cooperative (Green)	Regular communication, shared decisions, moderate trust.	Align 3–4 routines (bedtime, school rules, communication tone). Use shared calendars or joint family chats.
Hybrid (Yellow)	Partial cooperation, intermittent tension, limited collaboration.	Align 1–2 anchor routines (e.g., screen time, homework flow). Respect separate boundaries; keep topics strictly child-focused.
Parallel (Red)	Minimal contact, high conflict, or safety concerns.	Build unshakable rituals within your own home. Focus on emotional steadiness, clear structure, and transition predictability.

Every track can still raise resilient children.
When one home is unpredictable, **safety in your home becomes the nervous system's constant.**

Clinical Note

Children raised in one predictable environment and one unpredictable environment don't automatically become anxious—they adapt to the rhythm they can rely on. Your job is to make *your rhythm* their refuge.

Transition Planning—Keeping the Edges Soft

Transitions—those hand-offs between homes—are the predictable storms of co-parenting.
You can't stop the weather, but you can build the shelter.

For children, every exchange is a moment of reorientation. Their bodies shift between rhythms, tones, and rules. When those transitions feel calm and predictable, their nervous system learns: *"Change doesn't mean danger."*

Your role is to soften the edges of those transitions—not by perfect coordination, but through **intentional steadiness.**

Tools for Transition Support

Each of the following tools supports a specific aspect of emotional regulation—yours and your child's.

- **Bridge Item**
  A comfort object (stuffed animal, bracelet, journal, blanket) that always travels between homes.
  It acts as a *sensory anchor,* linking safety across two environments.

- **Visual Calendar**
  A physical or digital calendar marked with colors or stickers for each home.
  This reduces surprise and helps children externalize time, decreasing anticipatory anxiety.

- **Switch-Day Script**
  Keep goodbyes short, steady, and ritualized.
  Say: "I love you. I'll see you Friday. I'm here when you get back."
  Repetition is a nervous-system signal—predictable words equal safety.

- **Parent-to-Parent Log (If Safe)**
  Use a neutral co-parenting app for brief factual updates (e.g., "Homework complete; mild cold; slept well.")
  No opinions, emotions, or commentary. Facts only. The goal is clarity, not connection.

Activity 9.2: The Hand-Off Regulation Plan

Purpose
To create a structured, predictable response plan for the most vulnerable moments—
drop-offs and pick-ups.

Stage	My Action	Why it Matters (Trauma Lens)
1. Before Hand-Off	Use the 4-in/6-out breath for five full cycles before opening the car or front door.	Breath signals to your vagus nerve that the environment is safe, lowering activation before contact.
2. During Hand-Off	Maintain a neutral face and posture. Speak no more than three factual sentences (see Chapter 7).	Predictability in your tone keeps your child's amygdala quiet and models emotional containment.
3. After Hand-Off (The Pause)	Wait one minute before checking your phone or starting a new task. Repeat your mantra—"I did my job. My calm is their safety."	Post-contact regulation prevents re-entry into rumination or fight-flight mode.
4. Child Check-In Ritual	When your child arrives, start with a neutral fact-based question: "What are you reading?" "What made you laugh today?"	Shifts focus from emotional probing to relational ease; gives the child permission to land gently.

Integration Tip
Keep this plan printed in your car or saved as a phone note.
You can't control the exchange energy—but you can script your steadiness.

When You Can't Agree—Acceptance as Consistency

There will be times when your co-parent refuses to align. This may never change—and that truth hurts. But your power lies in **radical acceptance**: protecting your nervous system from the illusion of control.

- **Avoid Comparison Language**
  Never say, "At your mom's/dad's house…" Comparison forces the child to choose and breeds loyalty conflict.

- **Use Neutral Reassurance**
  "Different homes have different rules. You are safe and loved in both."
  This single sentence can rewire a child's sense of belonging.

- **Redefine the Win**
  Steadiness in *one* home is enough to raise a resilient child. Consistency in your emotional climate provides half the nervous-system stability they need.

Acceptance is not surrender—it's nervous-system alignment. It models peace in imperfection and teaches your child: *"I can be calm even when things aren't equal."*

Reflection and Commitment—The Consistency Compass

Consistency is not built in grand gestures—it's built in the quiet repetitions that teach the nervous system: *"This is what safety feels like."*
Each calm routine, each predictable transition, and each gentle repair becomes a compass point your child can return to when life feels uncertain.

You've learned how to stabilize communication, tone, and structure.
Now, you'll translate those insights into daily micro-commitments—the small, steady actions that create a sense of sanctuary in your home.

Activity 9.3: The Consistency Commitment

Purpose
To transform awareness into tangible action.
Use this activity as a living agreement with yourself—a short list of commitments that turn your regulation into rhythm.

Focus Area	Reflection Prompt	Your Response
1. The Anchor	What is one routine I can keep steady no matter what the co-parent does?	
2. The Adjustment	Where can I soften my expectations or release control of the other home?	
3. The Alignment	What is one shared topic I can clarify, confirm, or document this month (e.g., school, medical, travel)?	
4. The Affirmation	What single sentence do I want my child to remember about the feeling of safety in our home?	

Focus Area	Reflection Prompt	Your Response

Integration Tip

Keep your Consistency Compass visible—on your phone notes, fridge, or journal.
Return to it weekly. It's not a checklist; it's a grounding map.

Closing Thoughts

Every stable rhythm you hold—morning greetings, bedtime rituals, tone in transitions—writes an emotional blueprint of safety into your child's body.
They may not remember every word you say, but they will carry the *feeling* of your steadiness for life.

One day, your child will mirror your steadiness in their own storms.

That is your legacy of calm.

You've built steadiness into your communication and structure.
Your home now breathes with rhythm—predictable, safe, and clear. But even within that structure, ruptures will happen. Voices will rise, boundaries will bend, and emotions will spill over. This isn't failure; it's family.

The next chapter explores the art and science of *repair*—how to help your child recover from moments of conflict or inconsistency, and how to rebuild trust through your own accountability and regulation.

Repair is the heartbeat of resilience.
Consistency gives your child safety; repair teaches them that safety can return, even after it's lost.

PART IV: Child-Centered Protection

When One Parent Heals, the Whole System Begins to Breathe

"Children don't need perfect parents. They need adults who repair faster than they rupture."

Nahomie Julien, LCSW, CADCII, CAMSII, CDVSII

10

Repair and Resilience: Healing Your Child in the Middle

Introduction—You as Your Child's Buffer

You've spent the last chapters building a sturdy internal foundation: mapping your co-parenting reality, understanding your survival patterns, and mastering your regulation tools.
This inner work was not selfish—it was the most selfless act you could offer your child.

A regulated parent is a healing parent.
Your steadiness becomes your child's safety net—the buffer that absorbs the unpredictability of adult conflict and shields their developing nervous system from chronic stress.

The Illusion of Hiding Conflict

Children always know. Even without words, they read the emotional temperature of a room—the held breath, the clipped tone, the tension in your shoulders. Conflict energy cannot be hidden; it's transmitted physiologically.

When children sense tension without understanding it, their nervous system fills in the blanks—often assuming they are the cause.

The goal, therefore, isn't to eliminate conflict; it's to model recovery.

Your child's resilience depends not on your perfection, but on your willingness to **repair**.

Your Core Task—Modeling Recovery, Not Perfection

Your most critical parenting task during and after separation is not to prevent all stress, but to show what recovery looks like after rupture. Every family system experiences tension; what defines emotional health is how quickly and compassionately safety is restored.

Children learn resilience by witnessing repair—watching a parent apologize, self-regulate, and reestablish connection. In those moments, they internalize one of life's most powerful lessons: *Safety can return after conflict.*

Your Child's Need for Coherence

A child's developing brain depends on **coherence**—a narrative that makes emotional and cognitive sense. They need a story where the conflict belongs to the adults, not to them.

Message Type	Example	Impact on the Child
Coherent Message	"Mom and Dad are getting divorced because we couldn't agree on how to be partners, but we both agree on how to be your parents. Your job is to be a kid."	Promotes emotional safety and clarity; separates love from conflict.
Incoherent Message	"The divorce is because your dad/mom is difficult. You need to be happy at my house."	Forces the child into loyalty conflict; fractures their internal sense of safety.

Your regulated communication (see Chapter 7) is the delivery system for coherence and safety.

Every calm sentence you speak becomes a nervous-system message: *"You don't have to carry this."*

Integration Note (for Parents and Clinicians)
When parents narrate conflict with coherence and regulation, children's cortisol levels drop measurably faster after stress.
In therapy, invite parents to **rehearse the Coherent Message** until it feels natural. The body remembers safety when language aligns with calm.

Summary Thought
The foundation of repair begins with coherence. When your child can make sense of what's happening without feeling responsible for it, they stop trying to manage your emotions—and can finally return to being a child.

Your Power of Repair—The Antidote to Rupture

Repair is the single greatest act of love, accountability, and nervous-system leadership you can offer your child.
It is the action that follows every rupture—whether that rupture looks like yelling, anxious withdrawal, crying in front of them, or engaging in conflict within their earshot.

Repair communicates this essential truth:
Mistakes happen, but safety always returns.

Children do not need perfect parents; they need parents who know how to restore safety after disconnection.
Every repair you initiate teaches the developing brain a critical emotional skill—how to recover from relational stress without shame or avoidance.

Modeling Accountability—Your Trauma-Informed Apology

A trauma-informed apology focuses not on defending your intention, but on owning your impact and modeling regulation.
It shows your child that love is not fragile and that responsibility can coexist with kindness.

Many parents default to **two ineffective forms of apology**:

1. **The Minimizing Apology:** "I'm sorry you felt upset."
   → This centers the child's reaction instead of the parent's action.

2. **The Conditional Apology:** "I'm sorry, but you were being difficult."
   → This shifts accountability away from the adult and reinforces blame.

A trauma-informed apology repairs trust because it meets the child's nervous system where the rupture occurred—at the level of safety.

Your Three-Part Trauma-Informed Apology Framework

Part	Focus	Script Example (After Yelling)	What the Child Learns
1. Acknowledge Impact	Validate the child's experience without defensiveness.	"I see that I scared you when I raised my voice. That was not okay."	*My feelings are valid.*
2. Own the Action	Take full responsibility for your nervous system's reaction.	"My body felt really frustrated and overwhelmed, and I should have walked into another room to use my breath."	*Adults are responsible for their own emotions.*
3. State the Plan	Give the child a sense of safety through a concrete next step.	"Next time I feel that overwhelmed, I'm going to use my 4–6 Breathing Anchor before I talk. Thank you for forgiving me."	*I can trust my parent to fix their mistakes.*

This format is not just emotional—it's neurological.
When a parent repairs calmly, the child's amygdala (the brain's alarm system) settles, cortisol decreases, and their body re-learns that safety can return after fear.

Activity 10.1: Deep Dive—Drafting Your Repair Script

Goal

To internalize your three-part apology so it becomes a reflex, even during stressful moments.

Practice these three common scenarios until your language feels natural.

1. **Your Yelling Rupture**

   You lost your temper over a forgotten homework assignment.

   Write your full three-part apology after you've regulated yourself.

   Tip: Focus less on the content (the homework) and more on the emotional repair (safety and tone).

2. **Your Anxiety Rupture**

   Your child saw you crying or panicking after a difficult interaction with your co-parent.

   Draft the three-part apology that explains your emotional state as an adult feeling, not the child's fault.

   Example: "I was having big feelings about something between adults. You did nothing wrong. I took a breath, and now I'm okay."

3. **Your Criticizing Rupture**

   You said something negative about the co-parent, and your child overheard.

   Write the three-part apology that addresses the loyalty conflict directly and repairs the trust.

Example: "You heard me say something unkind. That was not fair to you or your other parent. I was upset, but I should not have said that. You never have to choose sides."

Integration Note (for Parents and Clinicians)

For clinicians: Invite clients to role-play their repair scripts out loud.

For parents: Practice saying your apology while making gentle eye contact and slowing your breathing.

The nervous system learns through repetition—the more calmly you repair, the faster your child's body learns to trust safety again.

Summary Thought

Repair doesn't erase the rupture—it rewires the memory.

Each time you return to your child with accountability and calm, you are literally teaching their body, *"Love can survive conflict."*

Your Child's Regulation Toolkit: Skills for Stress

You cannot directly regulate your child—but you can *co-regulate* with them.

You lend them your calm until their own nervous system learns to find it.

When you model steadiness, your child's brain and body borrow your regulation as a template for safety. Over time, those repeated moments become internalized—what neuroscience calls *interoceptive awareness*—the ability to notice and name what's happening inside the body.

Teaching Feelings Language—From Head to Body

Children first experience emotions through sensations, not words.

Helping them connect feelings to physical cues turns vague overwhelm into something understandable and manageable.

Your Prompt

"Tell me where you feel that worry in your body."

Your Child's New Vocabulary

"My tummy feels tight."

"My hands feel hot."

"My legs feel heavy."

This simple shift—from *thinking about* feelings to *noticing them in the body*—is one of the most powerful self-regulation tools a child can learn.

You practiced this skill in Chapter 3; now, you're teaching it forward.

Clinical Note

When children can name where a feeling lives in their body, the prefrontal cortex (reasoning brain) begins to reconnect with the limbic system (emotional brain). This is the neurological bridge between dysregulation and recovery.

Co-Regulating Your Child—Matching Their Zone

Just as you use specific tools for your own zones, you help your child differently depending on whether they are in *Hyper-Arousal* (too much energy) or *Hypo-Arousal* (too little energy).

Co-regulation is not about control—it's about **attunement**: matching their state so you can gently guide them back toward balance.

Child's Zone	Behavior (Signal)	Parent's Co-Regulation Tool (Lending Calm)
Hyper-Arousal (Anxiety, Tantrum, Clinging)	Fast heart rate, intense crying, frantic movement.	**Rhythm and Pressure:** Rocking, deep pressure hugs (if accepted), a steady, low voice, rhythmic counting aloud. Predictable rhythm tells their nervous system "You are safe."

Child's Zone	Behavior (Signal)	Parent's Co-Regulation Tool (Lending Calm)
Hypo-Arousal (Shutdown, Withdrawal, Numbness)	Flat voice, blank stare, heavy limbs, refusal to engage.	**Gentle Activation:** A short walk outside, a cool drink (temperature shift), naming colors in the room, or light, playful movement. Movement tells their body "It's okay to wake back up."

Clinician Note

When guiding parents, emphasize rhythm, breath, and tone. A parent's voice, breathing pace, and facial expression serve as biofeedback—each cue informs the child's nervous system whether connection or caution is required.

Activity 10.2: Deep Dive—Your Co-Regulation Game

Goal

To create a personalized Co-Regulation Game Plan for your child.
This plan helps both parent and child recognize triggers and match tools to zones with confidence.

1. Your Child's Hyper-Arousal Trigger

Name the situation that most often pushes your child outside their window (e.g., "transitions," "homework pressure," "separation goodbyes").

2. Your Child's Hyper-Arousal Tool

Identify one reliable tool that helps them calm down (e.g., "weighted blanket," "five minutes of quiet reading," "gentle back massage," "rocking on the swing").

3. Your Child's Hypo-Arousal Signal

Describe what shutdown looks like for them (e.g., "silence," "flat tone," "avoiding eye contact," "saying 'I don't care'").

4. Your Child's Hypo-Arousal Tool

Choose one gentle activation tool that helps them re-engage (e.g., "a sour candy," "jumping jacks for 30 seconds," "dancing to familiar music").

Integration Reflection

Once your plan is written, practice using one tool daily *before* stress arises. The brain learns calm through repetition, not crisis.

Therapeutic Tip

Invite your child to help design the plan. When they choose their own strategies, they experience agency—not correction—which strengthens self-trust and long-term emotional regulation.

Summary Thought

You don't teach calm through words—you teach it through presence.
Every moment you lend your steadiness; your child's body learns the same language.

Protecting Your Child from Loyalty Conflict

This is where your boundary work (Chapter 7) becomes a direct act of emotional protection.
Your child's nervous system cannot stay regulated if they feel responsible for keeping peace between two adults.
The task is not to make both homes identical—it's to ensure your child never has to choose, defend, or protect either parent.

Children thrive when they are freed from divided loyalty and given permission to belong fully in both homes.

The "Two Homes, Two Rules" Philosophy

Your child is not a traitor for adapting to different structures.
They are simply doing what emotionally intelligent children do—adjusting to survive in multiple environments.

Your role is to make that adaptation safe.
Explicitly grant them permission to love both parents and to follow each home's rules without guilt or secrecy.

Your Script
"At Mom's house, the rule is lights out at 9:00 PM.
At Dad's house, the rule is 9:30 PM. Both rules are okay. You just follow the rule for the house you're in. I trust you to do that."

This reassurance removes the hidden anxiety of having to secretly manage two sets of expectations.
It teaches your child a powerful truth: *different does not mean dangerous.*

Clinical Note
This approach strengthens attachment security. When children sense permission to attach

freely to both parents, their stress hormones (especially cortisol) stabilize, and they develop greater emotional flexibility.

Your Boundary—Never Triangulate

Triangulation is the most corrosive form of emotional enmeshment in co-parenting. It happens when a child is used as a bridge, a messenger, or a buffer between two adults in conflict.
Over time, it rewires their brain for hypervigilance and guilt, teaching them that love equals emotional labor.

A child must never be used to:

- Carry messages, documents, or payments between homes.

- Report on the other parent's activities ("What did Dad eat for dinner?").

- Serve as a confidante or emotional caretaker for a parent's pain.

Healthy parenting means taking the weight of adult dynamics off the child's shoulders and returning it to where it belongs—yours.

Activity 10.3: Deep Dive—Role-Playing Your Loyalty Boundary

Goal
To create clear, neutral scripts that remove your child from adult business while keeping connection and warmth intact.
Practice these scripts aloud so your tone stays calm and protective, not defensive.

1. The Report Scenario
Your child says, "Mom said you were 15 minutes late picking me up yesterday."

Your Regulated Response
(Neutral tone)

"Thank you for letting me know, but that's an adult issue for your mom and me to handle. You don't have to worry about that. Let's talk about your field trip."

Your Child Learns
"I don't have to carry tension between my parents."

---

2. The Emotional Question
Your child asks, "Are you sad we don't live together anymore?"

Your Regulated Response
(Compassionate tone)
"That's a big question. Sometimes I do feel sad—and that's okay. But I'm always happy and proud to be your parent. That never changes. You didn't cause that sadness."

Your Child Learns
"Sadness can exist without blame."

---

3. The Message Delivery
Your child hands you a note from the co-parent.

Your Regulated Response
(Gentle, steady tone)
"Thank you for bringing this to me. From now on, your job is just to enjoy being a kid. All adult notes go through the parenting app—that's my job to handle, not yours."

Your Child Learns
"I am safe from being in the middle."

Integration Note (for Parents and Clinicians)

- **For Parents:** Practice these responses before transitions. The nervous system learns safety through repetition, not reaction.

- **For Clinicians:** Use role-play to help parents regulate their tone; the words matter less than the energy. The goal is calm containment, not explanation.

Summary Thought

Every time you protect your child from the emotional crossfire, you repair their belief that love is safe. Your boundary isn't a wall—it's a shield made of steadiness, giving your child the freedom to just be a child.

Fostering Resilience: Your Long-Term View

Resilience is not about avoiding pain—it's about building the capacity to recover from it. Your child will face stress, disappointment, and loss throughout life; your task is to show them that those experiences can be survived and integrated, not feared or denied.

When you model calm accountability, your child learns: *"Safety can return, even after rupture."* This belief becomes the foundation for their emotional stability in adulthood.

Teaching Agency—Countering Helplessness

Divorce and family rupture can make children feel powerless, as if life happens *to* them instead of *through* them.
The regulated parent's goal is to **restore agency**—the child's internal sense of control and influence over their world.

When a child experiences appropriate agency, their brain moves from helpless freeze to engagement and confidence.
They stop bracing for life and start participating in it.

Ways to Build Agency:
- **Give Your Child Choices**
  Let your child choose what to pack, how to decorate their space, or what they'd

like to do after a stressful transition.
Choice communicates: "You still have influence."

- **Validate Effort, Not Perfection**
  "I know transitions are hard, and I'm proud of how you packed your bag yourself."
  Validation communicates: "You can do hard things."

Clinical Insight
Research in trauma recovery (Siegel, Perry, van der Kolk) shows that a sense of control—even in small, safe decisions—lowers stress hormones and increases resilience.
Agency is the antidote to helplessness.

Reflection—Your Legacy of Steadiness

The divorce or separation is part of your family story, but it does not have to be the *defining* part.
What defines the legacy is how you repair, rebuild, and remain steady in the aftermath.

Your consistent, regulated presence becomes the blueprint for your child's own future relationships—how they handle conflict, express emotion, and recover from rupture.
Your child will inherit not your perfection, but your pattern of repair.

Activity 10.4: Deep Dive—Your Legacy of Resilience

Goal
To clarify the emotional and relational lessons you are intentionally passing on.
This reflection helps you transform personal pain into generational healing.

1. Your Old Lesson
What was the most painful or unhealthy lesson about love, safety, or conflict you absorbed in your childhood or marriage—one you fear repeating?
Example: "Love means staying quiet to keep the peace."

2. Your New Lesson (Conflict)

What do you want your child to learn about conflict by watching how you use your regulation tools and boundaries?

Example: "Conflict can be uncomfortable, but it doesn't have to destroy connection."

3. Your New Lesson (Love)

What do you want your child to know about love and safety?

Example: "Love isn't earned through perfection. Safety can always be restored through repair."

4. Your Child's North Star

Write one short, powerful sentence that captures the essence of the resilience you hope your child carries forward.

Example: "Even when life shifts, I can find my balance again."

Integration Note (for Clinicians and Parents)

- For **parents**, read your North Star statement aloud once a week—out loud, with intention. Let your body hear it.

- For **clinicians**, encourage parents to write this statement on a card for their child's memory box or to include it in a bedtime ritual.

You are not just parenting your child; you are re-parenting your lineage. Every act of repair, regulation, and reflection builds a new inheritance—one rooted in steadiness, safety, and love that endures.

Closing Thoughts

You've learned to apologize without defensiveness, to co-regulate when emotions run high, and to repair ruptures with honesty and steadiness.
These skills form the foundation of psychological safety—showing your child that love is not perfection, but repair.

Now, the focus widens.
Up to this point, you've worked on calming the storm within yourself and rebuilding trust through your behavior. In Chapter 11, you will move beyond the *response* to the *understanding*—from managing your child's distress to recognizing the meaning behind it.

We'll explore how children experience divorce and co-parenting through their developmental lens—how their nervous system, emotions, and sense of self are shaped by the environment around them.
This next chapter will guide you in reading your child's signals with empathy, interpreting behavior as communication, and offering consistent presence even when they can't articulate what they need.

The goal is not to fix every feeling, but to understand the message it carries. Your steadiness will become the mirror through which your child learns that emotional truth can exist safely within connection.

11

Understanding & Supporting Your Child

Introduction—Returning to the Heart of Co-Parenting

You've built your structure: regulation (Chapter 4), communication (Chapters 7–8), and stability (Chapter 9).

Now we return to the reason this work exists at all: your child.

This chapter isn't about analyzing or fixing them. It's about developing deep empathy for what your child carries between two emotional worlds—and learning how to meet that weight with presence, curiosity, and steadiness.

Your task is not perfection; it's perception.
Children don't tell us how they feel; they *show* us. The goal is to learn to see behavior as communication rather than disobedience—to hear the message beneath the reaction.

Vignette—Maya's Silence

Nine-year-old Maya used to tell her mother stories about her day.
After the divorce, the stories stopped. When her mom asked, "How was school?" Maya shrugged, "It's fine."

Weeks later, in therapy, she whispered, "If I talk, someone gets mad."

Maya wasn't being defiant—she was being strategic. She had learned that her words could upset someone she loved.

So she traded truth for safety.

Children in divided homes often learn to edit themselves—to protect their parents from discomfort or conflict.

Your task is to build a space where your child's truth doesn't threaten your stability or their loyalty to the other parent.

When you respond to honesty with calm curiosity rather than defense, your child's nervous system learns: *It's safe to speak here.*

The Emotional Burden—What Your Child Might Be Feeling

Even when life appears peaceful, your child's internal world may be tangled with emotions they cannot name or regulate.

Some of these feelings are natural responses to rupture; others reflect the survival adaptations they've learned.

1. Loyalty Binds

When children love both parents, they may feel like they are betraying one to stay close to the other.

They become experts at emotional diplomacy—mirroring each parent's feelings to stay safe.

2. Grief

Children grieve not only the family that was, but also the imagined future that will never be.

Grief in children often appears as irritability, regression, or hyper-responsibility rather than tears.

3. Guilt and Shame

Even if told otherwise, many children believe they caused the separation or that they are a burden.

Their nervous system translates parental stress into personal responsibility: *If they're upset, it must be my fault.*

4. Caretaking and Role Reversal

Some children shift into adult-like roles, comforting a parent or acting as the "peacekeeper."
While this can look mature, it is an early form of parentification—the loss of childhood through emotional over-functioning.

Neuroscience Insight—Why Your Regulation Matters

Children's brains are wired with **mirror neurons**, which activate when they observe another person's emotional state.
This means your tone, body language, and breathing directly shape your child's nervous system.

When you speak in a calm, measured voice—even while feeling stressed—your child's mirror neurons register safety and downshift their internal alarm.
When your stress is unregulated, theirs amplifies.

Your regulation is not just your self-care—it is your child's emotional blueprint.
They learn how to handle uncertainty by watching how you handle yours.

Clinical Note (for therapists or facilitators):
When guiding parents, invite them to identify one visible way their body communicates safety to their child (steady tone, soft eyes, slow breath). Small physical signals often create the greatest emotional shifts.

Children thrive when their parents' nervous system is predictable.
They don't need you to solve every problem—they need to know your calm is available no matter the storm.
Your steadiness is not just love expressed; it's safety embodied.

Decoding Behavior—The Feeling Beneath the Action

Behavior is never random; it is communication in disguise.
When a child's world has been divided, emotions often surface through actions instead of words.
Your goal is not to correct the behavior first, but to respond to the *feeling* beneath it.

Children use behavior to say: *"I'm scared." "I'm sad." "Do you still love me?"*
When you decode the message rather than punish the symptom, you transform conflict into connection.

Your Feeling-Behavior-Response Map

Feeling Expressed	Behavior You Might See	Your Regulated Response
Grief/Loss	Crying, clinginess, baby talk, sleep disruption.	Offer extra reassurance. Repeat goodbye rituals. Validate sadness without trying to fix it. "It's okay to miss both homes."
Guilt/Shame	Over-apologizing, perfectionism, withdrawal, trying too hard to please.	Calm correction and explicit reassurance: "This isn't your fault. Not one part." Focus on effort, not outcome.
Anger/Fear	Defiance, tantrums, boundary-testing, aggression.	Name it ("You look furious"), hold steady (see Chapter 4), enforce the limit calmly, and circle back for repair later (see Chapter 10).
Confusion/Disorientation	Repeated questions, forgetfulness, low focus, zoning out.	Provide simple, consistent answers. Rely on visual aids like calendars (Chapter 9). Keep explanations short and concrete.
Loyalty Conflict	Avoidance of talking about the other parent, minimizing experiences.	Normalize love for both parents. Stay neutral. Do not ask probing questions about the other home. "You don't have to choose sides."

Clinical Note—The Nervous System View

Each of these behaviors reflects a **state shift** in the child's nervous system:

- **Hyper-arousal** (fight, flight): tantrums, defiance, over-talking.
- **Hypo-arousal** (freeze, shutdown): silence, withdrawal, flatness.

Your steady tone and predictable reactions help them return to the **Green Zone** (calm, alert state).
Remember: regulation first, guidance second.

Activity 11.1: When to Seek Extra Help

Even the most regulated parent needs professional partnership sometimes. Reach out to a licensed therapist, pediatrician, or school counselor if you observe any of the following lasting more than **2–4 weeks**:

- Persistent nightmares, sleep refusal, or major appetite changes.
- School refusal, withdrawal, or dramatic grade decline.
- Frequent unexplained stomachaches, headaches, or panic complaints.
- Intense guilt statements ("It's my fault") or comments about not belonging.
- Expressions of **self-harm, aggression, or hopelessness.**

Safety Note
If your child ever expresses immediate suicidal thoughts or intent, call **988 or local crisis services right away.**
Your calm action models that safety is never negotiable.

Behavior is the body's language for unmet emotional needs.
When you listen to the message beneath the behavior, you teach your child that even their hardest feelings can be met with understanding instead of fear.

Understanding Your Child's Developmental Needs by Stage

A trauma-informed lens asks us to meet the child where they are developmentally, not just chronologically.
Children don't all "grow out" of stress; some carry early survival patterns into adolescence.
Your job isn't to fix their age-specific behavior—it's to understand what it's trying to protect.

Ages 0–7: Attachment, Regulation, and Imagination

In early childhood, the caregiver's nervous system is the child's regulator.
Their emotional stability depends on your tone, rhythm, and presence far more than your words.

Stage	Needs & Stressors	Support Focus
Ages 0–3	Regulation is co-created through your body—heart rate, breath, and voice rhythm. Stress arises when routines change or separations occur suddenly.	Your body is their regulator. Offer physical comfort, slow touch, soft singing, and consistent bath/bed rituals. Use repetition to build predictability.
Ages 4–7	Magical thinking dominates ("It's my fault"). Big emotions, limited vocabulary. They test stability through behavior.	Provide simple, repeated explanations. Use visuals (like calendars) and play or art to help them express what words can't. Repair quickly when ruptures occur—repetition builds safety.

Clinician Note

For this age group, **predictability** (see Chapter 9) restores trust faster than logic or conversation.
Their prefrontal cortex (the "thinking brain") is often offline during distress.
Prioritize sensory and relational safety—not reasoning.

Ages 8–18+: Fairness, Identity, and Autonomy

As children move toward independence, they crave respect and control.
Their sense of self forms through comparison, fairness, and freedom—all of which can feel unstable during co-parenting transitions.

Stage	Needs & Stressors	Support Focus
Ages 8–12	Developing a strong sense of fairness; starting to compare homes and parents. They seek structure but resist control.	Normalize *both/and* emotions ("You can be mad at me and still love me"). Invite collaboration on routines to restore agency. Ask for their input when possible—this strengthens their sense of control.

Stage	Needs & Stressors	Support Focus
Ages 13+	Identity formation and privacy needs peak. Withdrawal often masks overload. Independence is protection, not rejection.	Ask—don't pry. Respect boundaries but remain predictably available. Your quiet presence (like offering a ride without talking) models emotional safety and consistency.

Clinician Note

Adolescents regulate through **autonomy and trust**. Attempts to control them increase resistance; reliability rebuilds connection.

Focus on tone and timing, not content—your calm availability is more influential than your advice.

Children of all ages need one message repeated in different ways: *"You are safe, and you are not responsible for our adult world."*

When your steadiness becomes predictable, their nervous system stops scanning for danger and starts growing toward freedom.

Empathy Mapping—Seeing Your Child's Life Through Their Eyes

Empathy is not about agreement; it's about attunement.

This exercise helps you use your stabilized self to step inside your child's world—to understand what they *see, hear, and feel* without judgment.

A trauma-informed parent learns to listen beneath the surface:
the silence, the sigh, the shrug.

When you can imagine their world through regulated curiosity, you stop reacting to behavior and start responding to need.

Activity 11.2: Deep Dive—Empathy Mapping Activity

Purpose

To map your child's emotional landscape and identify where their sense of safety may be strained or supported.

Complete one map per child and revisit it every few months; their emotional needs shift as their development progresses.

Prompt	My Child's Likely Experience	What I Can Stabilize in Response
What they see or hear about me	*(e.g., Mom sighs or tenses when Dad's name comes up.)*	**Stabilize:** Keep your tone neutral and words factual when the other parent is mentioned. "Different houses, same love."
What they hear about the other parent	*(e.g., Dad complains I'm too strict.)*	**Stabilize:** Never defend or over-explain. Say: "Different houses, different rules. You're safe to follow both."
What they might feel but not say	*(e.g., Fear of being asked to keep a secret; guilt about enjoying time with the other parent.)*	**Stabilize:** Explicitly state, "You never have to choose between us. You're allowed to feel happy in both homes."
What they might need more of	*(e.g., Comfort, autonomy, quiet connection, physical play.)*	**Stabilize (Commitment):** "I'll offer 15 minutes of quiet time or shared play after every hand-off."

Reflection—Integrating Your View

Empathy doesn't erase pain—it transforms perception.
Use these questions to deepen awareness:

1. What surprised me when I saw life through their eyes?

2. What part of their world might feel confusing or tense, even if I didn't mean to create that?

3. What small, predictable action can I take this week to make their emotional world steadier?

Clinical Note

Empathy mapping is not about guilt—it's about data.
You're gathering sensory and emotional information to improve *co-regulation patterns*.
Over time, this practice strengthens both your child's trust in you and your ability to stay grounded under stress.

When a child feels that both their truths can exist safely in front of you, their nervous system stops protecting and starts connecting.
Your empathy becomes their first safe mirror.

Co-Regulation, Sensory Tools, and Scripts

Children don't learn calm from our explanations—they learn it from our nervous systems.

Their sense of safety is built through rhythm, tone, and repetition, not logic or lectures. When you regulate yourself first, you become the external nervous system they borrow until theirs is ready to work on its own.

In co-parenting, this becomes sacred work: even when your world feels fractured, your steadiness becomes their map.

Your Sensory and Regulation Tools (When Words Fail)

When a child's body is flooded with stress, they lose access to reasoning. In those moments, the language that reaches them best is sensory—physical cues that say, *"You are safe; your body can rest."*

Each tool here draws on a different sensory system to support regulation. These are not tricks—they are biological interventions that tell the brain, *"The danger has passed."*

1. Deep Pressure (Proprioceptive Input)
Firm hugs, weighted blankets, or pushing palms into a wall provide grounding through muscle and joint compression. Pressure helps release oxytocin—the body's chemical of safety and belonging.

2. Rhythm and Repetition (Vestibular Input)
Slow rocking, swaying, drumming, or humming restores the body's natural rhythm. Repetition helps the nervous system predict what comes next, easing the fear of surprise that trauma so often teaches.

3. Focus and Orientation (Tactile or Visual Input)
Fidget toys, smooth stones, or the "Find Five Green Things" game bring the child's attention back to the present environment. By naming what they see or feel, their brain re-anchors in *now* instead of *then*.

Parent Reminder
Resistance is feedback, not failure. When a child rejects a calming tool, they're communicating overwhelm, not defiance. The goal is to adjust the intensity—to meet their window of tolerance, not force calm.

Your Language for Emotional Support (Scripts That Signal Safety)

When children speak from pain or confusion, they don't need explanations—they need nervous-system safety in words.
Each statement below translates regulation into language. The goal is not to fix the problem but to reflect security through tone and pacing.

Child's Statement/Situation	Your Regulated Response	Value Modeled
"I don't want to go to Dad's."	"It's okay to feel sad. I'll miss you too, and I know you'll be safe there. I'll see you [day]."	Empathy, Stability
"Mom said you were mean about the money."	"That sounds frustrating. We see things differently, but we both love you."	Neutrality, Boundary
Teenager withdraws or goes silent.	"You don't have to talk right now. I'm here and I'll check in tomorrow."	Respect, Predictability
"Why did you and Mom/Dad break up?"	"We learned we weren't good partners, but we're still your parents—that part will never change."	Honesty, Accountability
"It's my fault you're sad."	"You didn't cause this. Not one part. This was an adult decision."	Safety, Truth

The goal is *not* emotional agreement; it's containment. Your tone becomes the container for their fear. The steadier your delivery, the more quickly your child's nervous system mirrors your calm.

Supporting Without Triangulating (Holding Space, Not Sides)

When your child brings up the other parent, they are not inviting you into the conflict—they are checking whether you can hold both realities without collapsing.
Your response teaches them that love does not require allegiance.

- **Hold Space**—"That sounds frustrating. Thanks for telling me."
- **Stay Neutral**—"Every house has different rules. What helps you feel steady here?"
- **Set the Boundary**—Never ask for proof or detail. If something needs attention, follow up factually with the co-parent through the parenting app (see Chapter 7).

Therapeutic Reminder

Your neutrality is not silence—it's safety. When you resist the urge to react or defend, you teach your child that emotional honesty is not dangerous. That's how cycles of fear begin to end.

Your Final Commitment—From Pressure to Presence

Your child's body reads yours like the weather. They track your breath, your pace, the sound of your footsteps. Before you support their storm, you must first steady your own. (See your Core Regulation Tools in Chapter 4—your grounding is their forecast.)

This final exercise turns everything you've practiced—regulation, repair, empathy, and stability—into one embodied promise.
It isn't about perfection. It's about the moment-to-moment choice to replace pressure with presence.

Activity 11.3: Your One-Sentence Promise

Purpose
To integrate your growth into a single, observable commitment—a sentence that becomes your personal anchor when stress threatens to pull you off course.

You're writing not just a goal, but a nervous-system contract: how you want your child to experience *you* in the hardest moments.

Use these prompts to guide your reflection:

Draft 1—Your Wish
What do you hope your child feels when they are with you, even in conflict?
(e.g., "I wish they felt that my love never changed, even when I was tired.")

Draft 2—Your Regulated Commitment
Translate that wish into a steady, actionable promise you can embody.
(e.g., "I promise to take one breath before I respond, so my voice always feels safe.")

Final Version

I promise to...

(Write your one-sentence commitment here. Keep it visible—on a mirror, your phone, or inside a journal.)

Closing Thoughts

Your child will not remember every rule, every schedule, or every argument—they will remember how it felt to be around you.
They will measure love not by the absence of conflict, but by the consistency of your calm.

Your love becomes their steady room—the place where their feelings can stretch, breathe, and always return to safety.

You have learned how to see your child through the lens of regulation, empathy, and developmental understanding. You now know how to steady their body by first steadying your own, and how to turn conflict into coherence through language, tone, and presence.

But even with the best tools, there will be seasons when peace feels unreachable—when boundaries are tested, cooperation breaks down, or the other parent's behavior feels unsafe or unrelenting.

These moments are not proof that you've failed; they are proof that your nervous system and your child's are still doing their job—scanning for danger, trying to survive the storm.

Chapter 12 will help you navigate these storms without losing your steadiness. You'll learn how to recognize patterns of control and high conflict, how to protect your child's emotional and physical safety, and how to practice parallel parenting as an act of regulation—not retreat.

When calm connection isn't possible, **clarity and containment becom**

12

What to Do When it's Hard (Conflict, Control & Distance)

Introduction—When Peace Isn't Possible (Yet)

You've built your internal steadiness (Chapter 4), clarified your values (Chapter 6), and learned to set and hold your boundaries (Chapter 7).

But what happens when your co-parenting reality refuses to match your progress—when the system itself remains chaotic, unbalanced, or unsafe?

This chapter is for those seasons when peace is not mutual.
When one parent is working toward calm and the other thrives on control, avoidance, or conflict, cooperation cannot be the measure of success.

The goal now is not harmony; it's **containment**—protecting your nervous system, your child's safety, and the peace within your own home.

You do not need cooperation to create calm.
You need **strategy, clarity, and safety.**

Conflict doesn't mean you're failing; it means the environment still requires stronger boundaries and more deliberate regulation.

This chapter will help you shift from reaction to strategy—from trying to fix the storm to learning how to build shelter inside it.

Vignette—The Endless Text Thread (The Power of Silence)

Jordan's phone buzzed past midnight—another long thread of accusations, distortions, and demands.
The familiar surge hit: heat in the chest, racing pulse, the desperate urge to *explain*.

They typed, deleted, re-typed.
Then they stopped.

One breath in.
One breath out.

The reply, when it came, was simple:

"Please communicate through the parenting app. I'll respond in the morning."

That single line was not passive; it was powerful.
Jordan's silence was not withdrawal—it was **regulation.**
It was the body choosing safety over chaos.
Sometimes peace looks like not replying.

Your Quick Toolbox—When Conflict Won't Stop

These micro-tools are your first-response plan when the system refuses to de-escalate.
Each one reinforces containment and preserves emotional energy.

Tool	Action	Why it Works (Trauma Lens)
Shift Communication	Use written-only apps. Avoid text and phone, which bypass regulation and invite immediate reaction.	Written communication slows the feedback loop and lowers activation for both sides.

Tool	Action	Why it Works (Trauma Lens)
Protect Energy	No defending, no debating, no over-explaining.	Explanations feed the conflict cycle. Silence preserves clarity.
Set Script	Use low-engagement replies: "Noted." "Refer to the plan." "I'll review and respond later."	Predictable phrasing signals safety to your nervous system and disincentivizes escalation.
Ground First	One slow exhale (Chapter 4) before reading or responding.	Regulates the vagus nerve, anchoring you in the present before the threat loop begins.
Mantra	"I can't control them—I can control my peace."	Shifts locus of control inward; re-establishes agency.

Clinician Note

These tools are not avoidance. They are trauma-responsive containment strategies designed to restore physiological safety before cognitive processing.

Identifying Your Dynamic: High Conflict vs. Control

Not all conflict is created equal.

Some co-parenting systems are marked by differences in style, communication fatigue, or old emotional residue. Others are defined by **patterns of control, manipulation, or chronic disrespect** that keep your nervous system braced and your energy depleted.

Understanding which dynamic you're in allows you to stop reacting emotionally and start responding strategically. If every interaction feels destabilizing or unpredictable, you are likely in a **patterned system of power imbalance**, not a mutual disagreement.

Common Patterns of Dysregulation

Pattern	What It Looks Like	Parenting Impact	Nervous System Impact
Emotional Sabotage	Guilt-tripping, rewriting history, demanding loyalty, creating confusion.	The child learns instability and emotional inconsistency as normal.	Chronic hypervigilance, self-doubt, emotional fatigue.
Undermining Parenting	Contradicting your rules, late pick-ups, last-minute chaos, blaming you for structure.	The child becomes confused and tests boundaries to locate safety.	Exhaustion, over-functioning, frustration, self-blame.
Stonewalling	Ignoring messages, withholding responses, or creating chaos through silence.	Missed transitions, uncertainty, and inconsistent routines.	Heightened anxiety, irritability, and feelings of helplessness.
Child Triangulation	Using the child to carry messages, share adult details, or choose sides.	Emotional burden placed directly on the child; loss of innocence.	Protective overload, fight/flight activation, guilt response.

These patterns are not about miscommunication—they are about **control**. Recognizing this distinction allows you to stop negotiating for fairness in a system that depends on confusion to survive.

Activity 12.1: Red Flags—Conflict or Coercive Control?

Purpose
To differentiate between a difficult dynamic and an unsafe one.
If you constantly feel anxious, erased, or unsafe—even when nothing overtly "wrong" is happening—you may be experiencing coercive control rather than mere conflict.

Red Flag	What It Feels Like	Your Commitment (Boundary Practice)
Fear of Setting Boundaries	"If I say no, they'll punish me later."	I will speak to my safe person (Chapter 5) before responding or agreeing to anything.
Reality Rewriting/Gaslighting	"Did that even happen the way I remember?"	I will rely only on documented communication (app/email) for memory and clarity.
Reversal of Blame (DARVO)	"I'm suddenly the villain for naming the problem."	I will disengage immediately: "Noted. I'll revisit this tomorrow."
Power Imbalance (Financial/Time)	"They control the money, schedule, or access."	I will identify one concrete leverage point (lawyer, coach, support group) to reclaim structure.
Isolation/Disempowerment	"I feel smaller, uncertain, or afraid to speak honestly."	I will ground myself before any reply and seek validation from external, regulated sources.

If you find yourself repeatedly asking, *"Is this normal?"*—it probably isn't.

You are not overreacting; your body is responding to chronic, unresolved threats. These signs point to a pattern that requires external support, not more personal endurance.

Seek trauma-informed resources, legal advocates, or therapeutic support to help you stabilize your system before attempting further co-parenting collaboration.

Parallel Parenting—Your Strategic Distance

Parallel parenting is not a failure of collaboration—it is a **strategy of protection.** When contact repeatedly leads to chaos, disrespect, or control, the most regulated choice is distance.

Parallel parenting replaces emotional engagement with structure, creating enough space for stability to grow on both sides.

It is the practice of **loving your child without losing yourself.**

Parallel Parenting vs. Co-Parenting (The Essential Differences)

Category	Co-Parenting (Cooperative Goal)	Parallel Parenting (Distance Goal)
Communication	Frequent, flexible, open to discussion.	Written-only, factual, minimal, structured.
Decision-Making	Joint discussion and compromise.	Independent action within legal or documented limits.
Tone	Warm, conversational, collaborative.	Businesslike, neutral, non-emotional.
Contact	In-person when needed for logistics.	Avoided; use neutral locations or curbside drop-offs (see Chapter 8).

Parallel parenting is not withdrawal—it is **containment built on love.**

It's the recognition that proximity without regulation leads to harm, while distance with structure creates peace.

Clinical Reminder

For parents recovering from trauma, emotional neutrality *is not coldness*—it's safety. Parallel parenting is an adaptive nervous-system response that keeps both adults within their Window of Tolerance.

Minimizing Your Contact & Emotional Exposure

1. **Written-Only Contact**
   Written communication removes tone and time pressure. It also creates a factual record, reducing opportunities for manipulation.
   → Use the parenting app or email only. Avoid text messages.

2. **Grey Rock Method**
   The Grey Rock approach means becoming deliberately uninteresting in your communication.
   You offer no emotional "hooks" to engage or escalate.
   → Examples: "Noted." "Confirmed." "Refer to the parenting plan."
   These short, consistent phrases signal calm authority and stop the conflict cycle.

3. **Boundaries for Protection**
   People who thrive on chaos perceive calm as a challenge. When you enforce peace, expect pushback.
   → Remember: **Boundaries don't punish—they educate.**
   You're teaching the other parent (and your own nervous system) where peace lives.

Therapist Insight
The goal of parallel parenting is not to rebuild connection; it's to protect co-existence. Once safety and regulation stabilize, new communication patterns may emerge naturally—but they must never come at the expense of calm.

Documentation Without Obsession

Documentation is your safety net, not your identity. You document to preserve peace, not to relive pain. Excessive documentation can become its own trauma loop—keeping your nervous system anchored in vigilance rather than resolution. The goal is disciplined neutrality: **enough detail to protect, not enough to re-trigger.**

Your Documentation Focus

Record only what maintains clarity, safety, or legal consistency. Each entry should be brief, factual, and emotionally neutral.

Document Only When:	Example
There's a clear boundary violation (missed pickup, insults, or threats).	"Exchange occurred 30 minutes late. Child safely returned home."
Communication breaches the app or agreement.	"Received off-platform text. Redirected to parenting app."
The child's emotional or physical safety is impacted.	"Child reported being asked to relay message. Reassured and redirected."

Avoid over-documenting every frustration or rereading old messages. The act of documentation should close the loop, not reopen the wound.

Activity 12.2: Your Focused Documentation Log

Purpose
To capture only the necessary facts—cleanly, calmly, and consistently.

Date/Time	Incident (Facts Only)	Medium (App/Text)	My Regulated Response (Chapter 7 Script)	Child Impact (Objective Observation)
3/15 @ 7:30 PM	Parent arrived 30 minutes late for exchange.	App	"Noted. Child is now settled."	Child was anxious at drop-off; hid briefly, calmed with routine.
4/02 @ 10:00 AM	Message contained	App	"I will not respond to messages with	No direct child impact noted.

Date/Time	Incident (Facts Only)	Medium (App/Text)	My Regulated Response (Chapter 7 Script)	Child Impact (Objective Observation)
	insults and threats.		insults. I'll check back tomorrow."	

Personal Log

- My Log 3: _____

- My Log 4: _____

Goal

To document for peace, not for punishment. You are gathering clarity, not evidence of your worth.

Protecting Your Child from Emotional Fallout

Your child deserves a childhood—not a role in adult politics. They should never feel responsible for carrying, interpreting, or fixing the relationship between their parents.

Your regulation is their protection. Every time you respond calmly instead of reacting, you teach your child that love can exist without tension, and that safety can exist even in difference.

Your regulated nervous system (see Chapter 4) is their invisible armor.

Neutrality Scripts—Ending Triangulation

When your child brings home stories, questions, or emotional echoes from the other household, they are not betraying you—they are processing. Your job is not to explain, defend, or correct.
Your job is to **hold space, not sides.**

Use these scripts to model calm neutrality and preserve your child's emotional freedom.

Child Action	Your Neutralizing Script	The Message You Send
Delivering a message (e.g., about money, schedule, or complaints)	"Thank you for letting me know. That's not yours to carry—that's between grown-ups."	*I protect your childhood.*
Comparing households ("At your house, we can…")	"Different homes have different rhythms, and that's okay. Let's focus on what works best here."	*I am steady and clear.*
Asking big questions ("Why do you hate each other?")	"We are learning how to be better parents, even if we weren't good partners. You are safe to love us both."	*I protect your loyalty.*
Reporting conflict ("Mom/Dad said you did X.")	"That sounds hard to hear. I'm sorry you were in the middle of that. That's for me and Mom/Dad to figure out."	*You're not responsible for adult emotions.*

Clinician Insight

Neutrality is not denial; it's regulation in action.

When you refuse to be pulled into reactivity, you are rewiring your child's nervous system to associate calm with safety, not chaos with love.

Resisting the Urge to Correct the Narrative

You cannot control the version of yourself that lives in the other home.
You can only control the version your child experiences.

When children are exposed to blame or distortion, their nervous system registers the tension before their mind can make sense of it.
Your calm, steady presence repairs that distortion—not by defending yourself, but by **embodying** your truth.

Let Go of:
- Defending or proving your version of events.

- Over-explaining your decisions.

- Arguing through your child.

Anchor in:

- "My truth is in how I parent."

- "My tone teaches more than my words."

- "I lead with calm, not correction."

Your child's loyalty is not a prize to win—it's a **freedom to protect.** When you model this restraint, you're giving them permission to love without guilt, and to rest in the safety of your steadiness.

Therapeutic Reminder
The child's nervous system does not care who's "right." It only registers who feels safe.

Your Grief Release and Long-Term Steadiness

Sustained conflict requires sustained self-compassion. You cannot create peace while pretending you are not grieving. Parallel parenting, boundary enforcement, and emotional regulation often come with invisible losses: the loss of cooperation, the loss of being seen accurately, the loss of the dream that parenting could stay intact. To hold long-term steadiness, you must give yourself permission to **mourn what never was** and **release what no longer serves.**

Grief and Rage—Allowing Your Feelings

Grief and anger are not opposites; they are twins born from disappointment. Where there is rage, there was once hope. When you allow yourself to feel both, you stop turning pain inward. You are not weak for being angry, nor broken for still hurting. You are human, metabolizing a complex emotional system that has run on survival for too long.

Your Ritual for Release (Your Grounding Ceremony):

1. Write down what you are ready to release—the fantasy of teamwork, the wish for fairness, the anger that keeps circling.

2. Burn or bury it safely, or tear it into pieces and throw it away with intention.

3. As you do, say aloud: "I release what hurts. I keep what heals."

   This mirrors the **Stage 3: After-Conflict Ritual (see Chapter 5)**—a physical reset that signals completion to your nervous system.

Clinician Note

Rituals transform abstract emotion into embodied closure. They give the brain a sense of finality—a message that the loop can end.

Your Emergency Grounding During Conflict

When conflict spikes, your goal is not perfect calm; it is **sufficient regulation**—enough to keep you anchored in your body.

Use this list as a visible, rapid-access guide for moments of acute activation.

Trigger	Core Regulation Tool (Chapter 4)	Grounding Phrase (Chapters 4 and 8)
Panic/Overwhelm	Press feet firmly into the floor. Use the 5-4-3-2-1 sensory scan.	"I'm here. This is a moment, not my story."
Rage/Explosion	Cold water on wrists or face. Private physical discharge (Shake-Out or walk).	"This energy can move safely."
Freeze/Despair	Gentle activation: shake arms, stretch, jump once, call a safe person.	"My body can move again. I'm not alone."

You do not need full calm to respond well. You only need **enough safety to stay in your body.** Each micro-moment of regulation is a repair—a signal to your child's nervous system that safety can return, even when the world feels unpredictable.

Therapeutic Reminder
The opposite of dysregulation isn't serenity—it's presence.
Presence is the soil where resilience takes root.

Closing Thoughts

You have learned to regulate in the face of chaos, to protect your peace without apology, and to release the fantasy that cooperation is required for stability.
That is not failure—it is wisdom.
You now understand that calm is not something you wait for; it's something you create, breath by breath, boundary by boundary.

Grief has done its work. It has stripped away illusion and left behind what is real: your capacity to rebuild from the inside out.

In the next chapter, we will explore how to use that clarity to navigate one of the hardest realities of post-separation parenting—**when the other parent's behavior becomes emotionally unsafe or toxic**. Chapter 13, *Parenting with a Toxic Co-Parent*, expands your tools of protection and integrity. It will teach you how to recognize manipulation, preserve your dignity, and protect your child's emotional truth without escalating conflict. This is where survival transforms into strategy—where self-regulation becomes leadership

13

Parenting with a Toxic Co-Parent

Introduction—When Love is Used as a Weapon

You've built your regulation skills, boundaries, and internal calm. Now, you face the most complex challenge of all: maintaining that steadiness inside a system of ongoing manipulation and control.

Not every co-parenting relationship is merely "difficult." Some are emotionally unsafe, chronically destabilizing, and built on distortion. These systems don't seek cooperation—they seek control. They thrive on confusion, guilt, and exhaustion.

You cannot co-parent with chaos.
But you can protect your peace within it.

This chapter helps you name what's happening—without minimizing it—and build a structure that keeps you anchored, informed, and untangled from psychological control.

Vignette—Invisible Blame and the Erosion of Confidence

When Maya's co-parent accused her of "twisting words," denied obvious facts, and constantly interrupted, she ended the call feeling dizzy and ashamed.
She found herself rehearsing every line afterward, wondering, *"Was I the problem?"*

Gaslighting doesn't always burn; sometimes, it erodes—slowly grinding down your trust in your own perception.

This chapter helps you rebuild that trust, not through argument, but through anchored clarity. You will learn to name manipulation, document reality, and stop defending your sanity.

What a Toxic Co-Parent May Look Like (Expanded Patterns)

Toxic control rarely presents as rage alone. It often wears the mask of charm, competence, or "concern." Below are the most common patterns of manipulation and their psychological impact.

Pattern	Typical Behavior	Emotional Impact on You
Control Disguised as Concern	"I'm just thinking of what's best for the child…" (while overriding your decisions or demanding private information).	Erodes confidence; triggers guilt and helplessness.
Gaslighting	Denying facts, rewriting history, or minimizing your reality: "You're overreacting," "That never happened."	Creates confusion, shame, and self-doubt; disconnects you from your intuition.
Charm in Public, Cruelty in Private	Acts calm and composed in public, but attacks or blames you privately through texts, calls, or co-parenting apps.	Isolation, disbelief ("No one would believe me"), constant bracing.

Pattern	Typical Behavior	Emotional Impact on You
Weaponizing the Child	Uses affection or fear to make the child a messenger, spy, or source of validation.	Deep fear for the child's emotional safety; hypervigilance and guilt.
Endless Conflict Cycle (The Control Loop)	The predictable pattern: *Bait → Blow-up → Blame → Silence → Repeat.* (Also known as hoovering.)	Learned helplessness, exhaustion, collapse of trust in change.

Clinical Insight

Toxic dynamics operate like emotional malware—they install self-doubt, disrupt your internal system, and make you question your own "updates."
Recognizing manipulation is not judgment; it's protection. You're not overreacting—you're responding to chronic control.

Recognizing Coercive Dynamics (Clarity Over Diagnosis)

You don't need a formal diagnosis to protect yourself.
You need **clarity**—a clear understanding of the behavioral patterns that erode your safety, distort your perception, and keep your nervous system in a constant state of defense.

The goal here is not to label the other parent; it's to **restore your own internal map of truth**.

Core Destabilization Tactics

Coercive dynamics thrive on confusion. They manipulate time, memory, and emotion to keep you questioning yourself. Below are four of the most common tactics seen in high-conflict co-parenting systems and their physiological effects.

Behavior	How It Shows Up in Co-Parenting	Impact on the Nervous System
Gaslighting	Denies written agreements, dismisses documented conversations, and blames technology for "lost" messages.	Erodes trust in your own memory; forces you to over-monitor words and tone. Creates **hypervigilance** and self-doubt.
DARVO (Deny → Attack → Reverse Victim and Offender)	Accuses you of the exact behavior they just did (e.g., "You're the one starting fights").	Trains you to go silent; triggers **shame, confusion, and freeze or fight responses**.
Baiting & Withholding	Sends provocative messages, then withdraws or stonewalls; withholds critical information or delays key decisions.	Hooks your emotional regulation loop, causing **anxiety, urgency, and chasing behavior**.
Hoovering (Image Management)	Sudden charm, superficial apologies ("I'm sorry if you felt hurt"), or nostalgic gestures after conflict.	Reinforces the trauma bond; your brain mistakes **temporary relief** for safety, confusing chaos with connection.

Activity 13.1: Your Trauma Bonding & Self-Doubt Reflection

Purpose

To name the internal impact of these cycles without shame or self-blame.

1. **The Trauma Bond Check**
   Do you feel a strange "pull" or anxiety spike after silence is broken, even when the last interaction was painful?

→ This isn't proof you want them back—it's your nervous system seeking resolution.

Affirmation: "My body is searching for safety, not the source of the chaos."

2. **Identify and Reclaim**
   Coercive dynamics slowly shrink your world around defense.
   → List three things—people, hobbies, or values—that exist completely outside the co-parenting conflict.

   → These are your anchors of self beyond the system.

3. **Body Reflection**
   Where does this stress live in your body (jaw, chest, stomach, back)?

   → Place your hand there, breathe slowly, and whisper:
   "You're safe to rest for a moment."

Clinician Note

Gaslighting fatigue often mimics ADHD—scattered focus, disorganization, or memory slips.

These are not character flaws; they are **trauma responses**. Once your environment stabilizes, so will your attention.

Your Digital Safety and Disengagement Strategies

When you are dealing with a toxic or controlling co-parent, **digital safety and emotional detachment** are not luxuries—they are lifelines. Technology often becomes the new battlefield for control, intrusion, or manipulation. Protecting your digital space protects your nervous system.

Your Digital Safety & Tech-Abuse Hygiene

Your online systems deserve the same boundaries as your physical environment. Audit everything regularly.

Area	Protective Action	Why it Matters (Trauma Lens)
Passwords	Use strong, unique passwords and enable two-factor authentication (2FA) on all parenting apps, email, and social media accounts.	Prevents covert access and reclaims control over your data.
Location Data	Disable location sharing in photos, apps, and devices (especially for your child's school or home).	Eliminates digital tracking that can feed control or surveillance.
Documentation Storage	Keep copies of records and communications on a secure, encrypted drive—not a shared cloud or device.	Creates safety through separation; reduces exposure to tampering.
Co-Parenting Apps	Use the app *only* for factual, logistical updates. Never engage emotionally or argue in the thread.	Keeps communication legally clear and emotionally clean.

Remember: You don't need to win digital arguments—you need to win your peace.

Internal Grounding Tools: Your "Wall of Calm"

Emotional disengagement is not avoidance—it's mastery. These practices protect your body's energy field from being hijacked by conflict.

Anchor	Physical Action	Mental Action	Emotional Focus
Grey Rock	Sit or stand with steady posture; slow your movements (see Chapter 5).	Respond with a factual tone and minimal words.	*Detach from the bait; neutrality is protection.*
JADE Avoidance (Don't *Justify, Argue, Defend, or Explain*)	Pause before replying (minimum 30 seconds).	Delete the defensive draft.	*Dignity over explanation.*
Wall of Calm	Exhale through the soles of your feet; hands grounded on a stable surface.	Visualize a soft, light barrier around your body.	*Words slide off; I remain still.*
Mantra Breath	Hand over chest; one long inhale, one slow exhale.	Silently repeat: "This isn't new. My peace is mine."	*Choose courage over compliance.*

These anchors work because they shift the power from the interaction back into your body—your true safe space.

Activity 13.2: Your Decision Matrix for Disengagement

Purpose
To remove emotional decision-making in moments of activation and replace it with clarity and structure.

Situation	Engage (Brief & Factual)	Disengage/No Reply	Escalate Document + Consult Counsel
Logistics/Safety Facts (e.g., time changes, medication updates)	Respond briefly and factually.	—	—
Emotional Bait/Attacks (e.g., insults, blame, guilt-tripping)	—	Minimal or no reply.	—
Court Order Violations (e.g., late exchanges, withholding access)	—	—	Document and consult legal support.
Hoovering/Charm (e.g., flattery, nostalgic messages, "checking in")	Keep tone factual and detached. Wait 24 hours before replying.	—	—

Core Principles

Your calm is the rebellion.

Your boundaries are the revolution.

Disengagement is not surrender—it's self-respect in motion.

Protecting Your Child from the Fallout

You can't bubble-wrap your child, but you can build their internal armor through truth and emotional safety. When conflict spills over, your steady language becomes the shield that teaches them how to feel safe inside uncertainty.

Your Safety Language Scripts (Gentle Truths)

Children exposed to ongoing conflict absorb emotional signals even when no one speaks. Your goal isn't to erase tension—it's to give them reliable truths they can hold onto.

Situation	Your Script (The Protection)	The Core Message You Send
Child delivers a hostile message	"Thanks for telling me, but that's not something you need to carry. That's between grown-ups."	You are safe from adult problems.
Child says they feel guilty	"Real love doesn't make you scared or small. You don't have to protect anyone's feelings but your own."	Your feelings are valid.
Child echoes co-parent's insult (e.g., "Mom, you're being dramatic.")	*(Pause, regulate—see Chapter 4)* "I hear you're upset. Let's take a breath, then talk kindly."	We model health, not toxicity.
Child worries about your safety	"My job is to keep you safe—your job is to be a kid. I am strong, and I have help."	I am competent and secure.

Clinician Note
High-conflict parents may weaponize "alienation" when you set healthy boundaries. This is not alienation—it's protection.
Stay factual and child-focused; let documentation, not emotion, speak for you.

Grieving Your Illusion (Your Letter to Your Fantasy)

You can't heal if you keep pretending. To move forward, you must grieve your **illusion of cooperative parenting** and make peace with your reality.

Practice:

Write a *Letter to Your Fantasy*—a private letter that honors what you hoped for (mutual respect, shared effort, teamwork) but acknowledges the reality you now accept (safety, parallel parenting, distance, or limited contact).

Your Ritual of Release

Read the letter aloud, then burn or tear it safely while saying:

"I release the fantasy of who they were supposed to be. I keep the truth, my peace, and my boundaries."

This act closes the emotional loop and allows grief to transform into grounded acceptance.

Reclaiming Your Energy and Identity

Toxic dynamics shrink your life around survival. Reclaiming your identity is the act of expanding beyond defense—rediscovering who you are when you're not surviving someone else's chaos. When you stop explaining, defending, or proving, you begin healing.

Your Reinvestment Checklist

These are the foundational steps for rebuilding your selfhood and nervous system capacity.
Each one restores energy that chronic conflict once consumed.

Focus	Practice	Purpose (Why it Matters)
Schedule Joy	Block time for low-effort laughter, rest, or creativity.	Joy re-trains the nervous system to expect safety instead of danger.
Reinvest in Self	Reconnect with hobbies, art, or friendships unrelated to parenting or co-parenting.	Reclaims identity outside of survival roles.
Build Support Team	Surround yourself with trauma-informed professionals and friends who believe you without requiring proof.	Validation repairs the internal rupture caused by gaslighting and isolation.

You're allowed to take up space again.
Your peace is the legacy your child will inherit.

Reflection & Integration

Use these prompts as gentle guides, not tests. They are invitations to return to yourself—one truthful answer at a time.

1. **What am I no longer willing to justify or explain to the co-parent?**
    (This defines your new boundary.)

2. **What toxic cycle am I ready to leave—even if they stay in it?**
    (This defines your freedom.)

3. **What one action can I take this week to reclaim my identity outside of defense?**
    (Example: book a class, visit a friend, dance, rest, or start a new ritual.)

Clinician Note

Recovery after coercion requires re-expansion—widening what trauma narrowed. Each act of joy or rest is not indulgence; it's recalibration.

Closing Thoughts

You've rebuilt from the inside out.
You've learned to regulate, to set boundaries, to repair, and to rest.
Now comes the question that quietly follows healing:
"What does love look like now?"

When you've lived in survival mode, calm can feel foreign. Peace can even feel unsafe. Reclaiming your identity isn't just about who you are without conflict—it's about who you might become with connection.

Before you step forward, pause here and anchor what you've earned:

1. **I am no longer defined by what I escaped.**

2. **I am allowed to want more than peace—I can want joy.**

3. **I can choose relationships that align with my nervous system, not challenge it.**

Healing doesn't mean rushing back into vulnerability; it means entering new bonds with awareness, not amnesia.
You don't have to prove you're ready—you only have to stay regulated as you grow.

The next chapter shifts from survival of love to safety in love.
We will explore what it means to introduce new partners, navigate blended families, and protect your child's stability while honoring your right to joy.

You will learn how to:

- Assess readiness from a trauma-informed lens (for both you and your child).

- Create a stepwise introduction plan that builds trust, not confusion.

- Maintain the rhythm of safety you've established, even as new dynamics unfold.

The storm has passed. Now we rebuild—not the old structure, but a steadier, gentler one.

14

High-Stakes Co-Parenting Logistics: Public Events, Holidays, and Crisis Management

Introduction—Your Protocol Is Your Peace

You've built your internal regulation (Chapters 4–5) and established your communication boundaries (Chapters 12–13). Now, we move from **internal regulation** to **external execution**.

High-stakes moments—public events, holidays, and emergencies—are where the toxic co-parent dynamic often regains its power. These events operate inside what we call the **Conflict Funnel**. They combine **time pressure** with **emotional visibility**, forcing your nervous system back into survival mode.

Your protection plan begins here: **Pre-Decide** and rely on **Protocol Over Panic.**

This chapter serves as your operational guide. It translates calm intention into predictable action, protecting both your child and your emotional system under stress.

Mantra—*"The plan is the boundary that protects the moment."*

Your Three Enemies of Execution

Enemy	How It Manifests	Strategic Countermeasure
Time Pressure	Holidays, exchanges, or emergencies demand rapid decision-making, bypassing regulation (Chapter 5).	**The "If-Then" Rule:** Decide every step *before* the trigger occurs. Example: *"If they're late, I text once, then disengage."*
Ambiguity	Unclear logistics create emotional voids that conflict quickly fills (e.g., *"What do I do if they don't show?"*).	**Specificity:** Document every step, time limit, and consequence in writing. Structure is your stabilizer.
Public Visibility	Shared events and holidays often involve witnesses—inviting performance, provocation, or cruelty.	**The "Grey Rock Exit":** Keep tone flat, body calm, interaction brief. Prioritize your child and leave early if needed (Chapter 12).

Clinical Note

Public moments compress time and visibility—two of the brain's biggest stressors. Predictability activates safety; pre-planning replaces panic with purpose. When you pre-decide, your nervous system doesn't need to improvise under pressure.

Managing Shared Public Events

Shared events—such as school plays, graduations, ceremonies, and medical appointments—often carry unique emotional weight. They combine **social visibility** with **forced proximity**, creating a perfect storm of stress for both your nervous system and your child's.

Your goal is not cooperation; it's **predictability and separation.** You can attend the same event while protecting your peace.

Your Three-Zone Public Safety Rule

Create clear, physical boundaries in shared spaces to remove all potential for unplanned or unscripted interaction. Think of these zones as emotional armor made visible.

Zone	Protocol	Purpose
Zone 1: The No-Contact Zone (You & Child)	**Physical Barrier:** Keep an empty seat, bag, or a trusted ally next to you. Maintain a closed posture and focus on your child.	Ensures your attention stays child-centered while removing the *physical invitation* for contact.
Zone 2: The Neutral Zone (The Co-Parent)	Acknowledge their presence *once* (a nod, no words), then shift your focus back to your child or the event.	**Public Grey Rock (Chapter 12):** You're calm, polite, and disengaged. You observe without inviting.
Zone 3: The Buffer Zone (The Exit)	Pre-plan parking, seating, and walking route. Tell your child: "We leave immediately after the applause."	Prevents ambushes in foyers or parking lots. Ends contact the moment the event ends.

Your Scripts for Bystanders and Public Bait

Bystanders—teachers, coaches, or relatives—often try to "mediate," unaware of the dynamics. Meanwhile, a toxic co-parent may use **public baiting** to provoke you into visible distress.

Your script is your shield: brief, factual, and **JADE-free** (no Justifying, Arguing, Defending, or Explaining).

Situation	Co-Parent Tactic/Bystander Question	Regulated Response (JADE-Free)
Bystander Mediation	Teacher says: "Can't you two just sit together for the child's sake?"	"I appreciate the suggestion. For the child's stability, we stick to our current seating plan."
Public Baiting	Co-parent says loudly: "So glad I finally saw the child—since someone ignores my messages."	*No reply, or a calm glance away.* (Chapter 13—Silence is the defense.)
Forced Justification	"Why didn't you respond to my text about the costume?"	"Any logistical issue must go through the app. I'll check it later." (End conversation immediately.)

Activity 14.1: Your Public Event Safety Map

Purpose

To transform emotional dread into a concrete, repeatable plan for maximum protection and predictability during shared public events.

Action Item	Plan (Be Specific)	Ally/Buffer (If Applicable)
1. Arrival & Parking	Time I will arrive (___ min early/late): _____ Where I will park (near exit door): _____	
2. Seating Plan	My seat: (Aisle/Front/Back) Seat next to me for: (Empty/Ally Name)_____	
3. Communication Plan	The one person I will text before or after for support: _____	
4. Exit Protocol	Exact exit time: _____ (e.g., before final credits/immediately after applause). Route to car: _____	
5. Child Reassurance	The one thing I'll say to my child after the event: _____ (e.g., "You did great. I'm so proud of you.")	

Clinician Note

Shared events can awaken deep protective instincts and old grief. Preparation is not paranoia; it's regulation in action. Every pre-planned step lowers the body's arousal and protects your child's emotional safety from adult unpredictability.

Your Holiday Exchanges and Travel Protocol

Holidays and travel are high-pressure transition points where time, emotion, and control often collide. These moments test both your structure and your nervous system. The goal is not flexibility—it's **predictability with compassion.** Your strongest boundary is not confrontation—it's a **defined consequence** for violation, executed calmly and consistently.

Your Late Exchange Rule (Your Time Boundary)

Never wait indefinitely. Waiting is not patience—it's exposure to stress.
This plan protects your child's time, your emotional energy, and the integrity of your schedule. The late-exchange protocol must be **written, documented, and repeated without variation.**

Step	Protocol Action (Pre-Decided)	Rationale (Trauma-Informed Lens)
1. The Waiting Period	"I will wait 15 minutes (or as specified by court order) at the designated location."	Creates a *clear time container* for uncertainty, giving the nervous system a sense of control and closure.
2. The Single Communication	"At the 15-minute mark, I will send one factual message via the app: 'Exchange failed due to non-arrival by [Time]. I will be available again for exchange at [Next Scheduled Time/Day].'"	Keeps you in your thinking brain. One factual message prevents looping and protects against baiting (Chapter 13).
3. Departure and Documentation	Immediately leave. Log the event with the date, time, and a copy of the message.	Ends the exposure window; creates evidence without emotional residue. Documentation replaces argument.

Clinician Note
The brain interprets uncertainty as danger. Having a pre-decided "stop time" signals to your body that you are *safe to disengage.* This prevents overactivation and guilt-based second-guessing.

Your Travel and Information Boundaries

Toxic co-parents often use demands for excessive travel details to regain control or provoke defensiveness. Share **only** what is mandatory and legally required—no explanations, no extras.

Information Category	Status	Example of Acceptable Sharing
Mandatory (Safety & Access)	Must Share	Flight number, destination city, emergency contact, address where the child will be staying.
Optional/Bait (Justification & Control)	Do Not Share	Hotel confirmation, detailed itinerary, emotional reasons for the trip, photos, opinions on location.

Clinician Note—The 48-Hour Buffer

Build a 48-hour emotional cushion before and after major holidays or travel transitions. Avoid scheduling social events or emotionally heavy tasks in that window. Dedicate it to quiet regulation (Chapter 5) and steady reconnection with your child.

Your calm is their compass.

Activity 14.2: Your Holiday Exchange Protocol Checklist

Purpose

To automate high-stress transitions, shifting you from *reaction* to *protocol*.

Step	Completed Action	Check-In & Script
1. Pre-Exchange Prep	Review the court-ordered time and location.	**Self-Check (Chapters 4–5):** "I have my regulation tool ready."
2. Exchange Execution	Arrive on time. Wait 15 minutes if necessary.	**Handover Script:** "Everything's here. Goodbye." (3 words, neutral tone.)
3. Failed Exchange Protocol	Send the single factual message, then leave.	**Affirmation:** "I followed the plan. I protected our peace."
4. Immediate Reconnection	Begin post-exchange co-regulation activity.	**Child Script:** "I'm glad you're back. Let's start our quiet time."

Your Child's Medical and Crisis Management

A medical or safety crisis is the ultimate test of regulation. It requires **immediate, competent action** in real time while managing emotional overload and potential manipulation from the co-parent. Your focus must remain on the **child's safety**, not the co-parent's emotional demands.

Your Emergency Decision Hierarchy

Know who holds legal medical authority and establish a clear chain of communication before a crisis ever arises. In the moment, clarity protects calm.

Step	Protocol Action	Rationale (Trauma-Informed Lens)
1. Child First	Treat the medical situation (call 911, go to the ER). Focus only on the child and the medical staff.	Prioritizes immediate safety over emotional reaction or communication demands.
2. Legal Review	Confirm medical decision-making authority based on the court order.	Establishes the recognized legal boundary, preventing escalation or debate.
3. Single Factual Communication	Send *one* factual message via the co-parenting app (Chapter 12) only after the child is stable and accurate information is available.	Prevents emotional reactivity, avoids baiting, and blocks the **DARVO** cycle (Chapter 13).
4. Ignore Emotional/Logistical Bait	Respond only to factual questions about treatment or prognosis. Ignore demands for justification, doctor selection, or travel.	Protects your nervous system and ensures focus stays on the child, not conflict.

Your Need-to-Know Rule in a Crisis

In a crisis, panic can become a tool of control. Clarity about what to share—and what to withhold—keeps you regulated and legally safe.

Role	Information Is Required	Information Is Not Required
Medical Staff	All prior medical history, medications, and symptoms.	Divorce details, custody arrangement, or emotional commentary.
Co-Parent	Hospital name, child's condition, and basic medical status.	Doctor choice, detailed minute-by-minute updates, or emotional justification for decisions.

Clinician Note

Oversharing is often a trauma response—a nervous system seeking safety through explanation.

In medical crises, **containment is compassion.** You model grounded leadership for your child and protect your emotional bandwidth.

Activity 14.3: Your Crisis Communication Decision Tree

Purpose

A visual, step-by-step guide to manage a medical or safety emergency without defaulting to panic or reactive engagement.

Crisis Triggered

Child is ill, injured, or unsafe.

1. Stop & Regulate (Chapters 4–5)

Take three slow breaths.

Ask yourself: "What is the single most factual step I need to take right now?"

2. Act: Safety First

Address your child's immediate physical need (ER/call 911).

This comes before any communication or documentation.

3. Check Stabilization

Is your child stabilized (out of immediate danger)?

- **No:** Repeat Step 1.

- **Yes:** Move to Step 4.

4. Communicate (Chapters 12–13)

Draft **one** factual message.

- **Content Check:** Is it factual, brief, and app-based? Does it contain *zero emotional justification*?
- **Factual Message Example:**
  "*[Child Name]* is at *[Location/Hospital]* for *[Factual Reason]*. Condition is stable. Update will follow."

5. Set Your Boundary

For the next 24 hours, you will only respond to factual questions about treatment and logistics.
No defense, no debate.

Clinical Integration Note

During crises, the nervous system defaults to survival mode—fight, flight, or freeze. This structure restores your **prefrontal control**, letting calm action replace chaos. You're not shutting out the other parent—you're protecting the safety hierarchy: **Child first. Facts next. Emotion last.**

Child-Centered Logistics—Preparation and Repair

The adult protocols protect the structure, but your child's nervous system needs something more—your attuned presence. Even the most organized plan cannot soothe a child's hidden fears: loyalty binds, guilt, or the somatic stress of sensing adult conflict.

This section helps you **prepare the child before stress** and **repair safety afterward**, transforming high-stakes moments into lessons in resilience.

Your Pre-Event Briefing—Giving Your Child Power

Children find safety through agency. When you give them language and small choices, you restore their sense of control in moments that might otherwise feel overwhelming.

Strategy	Actionable Script for the Child	Purpose (Regulation Lens)
The Permission Script	"I want you to focus only on the game/play. You don't have to worry about who's talking to who. That's my job."	Decouples the child's emotional state from adult conflict, letting them stay in their own lane of joy.
The 'Code Word' Escape	Agree on a discreet cue or phrase (e.g., "I need a drink of water," or a shoulder touch) for when the child feels trapped or anxious.	Creates an immediate, safe exit from emotional overload without drawing public attention.
Loyalty Affirmation	"The love we share is yours alone. No adult can ask you to choose sides or carry messages. That's not your job."	Counters loyalty binds, and protects the child's integrity in triangulated dynamics (Chapter 10).

Post-Event Repair and Re-Regulation

The first hour after a stressful event is your window of influence. During this time, your child's body decides whether the world is safe again. The goal is **physical reconnection before emotional discussion**.

Action	Detailed Protocol	Rationale (Somatic Repair)
Immediate Reconnection Ritual	Spend the first 30–60 minutes in **uninterrupted, low-stimulation time**: reading, music, or quiet play. Avoid questions or debriefing.	Re-establishes *felt safety*: the body learns "the event is over, and my anchor is here."
The Repair Script	"I saw that was stressful. I'm proud of how steady you were. That stress is done now. We are safe. Let's do our calming breath together."	Names the experience, validates emotion, and co-regulates through shared breath. The body discharges the tension through connection.
Sensory Anchor (Chapter 2)	Use a repetitive cue that signals 'safe home time': a weighted blanket, incense, or a calming activity like stacking blocks.	Pulls the child from the analytical brain (worry) into the sensory brain (safety). Predictability restores stability.

Activity 14.4: Your Child's Post-Stress Safety Plan

Purpose

A quick-reference map for your child's most vulnerable moments—ensuring every stress response ends with repair.

Vulnerable Moment	Pre-Plan: Child's Safety Tool	Post-Plan: Parent's Reconnection Ritual
Public Event/Ceremony	Code Word: _____ (signal for anxiety)	Ritual: _____ (e.g., two chapters of favorite book).
Difficult Exchange	Affirmation: _____ (e.g., "I'm safe with Mom/Dad now.")	Activity: _____ (e.g., 10 minutes of low-stimulus play or drawing).
Crisis/Scare	Body Anchor: _____ (e.g., hand on chest/stomach).	Repair Script: : _____ (e.g., "I'm proud of you. We are safe now.")

Activity 14.5: Your Regulation Recovery Audit

Purpose

To integrate self-awareness into your logistical plan and identify emotional blind spots before high-stakes events.

Reflection Area	What I Noticed	My Core Regulation Tool (Chapter 4)	Adjustment for Next Time
Before the Event	(How did my body feel while preparing?)		
During the Event	(Where did I feel the first sign of activation?)		
After the Event	(What stayed in my body after it ended?)		

Reflection Area	What I Noticed	My Core Regulation Tool (Chapter 4)	Adjustment for Next Time
With My Child	(Did I model calm or urgency?)		

Clinical Integration

This tool trains interoception—the ability to track your body's internal signals—which is the foundation of trauma recovery and calm decision-making.

Reflection—The Meaning of Predictability

Use this as an emotional check-in after completing your protocols.

1. When I think of "structure," do I associate it with safety or control?

2. What emotion do I feel most often before shared events—anxiety, guilt, fear, anticipation?

3. Which part of my plan feels most empowering, and which feels most rigid?

4. What would it look like to bring compassion, not just compliance, into my protocol?

Your Final Action & Integration

This chapter is your final line of defense against the chaos of high-conflict co-parenting. These protocols are not about control—they are about execution. Calm, predictable execution communicates **safety** louder than any words.

Reflection Prompts—Your Protocol Mindset

1. **Future-Pacing**
   What is the next high-stakes event you will face?
   Identify the single most predictable conflict point—and write your one-sentence **Grey Rock Protocol** for it.

2. **My Protocol Test**
   Think of your most recent exchange. Did you follow the Late Exchange Rule or get pulled into emotional reactivity?
   What's the one refinement you'll commit to next time?

3. **My Child's Anchor**
   What's the simplest **Post-Event Repair Ritual (V.B.)** you can make non-negotiable this week?

Closing Thoughts

Your ability to execute a plan in moments of chaos is the living proof of your healing. You are not just building boundaries—you're building a **fortress of predictability** your child can lean on.

"You don't have to be loud to be powerful. Your consistency is your authority."

You now have structure—not just for communication, but for crisis. You've learned to transform uncertainty into protocol and emotional chaos into calm execution.

Yet even the strongest systems of safety eventually meet the human need for connection.

In the next chapter, we expand beyond protection into *reconnection*—exploring how to build new love, family structures, and blended stability without disrupting the nervous system you've worked so hard to steady.

15

Introducing Your New Partner & Blended Family Transitions

Introduction—Love After the Storm

After navigating separation and rebuilding internal steadiness, you are standing at a new threshold—the possibility of love again.
For many, this step feels like sunlight breaking through after years of conflict, loss, and healing. Hope returns, but so does complexity.

When you are a parent—especially after divorce or a high-conflict co-parenting dynamic—love cannot rush the nervous system that's still learning safety. The work now is not to find *new excitement*, but to build *new steadiness*—for both you and your child.

This chapter is your guide to moving forward with compassion, clarity, and pacing that honors everyone's capacity. Love that truly heals does not demand speed; it demands respect for each nervous system involved.

Your Core Principle—Safety Sets the Pace

Your child has already weathered one major change—the loss or redefinition of family structure. Introducing a new partner is not a "fresh start"; it's another shift in the emotional ecosystem they depend on for security.

Your responsibility is to manage the tempo of transition so that your child's body—and your own—have time to adapt. Your new partner is entering a living, breathing system built on resilience, routines, and the hard-won sense of safety you've established since the separation.

Every introduction, conversation, and milestone must serve that safety first.

Mantra—"Love grows slowly when it's safe enough to stay."

What You Will Learn

In this chapter, you will explore both the emotional and practical scaffolding for integrating new love into family life without destabilizing the system you've worked so hard to rebuild.

You'll learn how to:

- **Assess genuine readiness** for introductions—emotionally, developmentally, and relationally.
- **Prepare your partner** for the sacred role of *waiting*—being present without pressure.
- **Communicate with honesty** and age-appropriate clarity.
- **Navigate loyalty binds and triangulation** when children or co-parents react from fear, not malice.
- **Handle scrutiny and boundary testing**—both from co-parents and the legal system—with calm documentation and predictable responses.
- **Create rituals and rhythms** that allow blending or coexistence to happen naturally, without force.

Before you invite anyone into your child's world, pause. Readiness isn't about time passed—it's about nervous systems healed. The next section will walk you through the internal and relational signs that signal true readiness—for you, your child, and your new partner—to begin a slow, stable introduction process.

Readiness Assessment—Pacing for Protection

There is no universal calendar for readiness—only regulation and relational stability. True readiness isn't measured by how much time has passed; it's measured by how grounded, stable, and emotionally predictable your home has become.

This process protects both you and your child from premature transitions. Readiness is protection.

Your Comprehensive Readiness Checklist (Scoring & Interpretation)

Use this checklist as a self-assessment tool, not a judgment.
Complete it when you are calm, honest, and willing to look at your current ecosystem as it is—not as you hope it to be.

Rate each factor from **0 to 2**
(0 = No, 1 = Partly, 2 = Yes)

Factor	Question & Rationale	Score
1. Time Since Transition	Has it been at least 12 months since the final separation or stabilization of conflict? *Rationale:* The family system needs time to establish a "new normal."	☐
2. Relationship Stability	Is this partnership fully established, committed, and beyond the "honeymoon" phase? *Rationale:* Introductions should be reserved for long-term, emotionally mature relationships—not early dating.	☐
3. Motivation Check	Am I introducing this person out of love and grounded connection—or loneliness, relief, or spite toward my ex? *Rationale:* Emotional needs must be met outside of new partnerships before introducing one to your child.	☐
4. Child's Stability Baseline	Has my child maintained steady sleep, appetite, mood, and performance for at least 3–6 months? *Rationale:* A major stressor should never coincide with a new introduction.	☐
5. Partner Empathy	Does my partner understand the child's emotional history—including trauma, conflict, or grief—and show patience with the process? *Rationale:* The ability to wait is more important than eagerness to bond.	☐

Factor	Question & Rationale	Score
6. Co-Parenting Stability	Are communication systems (Chapters 12–13) strong enough to withstand potential reactions from the other parent? *Rationale:* A new relationship will test boundaries; stability must come first.	☐
Total Score:		/12

Score Interpretation

- **10–12 (Green Light):** Proceed gently. Plan a neutral, low-stakes first meeting.
- **7–9 (Yellow Light):** Slow down. Identify the lowest factor (usually your motivation or child's stability) and address it before introducing anyone new.
- **≤6 (Red Light):** Pause. This is not the right time. An introduction now risks destabilizing the child's sense of safety and trust.

Your Nervous System Lens—Is this Safe?

Children who have endured instability, loss, or chronic conflict (see Chapter 13) carry a *high-alert nervous system.*
When faced with a new adult, their body silently asks one question:

"Is this person a replacement, a threat, or an additional source of safety?"

Your pacing answers that question more clearly than your words ever can.

- **Pacing Answers**
  "This is safe. This doesn't change us."
  Slow, steady exposure, consistent routines, and emotional predictability communicate safety through action.

- **Rushing Answers**
  "This is chaos. I might lose you."
  Rapid overnights, emotional labeling ("They love you too!"), or sudden role changes can overwhelm a child's still-recovering system.

Clinician Note

Most children need **12–24 months** of stability after divorce or major transitions before they are ready to integrate new attachment figures.

The Stability Window: 12–24 Months of Repair

Most family therapists and trauma specialists recommend a **stability window** of 12–24 months after final separation or high-conflict resolution before introducing new partners. This is not a punishment or a delay tactic—it's nervous system science. Healing attachment systems takes time, structure, and predictability.

Use your therapist's guidance, your own self-awareness, and your child's **somatic cues**—sleep, appetite, eye contact, tone—as your compass. When in doubt, follow the body over the calendar.

Reflection—Love After Loss: Your Inner Inventory

What am I hoping this new love will repair that only I can heal?

Which part of me still believes safety must be earned through performance or closeness?

How will I measure success—by my child's comfort, my partner's enthusiasm, or my own calm?

Preparing Your Ecosystem—Your Partner and Child

The introduction phase is less about the *event* and more about the *ecosystem*—the emotional readiness of your partner, your child, and yourself. You are preparing not for a single meeting, but for a gradual adjustment that protects the attachment systems involved.

Your Partner's Guide to Waiting (Attunement vs. Intrusion)

Entering your child's world is not a moment—it's a process. The greatest gift a new partner can bring is patience. Their role is not to *enter* quickly, but to *attune* slowly. Each interaction should protect your child's sense of safety, not rush their acceptance.

Do (Role—Supporter & Friend)	Don't (Role—Parent or Rival)
Follow the child's lead. Let them set the pace and initiate contact or conversation.	**Seek instant closeness.** Avoid forced hugs, big gifts, or over-the-top praise.
Ask, "What helps them feel safe?" Debrief with you after each interaction to learn your child's boundaries.	**Post about the child online.** Maintain privacy and avoid public sharing; this protects both the child and co-parent boundaries.
Keep meetings short, kind, and neutral. Shared activities like a park visit or simple meal keep things light.	**Discipline or correct early.** Your partner's role is *bonus adult*, not replacement parent.
Model the peace you want to create. Be calm and respectful of the co-parent's home and rules.	**Compare to the co-parent.** Never speak negatively about the other parent, even if the child does.
Quote to share with your partner: "A child doesn't need a perfect new adult— just one who knows how to wait."	

Clinician Insight
Early-stage introductions should look more like parallel play than family bonding. The nervous system needs *familiarity* before it can build *trust*.

Activity 15.1: Your Blended-Readiness Reflection Map

Purpose
To transform the psycho-educational "Readiness Assessment" into a reflective, embodied process.

Reflection Prompt	My Honest Response	My Regulation Plan (Chapter 5)
What emotion arises when I imagine my child meeting my new partner?		
What fear or fantasy most drives my pacing (loneliness, excitement, guilt)?		
What body cues tell me I'm ready/not ready?		
What does *safety* mean for me and my child in this season?		

Clinician Note
This map trains metacognition—helping parents read the signals of readiness as somatic information, not moral judgment.

Communication—Honesty Over Hype

Your tone and pacing will shape the child's perception more than your words. Honesty regulates; hype destabilizes. Keep all explanations rooted in simplicity and emotional truth.

Age Guidance	Key Messages & Example Scripts
Ages 3–6 (Concrete Thinkers)	**Focus:** *Meeting a friend.* Script: "I have a friend named [Name] who is special to me. We're going to meet them at the park for a few minutes." *(Keep it about your calm feelings, not the child's reaction.)*

Age Guidance	Key Messages & Example Scripts
Ages 7–12 (Loyalty Bind Stage)	**Focus:** *Your consistent relationship.* Script: "I've been spending time with someone named [Name], and I'd like you to meet them when you're ready. This doesn't change how much time we spend together." *(Acknowledge the child's fear of loss directly.)*
Ages 13+ (Autonomy Stage)	**Focus:** *Respect for their timeline.* Script: "I've been in a relationship with [Name] for [duration]. Would you like to meet them soon, or later? I'll follow your lead." *(Offer agency—this invites connection through choice.)*

Your Tough Question Scripts

Children often test new emotional territory through direct questions. These moments are not challenges—they're bids for reassurance.

- **Child:** "Are they my new Mom/Dad?"
  You: "No. You already have [Parent's Name] and me. [Partner's Name] is a new adult who cares about us both. They're someone who will be kind and respectful to you."
- **Child:** "Will they come to my events?"
  You: "Not yet. We're taking this slowly. You'll decide with me when that feels right."

Clinician Note
When you answer without defensiveness, you model emotional safety. The goal is not to create *acceptance*, but to remove *alarm*.

Activity 15.2: Your Partner Preparation Checklist (Attunement Plan)

Purpose
To support structured conversations with your new partner so they can join the system without intrusion.

1) Schedule a 30-minute talk with your partner.
2) Review each statement aloud and have them answer "Ready," "Learning," or "Not Yet."

216

Statement	Response
I understand the child's history and current sensitivities.	
I am comfortable waiting months before being introduced.	
I know the child's parent remains the central attachment figure.	
I will not post or discuss the child online.	
I'm open to feedback after each interaction.	

Afterward, journal: *What did their responses reveal about my pace, boundaries, or fears?*

Managing the Aftershock—Your Child's Emotional Responses

Big feelings after introductions don't mean failure—they mean the body is processing change.
Your child's behavior is always communication, not defiance. Every reaction is a nervous system response searching for safety.

Deciphering Your Child's Reaction

Each behavior tells you what their body believes about safety in this new context.
Your role is to respond to the feeling underneath, not the surface behavior.

Reaction	Possible Meaning	Parent Response (Attunement)
Withdrawal/Quietness	Overwhelm, loyalty bind, or fear of disappointing you.	**Quiet reassurance:** "I see you're quiet. You don't have to feel any certain way. I'm here, and we're just spending time together."

Reaction	Possible Meaning	Parent Response (Attunement)
Clinginess/Regression	Fear of losing you or fear of the new partner taking your attention.	**Extra connection:** Schedule sacred one-on-one time before and after visits. Anchor them in your consistent presence.
Anger/Defiance	Grief disguised as anger, or stress discharge; testing whether your boundaries still hold.	**Steady boundaries:** "I hear you're angry. We can talk about this when you're calm, but this is a choice I've made." *(Do not defend your choice.)*
Over-Eagerness/People-Pleasing	Anxiety masked as performance; fear of rejection by the new adult.	**Slow the pace:** Reduce the intensity and duration of interactions. Protect their authenticity over "good behavior."

Clinician Note—Body First

Children process distress through their bodies—sleep disruption, appetite changes, stomachaches, regression in independence. If these occur, **pause introductions** and **restore predictability** for at least 1–2 weeks. Familiar routines re-teach the body that safety has returned.

Loyalty Binds and Triangulation Management

This is one of the most delicate and crucial dynamics in post-divorce family systems. A child caught between loyalty to one parent and affection for a new adult experiences chronic stress. Your goal is to **separate loyalty from love**—allowing your child to feel free to care for both.

Your Core Goal

Decouple your child's loyalty to their other parent from their freedom to enjoy their relationship with your new partner.

Steps for Supporting Dual Bonds

1. **Validate Dual Feelings**
   Script: "You can love Daddy and still enjoy being around [Partner's Name]. Those feelings don't take away from each other."
   Purpose: Validates ambivalence and teaches emotional integration rather than secrecy.

2. **Affirm the Parent–Child Bond**
   After an introduction, immediately carve out **30–60 minutes of one-on-one parent/child time.**
   Use physical proximity and consistent attention to anchor safety.
   Script: "You'll always have this time with me. [Partner's Name] didn't take that away."
   Purpose: Confirms permanence and stabilizes attachment security.

3. **Grey Rock the Co-Parent (Child Reports Conflict)**
   If your child shares negative comments or emotional content from the other parent, respond with calm neutrality.
   Script: "That sounds like a grown-up problem. That's between [Co-Parent's Name] and me. You don't have to carry or fix it."
   Then, **end the conversation** gently but firmly to prevent emotional triangulation.
   Purpose: Protects the child from adult emotional weight while modeling emotional boundaries.

Navigating Your Ex-Partner Dynamic (Protection, Not Permission)

You do not owe your ex-partner approval. You owe them **clarity, safety, and compliance with the law—nothing more.**

The introduction of a new partner often activates your ex-partner's deepest fears of replacement or loss of control. Your goal is to stay anchored in **protection, not permission.** You protect peace by staying in the lane of law and structure, not emotion.

Your Co-Parenting Approach (Boundary Triage)

Each co-parenting relationship requires a unique communication strategy. Your response should always be proportional to the level of safety and cooperation in the dynamic.

Co-Parenting Type	Your Response Strategy	Documentation Focus
Collaborative	**Brief heads-up:** "I've started dating someone committed and plan to introduce them to the kids in a few weeks. I'll let you know the date of the first meeting." *(Share minimal details; keep tone factual and professional.)*	**Optional:** One short note confirming communication suffices.
High-Conflict	**Minimal info, maximum boundary.** Only disclose if legally required. Script: "I'm in a committed relationship and will be following the introduction guidelines outlined in our plan." *(No elaboration, no engagement.)*	**Required:** Log every reaction—include date, time, and direct quotes to identify control or disparagement patterns.
Litigious/Controlling	**Consult counsel first.** Review your court order for morality or non-disparagement clauses before making introductions. If needed, notify only through counsel.	**Critical:** Each communication should be vetted and logged to avoid manipulation or future weaponization.

Clinician Note

When safety or control issues exist, *transparency should always flow upward*—to professionals, not to the ex-partner. Oversharing with an unsafe person is not co-parenting; it's self-exposure.

Your Legal and Digital Safety Triggers

Protecting your peace includes protecting your digital footprint and legal compliance.

- **Review Your Order**
  Know your state's specific language around introducing new partners, overnight visits, and supervision.

- **School List Protocol**

Only list your new partner as an emergency contact once there is a defined legal role or long-term commitment.

- **Digital Hygiene**
  Assume every screenshot could end up in court. Write and store all communication accordingly.

- **Boundaried Transparency**
  You owe honesty to your child's truth—not to your co-parent's volatility.

Mantra—"I owe transparency to the law and to my child's truth, not to someone else's chaos."

Blending or Co-Existing—The Art of Slow Integration

True belonging is not built in milestones—it's built in *moments*.
Slow integration gives your child's body, mind, and heart time to believe that safety still exists, even as life expands.

This phase isn't about forming a "perfect blended family." It's about defining what form of connection feels **safe, sustainable, and aligned** for your unique system.

Defining Your New Family Form

Every family system after divorce or separation finds its own rhythm. Naming your structure gives clarity—and clarity is what the nervous system craves.

Form	Meaning & Pacing	Child's Felt Safety
Fully Blended	Shared home, finances, and caregiving. *(The slowest and most complex path.)*	Requires years of predictable safety and emotional stability before cohabitation.
Parallel Partners	Separate homes; the partner supports your parenting rhythm without stepping into it.	Often the safest path to stability; preserves the parent-child attachment.
Bonus Adult/Friend	The partner is a consistent, non-parental adult who offers warmth,	High safety, low confusion. This form works well for

Form	Meaning & Pacing	Child's Felt Safety
	presence, and support—without taking on discipline or decision-making.	children still building post-divorce trust.

Clinician Insight

"Blending" is not a moral upgrade—it's a pacing decision. The slower the integration, the more the nervous system trusts it.

Your Rituals of Integration—Translating Change Into Consistency

Rituals are the nervous system's love language. They say what words can't: *You are safe here. This new adult fits into our predictable rhythm.*

Here are key rituals to anchor steadiness:

- **Hello/Goodbye Phrase**
  Use a fixed phrase for the partner's arrivals and departures—something simple and repeatable.
  Example: "See you tomorrow, [Name]."
  Predictable words regulate unpredictable emotions.

- **Quiet Time Post-Visit**
  After any visit with the new partner, reserve **30–60 minutes** of quiet, low-stimulation time for just you and your child.
  Example: reading, coloring, or slow breathing.
  Purpose: Gives the body space to decompress and reaffirm secure attachment.

- **Shared Mini-Traditions**
  Build small, low-stakes traditions that include the new partner.
  Example: Saturday pancakes, a short walk, a specific card game.
  Simple consistency outperforms grand gestures.

- **One-on-One Parent Time**
  No matter how well integration goes, your child needs **uninterrupted, non-negotiable time** with just you every week.
  This isn't exclusion—it's reassurance: "Our bond doesn't shrink as our world grows."

Your Final Safety Measures

Love after loss doesn't need an audience to be real. Public exposure—especially online—invites emotional risk for both you and your child. This stage is about keeping sacred what's still growing, while ensuring your digital life supports your legal, emotional, and family safety.

Your Digital Boundaries & Privacy

Digital restraint is not secrecy; it's safety. Protect what is private until it is stable enough to be shared.

- **Social Media Review**
  Check your parenting plan for clauses about social posting. Avoid real-time tagging, location sharing, or posting images of your child without explicit permission.

- **Teen Consent**
  Always ask your teen before sharing or tagging. Respect their digital boundaries as you would want yours respected.

- **Partner's Profile**
  Ensure your new partner understands that no photos, updates, or public references to your child should be shared until long-term stability—or legal approval—is established.

Clinician Note
Treat every online interaction as part of the public record. If you wouldn't want to explain it in court or in therapy, don't post it.

Reflection & Planning Self-Check—Steady Is Safe

You are not putting your heart on hold—you are protecting it long enough to build something sustainable. Each reflection question below invites you to ground love in steadiness, not speed.

Reflection Prompts (Write these out)

1. Your Child's Experience

What do I want this to *feel* like for my child—safe, fun, normal, not rushed?

_____

_____

_____

2. Your Partner's Role

Is my partner acting as a supporter (healthy) or as a second parent too soon (intrusive)? What boundary do I need to restate with them?

_____

_____

_____

3. Your Co-Parent Buffer

How can I apply the Grey Rock method (see Chapter 12) to prevent my co-parent's emotions from entering my home? (e.g., *Script:* "Noted. I won't be discussing my personal life.")

_____

_____

_____

4. Your Self-Check

What am I grieving—the ease of dating, the fantasy of simplicity, or the illusion of closure?

_____

_____

Signs You're Integrating Well

- Your child still comes to you first for comfort and discipline.
- Your partner waits for the child's invitation before engaging ("Would you like me to join this game?").
- Home routines feel rhythmic and predictable, not chaotic.
- The co-parent's opinions no longer control your nervous system (see Chapters 12–13).
- Love feels *spacious*—not divided, not secret, not rushed.

Closing Thoughts

Introducing a new partner isn't about filling the space of what was lost—it's about expanding the circle of what's safe, steady, and possible for your child. It is love that expands, rather than replaces.

Love after divorce or conflict is not proof of moving on; it's evidence of healing. It's the moment when your nervous system begins to trust peace again.

When you lead with truth, patience, and regulation, you're not just building a new relationship—you're modeling emotional intelligence for your child. You're teaching them that love and stability can coexist, that new bonds don't erase old ones, and that safety can grow in more than one direction.

Parent Reflection
"Every healthy love begins with self-trust. When I protect my child's pace, I protect my own."

Love that honors safety is never rushed, loud, or performative—it's quiet, rhythmic, and believable.

"Connection without pressure becomes belonging.
Belonging without fear becomes home."

By slowing love to the speed of safety, you've built the scaffolding for expansion without collapse.
The next step is protection—not just of emotional space, but of psychological integrity.
Chapter 16 to start Part V moves from emotional integration to *defense of the system itself*—

teaching how to shield your child's mind and self-worth from manipulation, triangulation, and power games that threaten the safety you've rebuilt

PART V: Integration and Sustainability

Coming Home to the Self You Were Before Survival Took Over

"Redemption isn't about erasing what happened. It's about reclaiming the parts of you that learned to survive it."

NJ

16

Protecting Your Child Against Manipulation

Introduction—When Love Gets Twisted

After establishing new connections safely in Chapter 15, we turn to the paramount need: **protection**—guarding your child's emotional clarity when adults behave unfairly.

Manipulation occurs when a child is drawn into emotional labor they were never meant to perform—managing an adult's moods, protecting their secrets, or serving as a messenger. These roles distort safety. They teach the child that love must be earned through loyalty, silence, or emotional caretaking.

Whether overt or subtle, manipulation rewires a child's nervous system. Their body begins to brace for guilt, freeze in confusion, or over-function in an effort to keep the peace.

Clinical Insight
This is not a moral failure of the manipulative parent—it is often an unhealed trauma pattern. But the impact on the child is always greater than the parent's intent.

You can't control what another parent says, but you can shape what your child believes about themselves.

Your work is to help your child unlearn the hidden message: *"Love is conditional and heavy."*

What Manipulation Looks Like to a Child

Children sense distortion long before they can describe it. Their behavior—withdrawal, people-pleasing, or sudden anxiety—is often the nervous system's attempt to restore balance when the emotional truth doesn't match the spoken one.

Manipulative Pattern	Example of Adult Behavior	Hidden Lesson to the Child
Guilt-Tripping	"If you really loved me, you wouldn't be happy at the other house."	*Love means pleasing others.*
Emotional Withdrawal	Coldness or silence after a visit with the other parent.	*Affection is conditional on my choices.*
Bribery/Over-Praise	Excessive gifts or "special treatment" for loyalty or secrets.	*Stuff equals safety and conditional approval.*
Triangulation	"Tell your dad he owes me money."	*I exist to carry adult problems.*
False Blame/Shame	"You made me feel this way when you told them that."	*I'm responsible for adult pain.*

Clinician Note

These behaviors often stem from a parent's own unprocessed grief, abandonment wounds, or attachment trauma. But for the child, the result is internalized confusion: *"Am I loved for who I am, or for what I protect?"*

A Child's Internal Impact—Rewiring for Safety

Manipulation rewires a child's nervous system for survival, not for safety. Instead of learning that connection is reliable, they learn that love comes with conditions. Their body becomes fluent in scanning for tone, tension, and danger—constantly predicting, protecting, and performing.

Your calm presence is the antidote. Each regulated response you offer tells their nervous system, *"You don't have to perform here. You're already safe."*

Your steadiness doesn't erase the manipulation; it retrains the brain toward safety.

Activity 16.1: Your Manipulation Impact Inventory

Purpose
To track behavioral, emotional, and physical signs of manipulation while staying focused on healing rather than proving.

Observation Area	Signs I've Noticed	Possible Manipulation Source	My Regulation or Response Plan
Mood & Emotion	(e.g., withdrawal, guilt, tension after visits)		
Behavior & Language	(e.g., "You always yell at Dad.")		
Body & Sleep	(e.g., nightmares, stomach pain, restlessness)		
Relationship Shifts	(e.g., sudden rejection, secrecy)		

Clinical Insight
This tool transforms documentation into a **healing log**—a way to observe without reacting, creating an evidence-informed emotional map for therapy and parenting consistency.

How Manipulation Changes a Child's Core Beliefs

These children internalize messages that shape their worldview—not through words, but through nervous system memory. Healing begins when you name what's happening, without blame, and help the body unlearn survival as its only language.

Impact	Observable Signs	Core Belief Learned
Hypervigilance/Shutdown	Watches every mood, over-apologizes, or goes silent when tension rises.	"I must stay alert to survive."
Blurred Boundaries	Absorbs others' sadness or guilt; becomes the emotional manager.	"My job is to fix and manage you."
Split Loyalties	Acts like two different children between homes; hides one parent's love from the other.	"I can't be whole anywhere."
Shame Core	Perfectionism, guilt, self-blame, or an exaggerated sense of responsibility.	"Love is performance. I am the problem."

Clinician Note

The child's symptoms—anxiety, regression, perfectionism—are not misbehavior; they are survival strategies. Their body is adapting to emotional unpredictability. Your role isn't to correct the behavior; it's to restore safety until the behavior no longer serves a purpose.

The STOP Skill Protocol (When Your Child is Activated)

When your child is triggered—crying, withdrawing, or lashing out—your regulation must become their external nervous system. This 60-second intervention interrupts the survival loop and reorients them toward safety.

S—Stop.
Drop what you're doing. Freeze your reaction. Eye contact off. You are switching from "fixing" to "anchoring."

T—Take a Breath.
One slow exhale signals your own nervous system: *pause before protecting*. (See your Core Regulation Tools in Chapter 4.)

O—Observe.

Notice where you feel the pull to react (tight chest, clenched jaw, racing heart). Awareness rewires impulse.

P—Proceed with One Steady Sentence.

Deliver a short, calm connecting statement:

"You're safe to tell me that. We can slow down."

Avoid lecturing, correcting, or asking questions. Your tone—not your words—is the repair.

Bridge to Protection

True protection isn't about controlling exposure; it's about counteracting distortion.

Protection = Truth told calmly by a regulated parent.

Every time you model steadiness, you become the predictable signal that safety still exists in their world.

Teaching Your Child Inner Clarity—Using Questions as Bridges

The most powerful protective skill you can teach your child is **discernment**—the ability to separate *their truth* from someone else's emotion. Discernment is not defiance; it is self-trust. When you help your child locate what's real inside them, you are rebuilding their **emotional immune system**—the capacity to filter what enters their heart.

These questions are not interrogation tools. They are gentle bridges—invitations that guide the child from confusion back to inner safety.

Questions to Build Your Child's Emotional Immune System

Gentle Prompt	Why it Matters/Core Skill Built
"Where do you feel that in your body?"	**Anchors Emotion to Sensation.** Helps them link emotional discomfort to a physical cue, teaching that their body holds trustworthy information.
"Is that your thought, or something someone else told you?"	**Builds Discernment.** Teaches them to recognize when external influence is shaping their internal experience.
"Did that feel kind, confusing, or something else?"	**Normalizes Complexity.** Gives permission to experience mixed feelings—about both parents—without shame.
"What would help you feel safe right now?"	**Restores Agency.** Allows the child to take small ownership of their environment when they feel powerless.
"Can we pause and check again later?"	**Teaches Emotional Pacing.** Shows that truth doesn't need to be rushed; it grows safer with regulation.

Clinician Note

These questions activate the prefrontal cortex—the thinking, reasoning brain—and quiet the amygdala (the threat center). Over time, your calm tone rewires "What's true?" from panic to curiosity.

Your Scripts for Repair & Resilience (Calm Truth)

When distortion or manipulation enters your home, your tone is the medicine. The goal is not to *disprove* the distortion but to '*outsteady*' it.
Each response below centers your child's lived experience—not the other parent's behavior.

Situation	Regulated Response (Centered in Child's Experience)
Child repeats a distortion or lie	"That sounds confusing. Let's check what feels real for you and me here."
Child feels guilty or torn	"You don't have to choose. You get to love both of us—and still have your own feelings."
Child refuses affection or pulls away	"It's okay to need space. Even when it's hard between us, I'm still your safe place. I'm here when you're ready."
Child uses a manipulative tone (Trauma Re-enactment)	(Use STOP Skill first.) "I hear the anger. When we use kind words, we can talk about it."

Activity 16.2: Truth-Telling Scripts

Purpose
To rehearse consistent, safe language that neutralizes manipulation and anchors calm truth.

Example Prompts:
1) "It's okay if you love both homes."
2) "That sounds confusing; I'll help you sort it out."
3) "No one can make you choose. You belong to both of us."

Practice Area

Clinician Note
Use a steady cadence. Your predictability becomes the nervous-system cue for safety.

Vignette—The Walk Home

Eight-year-old Milo whispered, "Dad said you don't love him."
His mother paused, taking a slow breath. "That must've felt strange to hear. I love him differently now—and I always love you the same." She exhaled.
You don't have to fight the story; you only have to 'outsteady' it.

Therapeutic Reminder
Your child doesn't need you to defend the truth—they need you to *embody* it. Each calm correction re-establishes the nervous system truth: *safety exists here.*

Your Protection Strategy—Neutrality and Documentation

Protection doesn't mean silence—it means holding the truth steady without pulling your child into adult battles.
Neutrality is not avoidance. It is your nervous system saying, *"We can stay truthful without joining the storm."*

Reflection—Protect Without Policing

1. What emotion arises when my child repeats something untrue or confusing?

2. Do I rush to "correct," or can I stay still and model calm?

3. How do I know I'm protecting versus defending?

4. What ritual (hug, phrase, bedtime pattern) rebuilds trust after tension?

Clinical Framing

This reflection strengthens **self-attunement**—the difference between regulating *for* your child and reacting *through* them.

How to Stay Neutral While Still Protecting Your Child

Your goal is to correct distortion without assigning blame. Each time you speak calmly, you model to your child that truth can exist without shame, anger, or sides.

Protective Action	What to Say (Neutral Script)	What Not to Say (Disparagement)
Address the Lie	"That sounds confusing. Here's what's real in our home."	"That's a lie."/"They always do this."
Protect Loyalty	"You're allowed to love us both. That's your choice."	"Pick a side."/"They're trying to turn you against me."
Contain Messages	"That's not something you need to carry or worry about."	"Don't tell them what we talked about."

Clinician Note

A neutral correction rewires the child's sense of truth as safe—not explosive. This helps rebuild the link between honesty and safety in their body. The goal isn't to "fix the story," but to keep the home emotionally predictable.

Your Debrief Worksheet (Focus on Repair)

This tool helps you process conflict without reactivity and identify what your nervous system needs next.
Use it after every emotionally charged exchange.

Prompt	Your Notes
1. Trigger Event:	Example: Child returned 3/15 and said, "Mom said you always forget."
2. My First Body Reaction (Chapter 4):	Example: Tight chest, heat rising, urge to defend.
3. Regulated Response I Used:	Example: STOP skill—paused, said, "That sounds confusing," and made tea.
4. What Worked/Didn't Work:	Example: The pause worked. Following up later was too complex.
5. One Truth to Reinforce Next Time:	Example: "You are the center of my world; I always put you first."
6. My Plan for Self-Care/Discharge (Chapter 4):	Example: 10 minutes of journaling and a shower.

Clinical Insight

Processing your reaction after—not during—protects your child from witnessing your repair process while still ensuring that your nervous system integrates the event instead of storing it.

Your Safety Sidebar—When to Escalate

If manipulation escalates into abuse or isolation, immediate, trauma-informed action is required.

- **Mandatory Reporting**
  If the child discloses fear, threats, or physical harm, you have a legal and ethical duty to report. Believe them. Don't interrogate; record their exact words and the time.

- **Legal/Clinical Next Steps**
  If chronic manipulation causes emotional harm (e.g., alienation, anxiety, extreme loyalty conflicts), document the behavioral patterns (Chapter 12) and consult a trauma-informed clinician or family law expert.

  Mantra—*Protect with facts, not fear.*

Truth documented calmly is more powerful than truth delivered in panic.

Your Final Guardrails—Digital and Relational Boundaries

Boundaries are the final layer of protection between your child's nervous system and the ongoing waves of manipulation or confusion.
Digital and relational boundaries don't isolate your child—they create *clear containers of safety* where connection can grow without intrusion.

When you manage these boundaries with calm consistency, you teach your child:

"Privacy is protection, not secrecy."

Your Device & Privacy Guardrails

Digital devices are often the most common—and subtle—entry points for manipulation. Each safeguard below reduces your child's emotional exposure while reinforcing digital trust and autonomy.

- **Disable Location Sharing**
  Turn off all location tracking on shared cloud albums and apps.

  > *Why it matters:* Surveillance fosters anxiety and erodes safety; privacy restores peace.

- **Privacy Lesson**
  Teach your child, *"There are no secret recordings in our home. If something feels scary or secret, show me right away."*

  > *Why it matters:* Builds discernment around healthy transparency versus emotional spying.

- **Screen Time Boundary**
  Ensure your child has uninterrupted, phone-free time when in your home—without pressure to constantly update or contact the other parent.

  > *Why it matters:* Creates emotional decompression space; reestablishes your home as a sanctuary.

Clinician Note
Digital intrusion activates the same part of the brain as physical threat (the amygdala). By separating digital time from emotional time, you give the nervous system permission to rest.

Your Boundaries for Extended Relatives

Well-meaning relatives can unintentionally reopen the child's loyalty conflicts. Equip them with language that keeps curiosity from becoming pressure.

Script
"Please don't ask [Child] about the other home or the conflict. Follow our lead—ask how they feel, what they're learning, but not for details about the co-parent."

Why it Matters
This preserves the child's emotional autonomy and teaches the wider family system how to support stability instead of feeding division.

Your Outcome Signals—How You'll Know it's Working

You'll know your guardrails are regulating, not restricting, when these subtle but powerful shifts appear:

- Fewer "testing" statements from your child—quicker returns to calm after conflict.

- Sleep and mood stabilize within 24–48 hours post-visit.

- Your child begins using "I feel…" instead of "They said…" language.

- You respond slower, softer, and more strategically.

Healing is rarely loud—it looks like longer pauses, fewer explanations, and steady repetition of safety.

Closing Thoughts

Protection is not war; it's endurance. It is the quiet work of holding your ground so your child can find theirs. Every time you stay calm in the face of distortion, you teach your child that peace is possible—even inside chaos.

Truth held calmly becomes louder than manipulation ever will.

You can't silence every falsehood, but you can embody the truth your child will one day recognize as home. Your steadiness—repeated, gentle, unshakable—is the shelter they'll return to long after the noise has passed.

You've practiced separating confusion from danger and protection from control. These pages taught you to transform fear into clarity and defensiveness into grounded truth.

The next chapter moves into *Financial and Power Dynamics in Co-Parenting*, where we'll examine how money, leverage, and dependency shape emotional safety—and how to restore dignity and fairness without losing your calm

17

Financial & Power Dynamics in Co-Parenting

Introduction—When Money Stops Being Neutral

Money isn't just about numbers or bills—in co-parenting, it's deeply emotional. It represents **safety, shame, and control**. After separation or conflict, financial exchanges often shift from support to leverage—a silent battleground disguised as obligation.

You've learned to hold your emotional truth steady under manipulation. Now, you'll learn to hold your *financial peace* with the same steady hand.

This chapter helps you **reclaim your dignity and stability** when finances are used as a form of control. Your power is not in your pay stub—it's in your presence and planning.

"Your receipts aren't your worth."

Even when your financial situation feels fragile, your value is non-negotiable.

Your Emotional Toll—Regulating Your Money Trigger

Financial stress lands first in the body, not the budget. When you receive a late payment, a shaming message, or a manipulative demand, your nervous system reacts before your rational brain does.

Typical Emotional Reflexes and Their Hidden Needs

- **Guilt/Shame**
  The body's call for *validation*—proof that your effort and survival count.

- **Over-Compensating**
  The nervous system's plea for *permission to pause* without fear of being judged irresponsible.

- **Avoidance/Freeze**
  The core need for *safety* to look at financial details without spiraling into panic.

Clinician Note
Financial triggers often awaken trauma tied to scarcity or self-worth. Regulating before reacting allows you to reframe money as a tool, not a test.

Activity 17.1: Your Money Trigger Map

Purpose
To help parents identify the link between financial stress, body sensations, and childhood associations.

Trigger Situation	Body Sensation	Old Narrative ("I must …")	New Regulated Message
Late payment/unmet obligation	Chest tightness, shallow breath	"I can't trust anyone."	"I can regulate first, then decide."
Shaming comment ("You depend on me")	Heat in face, clenched jaw	"I need to prove myself."	"My worth isn't for sale."

Trigger Situation	Body Sensation	Old Narrative ("I must …")	New Regulated Message
Financial demand	Numbness, fatigue	"I have no power."	"I can pause and plan."

Clinician Note

Use this tool as a somatic bridge—it transforms money from a moral stressor into neutral body data.

Your 60-Second Money STOP Protocol

When the financial trigger hits—a text, an invoice, or an accusation—your goal is to regulate, not react. You're not managing money; you're managing adrenaline.

S.T.O.P. in Practice

1. **S—Stop:** Do not reply, transfer, or even open the app. Pause all movement.

2. **T—Take one long exhale:** Let your breath reset your heart rate before your mind engages.

3. **O—Observe your body:** Notice and name what's happening—*"This is panic, not proof."*

4. **P—Proceed with one factual sentence (or none):** Delay response by 30 minutes or more.

   Mantra—*"Regulation is the budget line that makes every decision cheaper."*

Every calm decision saves energy, time, and self-respect.

Recognizing Economic Abuse and Financial Power Plays

Money becomes toxic when it stops being a resource and becomes a **weapon**—used to punish, provoke, or prove superiority. When financial control is used to induce fear, guilt, or dependence, it becomes a form of **domestic power**, not partnership.

This section helps you name what's happening so you can stop internalizing blame and start building protection. Financial safety begins with clarity, not confrontation.

Financial Power and Control Tactics

Economic abuse rarely announces itself. It hides inside "practical concerns" and "justifications"—until you start to feel smaller, scared, or indebted.

Power Play	Example of Behavior	Emotional Effect on You
Withholding Support	Late, missing, or partial payments; demanding receipts for every expense.	Triggers panic and scarcity; keeps you in survival mode.
Gift Leverage	Lavish gifts to the child to "win" loyalty or create imbalance.	Creates loyalty confusion for the child; breeds resentment and guilt in you.
Financial Shaming	"I'm the real provider."/"You'd be nothing without my money."	Destroys self-worth; fuels defensiveness and shame.
Court Weaponization	Excessive documentation demands, threats of legal action over trivial issues.	Causes hypervigilance, fear of making mistakes, and decision paralysis.
Forced Debt/Credit Damage	Opening accounts in your name, sabotaging employment or financial documents.	Instills chronic anxiety and long-term instability.

Clinician Note

Economic abuse erodes your sense of safety by making survival feel conditional. Treat these tactics as safety threats—not relationship problems.

Activity 17.2: Your Financial Boundaries Audit

Purpose

To identify which financial boundaries are being violated and to script regulated responses.

Boundary Area	Violation Example	My New Boundary Statement	Enforcement Plan
Payments/Support	Late or partial payments	"I'll log and address this through the app only."	Document + no debate
Purchases/Gifts	Competitive spending	"Our home focuses on connection over cost."	Reframe for child
Documentation	Excessive receipt requests	"Records are filed through counsel per agreement."	Copy to folder monthly

Reflection Prompt

Which boundary drains you the most, and which one restores you most when held?

Activity 17.3: Your Financial Safety Plan: Building Your Ally Network

Purpose

To create a practical safety net that separates your stability from the co-parent's control. This is about *structure over panic*—taking one protective action at a time.

Area	One Action Step This Month	Due Date	Ally/Resource
Ally Path	Identify one legal aid group or domestic violence economic advocate (DV Econ Program/Social Worker).		[Name/Number]
Digital Hygiene	Set up **two-factor authentication** for all financial apps, banking, and communication accounts.		[Password Notes]
Documentation	Create a **secure folder** (digital or physical) for all financial logs, receipts, and communications.		[Location]
Autonomy Step	Research one **job training, benefit, or credit repair resource** that increases independence.		[Resource Name]
Rest/Regulation	Schedule one **block of rest or joy** each week (see Chapters 4–5). Rest is resistance.		[Date/Time]

Action Step

Your first move is to identify one **Ally Path** this week—call a legal aid line, domestic violence advocate, or trusted social worker. You don't need to fight alone; you just need one informed witness to start the safety chain.

Responding to Financial Bait (Your Dignity Script)

Financial manipulation is one of the most common forms of post-separation control. The co-parent may use financial topics to provoke emotional reactions, disguise power plays as "logistical questions," or collapse boundaries through guilt.

Your task is not to win the argument—it's to protect your peace and preserve documentation.

When you respond with **factual neutrality**, you convert chaos into evidence and dignity into defense.

Core Reminder

Every unnecessary reply is an invoice on your nervous system.

Your Financial Disengagement Scripts

Each script below transforms reactivity into calm authority.
Your goal—**one factual sentence, no justification, no debate.**

Trigger	Common Reactive Impulse	Regulated Reclaim Script (Factual & Neutral)
Late Payment/"I won't pay."	Panic texting, arguing about fairness.	"Please confirm the payment date for [Month]. If payment is not received by [Date], I will document it as an arrears violation." *(Limit to one message.)*
Extravagant Gifts/Comparison	Defending your limited budget or feeling inferior.	*(To co-parent)*: No reply. *(To child)*: "That was a fun trip! We do things differently here, and that's okay. Our memories cost nothing."
"You owe me money/access."	Arguing for self-worth or fairness.	"Support payment is distinct from access time. All exchanges will follow the parenting plan."
"Send receipts for everything."	Over-explaining your purchases.	"All requested financial records are filed appropriately. Please direct future requests through counsel, as agreed."
"You're financially irresponsible."	Paragraphs of justification, defensiveness.	*Do not reply.* If absolutely necessary: "This exchange is documented. I will limit

Trigger	Common Reactive Impulse	Regulated Reclaim Script (Factual & Neutral)
		communication to factual, logistical matters."

Clinician Note

Financial bait is not about the bill—it's about your emotional currency.
Refusing to engage is not avoidance; it's regulation.

Reflection—Your Emotional Cost Ledger

1. What interaction costs me the most energy?

2. Which conversation actually earns me peace?

3. If my calm was money; how would I spend it more wisely?

Clinician Framing

This reflection links **economic regulation** with emotional budgeting—a reframing that's deeply effective in trauma-informed financial coaching.

Your Digital Finance Hygiene & Communication Protocol

When your finances and communication overlap, boundaries must become procedural. Think of your phone and your inbox as *legal spaces*, not emotional ones.

Co-Parenting App & Messaging Tips

- **Assume every message is read by a judge.**

- **Subject Lines:** Always factual (e.g., *"Child Support Payment—October"*).

- **Length:** Limit to three sentences or less.

- **Content:** One topic per message. Avoid sarcasm, opinion, or emotional appeals.

- **Tone:** Neutral, dry, and recorded.

Court-Safe Documentation Practice

- Log every financial exchange, insult, or delay verbatim.

- Record the *observed emotional effect* (yours or the child's) factually, without interpretation.

- Store these records **outside** the co-parenting app—on a secure, offline drive or encrypted folder.

> **Mantra**—*"My silence is structure. My documentation is peace."*

Talking to Your Child About Money Without Shame

Your child will notice differences. They'll compare houses, toys, vacations, and tone. Your calm response is the anchor that turns comparison into stability—teaching them that **security comes from connection, not cash.**

Money conversations are never really about numbers; they're about safety, belonging, and worth.

This section helps you reframe those moments into quiet lessons of resilience and truth.

Messaging Safety Over Scarcity

Children absorb your energy long before they understand economics. When you speak about money, your tone becomes their financial nervous system.

Use phrases that emphasize sufficiency, dignity, and connection:

Message	Purpose
"We do things differently here."	Teaches autonomy and respect; separates self-worth from possessions or comparison.
"We have everything we need right now."	Centers emotional safety over financial fear; grounds the child in sufficiency and presence.
"Money is my job, not yours."	Removes financial burden and loyalty pressure from the child.
"Memories cost nothing."	Shifts focus from material value to shared experience. Connection becomes the measure of abundance.

Clinician Note

A child's sense of "enough" is borrowed from your nervous system. When you sound steady, their body learns that scarcity is not danger—it's simply difference.

Activity 17.4: Your Child's Money-Message Map

Purpose

To track the child's exposure to money talk and reframe it into security language.

Situation	Child's Possible Thought	My Regulated Reframe	Frequency (Weekly/Monthly)
Overhears financial argument	"We're broke/in trouble."	"Adults are sorting adult things. You're safe."	
Sees unequal gifts	"Dad loves me more."	"Different homes, same love."	
Hears complaint about support	"I cause problems."	"Money is grown-up stuff—your job is to be a kid."	

When Your Peers or Co-Parent Highlight Differences

Children may come home carrying comparison—or confusion.
A gift from the other household might feel like proof of love. A peer might say, "You don't have as much." This is not a test of your finances; it's a test of your steadiness.

Script (Gentle Reframe)
"It's okay to love that new toy—and it's also okay if someone else has more stuff. You're not less; you're loved. Let's plan something small that feels like *us*—our kind of fun."

This validates their excitement without feeding material competition. You model peace without pretense.

What Not to Put on Your Child

Children are never meant to carry the weight of adult math. Avoid disclosing the amounts of support, arrears, or "who pays what."

Anchor Phrase
"Money things are for adults. Your job is to be a kid."

Even when under pressure or scrutiny, your restraint is protection. Each time you shield your child from adult financial tension, you rewire their nervous system for trust—not fear.

Your Financial Dignity and Emotional Wealth

Financial dignity means recognizing both your effort and your reality. It's the quiet, grounded belief that your worth is not measured by your income, your receipts, or your ability to match another household's spending.

Money mirrors power systems—gender inequity, care labor, disability, and burnout—all of which can distort your sense of 'enoughness'. Reclaiming financial dignity is not about earning more; it's about **disconnecting your worth from external validation** and realigning it with truth, stability, and care.

Activity 17.5: Your Abundance Practice Planner

Purpose
To translate emotional-wealth concepts into daily practice.

Day	Small Act of Calm ("Emotional Deposit")	How It Felt	Child's Reaction/Reflection
Monday	Ate dinner without phone notifications	Grounded	Smiled more at table
Wednesday	Shared story from childhood about gratitude	Warm	Asked for more stories

Mantra

Write a sentence you'll repeat this week when scarcity shows up:

_____

_____

Your Abundance Reframe

These phrases serve as internal anchors—brief mantras that rewire scarcity thinking into emotional sufficiency. They don't change your budget; they change your relationship to it.

Anchor Phrase	Intention/Self-Validation
"I give what I have—it's enough."	Releases the compulsion to over-give or over-prove. Replaces guilt with presence.
"My worth isn't for sale."	Reinforces that love, loyalty, and access cannot be purchased or bargained for.
"Our home is rich in calm."	Redefines wealth through regulation—where peace, predictability, and care become the true assets.

Clinician Note

A scarcity mindset is a nervous-system state, not a moral failure. Every calm breath around money teaches the child that security is something we feel, not something we spend.

Non-Monetary Rituals (Calm is a Currency)

Emotional wealth is built in ordinary moments. It's the rituals that create continuity when finances fluctuate.

- **Low-Cost Joy**
  Create two small, recurring rituals—like Saturday pancakes, evening reading, or a shared gratitude jar. These are deposits into your child's emotional bank account.

- **Care is Support**
  Acknowledge that for many (especially non-custodial parents or caregivers managing systemic barriers), care itself is a contribution.
  Time, reliability, and emotional presence carry financial value.

  Care is currency. Consistency is compound interest.

Closing Thoughts

Calm isn't free—it's earned through regulation, boundary-setting, and repair.
But once you have it, it multiplies

Every calm reply, every bedtime story uninterrupted by chaos, and every regulated hand-off builds wealth your child will inherit—the wealth of safety.

Closing Mantra
"Calm is a currency; I spend it on stability."

You've reframed money from a weapon into a window—a mirror reflecting your values, boundaries, and nervous-system steadiness.

Chapter 18 deepens that same principle through the lens of culture and meaning. You'll explore how **spiritual and cultural anchors** sustain regulation across generations—building safety not from numbers, but from belonging.

18

Your Spiritual & Cultural Anchors in Co-Parenting

Introduction—Returning to Your Roots

After navigating the external storms— conflict (Chapter 13), logistics (Chapter 14), and finances (Chapter 17)—we now turn inward, toward the soil that steadies it all. When external chaos dominates, the spirit hungers for ground.

Co-parenting, especially after trauma, loss, or chronic conflict, can leave you feeling spiritually **untethered**—disconnected from your sense of meaning, ritual, or community. The goal of this chapter is not religious doctrine; it's **sacred regulation**—remembering what keeps you and your child connected to love, rhythm, and belonging.

"You don't need a temple to be sacred—just presence."

This is about rebuilding the invisible architecture of your home: the small rituals, values, and traditions that remind your family, *we belong to something larger than the conflict.*

What Counts as Spiritual or Cultural Anchors

Anchors are anything that bring stillness, memory, or belonging to the body and soul. They are consistent rhythms that signal safety and continuity across homes.

Anchor Type	Examples of Practice	Nervous System Impact
Spiritual	Prayer, meditation, mindful breath rituals, ethical readings, morning affirmations.	Signals presence and regulation; quiets the sympathetic nervous system.
Cultural	Language, food traditions, specific music, honoring ancestral or seasonal holidays.	Fosters belonging; reinforces intergenerational identity and lineage.
Personal	Nature walks, art or creativity rituals, gratitude lists, specific bedtime routines.	Connects the individual to their internal rhythm; restores stillness.

Clinician Note—Safety Before Symbolism
For trauma survivors, even meaningful rituals can trigger past harm.
Introduce any anchor slowly and only with genuine consent.
The goal is safety before symbolism, and presence before practice.

Why Anchors Matter in Co-Parenting

When families fracture, time and geography may split—but shared rituals rebuild continuity.
Anchors give your child something stable to return to, no matter whose house they wake up in.

A bedtime prayer, a song sung the same way, a shared meal every Sunday—these are more than routines; they are the nervous system's promise that love still has a rhythm.

When your child experiences that rhythm, their body learns:

"Change is real, but I am still held."

Activity 18.1: Your Anchor Mapping Worksheet

Purpose
To identify the anchors that regulate *you* versus those that regulate *your child*, and to assess how each one shows up across homes.

Anchor Type	Current Example	Who It Regulates (Me/Child/Both)	Sensory or Emotional Cue	Consistency Across Homes
Morning Ritual	Quiet coffee + 4–6 Breathing Anchor	Me	Smell, sound	Only my home
Mealtime Blessing	"Grateful for today"	Both	Tone, routine	Both homes
Storytime Song	Same song before bed	Child	Rhythm, melody	My home only

Clinician Insight
Mapping where regulation *lives* allows you to see gaps in rhythm and consistency. When anchors align across homes, children internalize *continuity* even through separation.

Navigating Belief Differences Between Your Child's Homes

Different faiths, traditions, or levels of belief don't have to divide your child. Handled with gentleness, these differences can actually **expand their worldview** and teach them the language of empathy.

Your child doesn't need you and your co-parent to share rituals—they need to know that **both homes are safe for curiosity** and that they will not be asked to choose between the people they love and the beliefs they are learning to understand.

When you model calm respect across differences, you give one of the most enduring gifts your child can receive—the ability to hold multiple truths without fear.

Your Scripts for Shared Respect (Modeling Tolerance)

These phrases help anchor the message that identity, faith, and belonging are not competitions—they are invitations to understanding.

Situation	Script for Shared Respect	Core Lesson for Child
Naming Differences	"In this home, we believe [X], and your other parent may believe [Y]—and that's okay."	My home is safe for curiosity.
Handling Curiosity	"You can ask questions, read, explore, and think about both. You don't have to choose what you believe right now."	My thought process is respected.
Holiday Harmony	"We're celebrating [Holiday Name] today. We focus on gratitude and generosity here—just like you did at the other house."	Values can be shared across differences.
Managing Conflict	(If the co-parent criticizes or mocks your beliefs) "That's how they see it. Here, we honor all paths. Let's focus on what we're practicing together."	I can protect my peace without judging others.

Clinician Note—Modeling Curiosity, Not Conversion
When you respond with openness rather than defense, you regulate both nervous systems.
Children learn safety from tone, not theology.

When Your Spiritual Path Feels Lost

Even adults can feel spiritually homeless after divorce or trauma. Grief for lost rituals, disconnection from faith communities, or the exhaustion of rebuilding can leave you spiritually numb. But meaning doesn't require perfection—it begins with one intentional breath.

If You're Feeling…	Try… (The Bridge to Practice)
Spiritually Numb	Take one slow breath of gratitude or light a candle. Let that one action be enough for today.
Relearning Tradition	Ask: "What did my ancestors or my people do to find comfort before formal religion?" Rediscover cultural wisdom that predates perfectionism.
Seeking New Meaning	Blend old and new. Invent a small ritual—a song, a daily walk, or a shared prayer—that feels authentic. Invention can still be sacred.

Clinician Note—Religious Trauma Recovery

If faith was once a source of harm, healing may begin outside traditional structures. Work with trauma-informed spiritual directors or therapists to build a sense of safety before rebuilding belief.

The goal is **agency**, not compliance; **connection**, not conversion.

Reflection—Your Practice of Meaning

1. What tradition or memory once made me feel safe in my body?

2. What part of that practice can I reclaim without pressure?

261

3. What does "sacred" mean to me today—in one sentence?

_____

_____

_____

4. How can I teach that definition to my child through action, not words?

_____

_____

_____

Clinician Note
This reflection transforms spiritual recovery from an abstract goal into a sensory-based practice.
Safety precedes belief; regulation precedes ritual.

Practices that Ground and Heal (Your Safety Rhythm)

You don't need grandeur; you need rhythm. Healing after chaos begins with predictable, sensory practices—the gentle repetitions that tell your nervous system, _"You are safe enough to rest."_

These grounding rituals restore what trauma fractured: the sense of continuity between the body, the moment, and meaning itself. They are small, repeatable gestures that anchor your day, regulate your physiology, and quietly build resilience for you and your child.

Trauma-Sensitive Grounding Practices

Each of these simple practices works directly with the nervous system's language— breath, touch, sound, and repetition. Choose one or two that you can return to every day without pressure. Consistency, not complexity, is what heals.

Gentle Practice	Detailed Action	Nervous System Purpose
Vagus Breathing	Use the 4-in/6-out breath (Chapter 4) while silently pairing each exhale with: "Inhale: *Held.*"/"Exhale: *Here.*"	Activates the parasympathetic system; signals safety and calm through extended exhale.
Sensory Anchor	Light a specific candle, touch soil, hold a stone, or listen to a slow drum rhythm.	Redirects awareness from internal chaos to physical presence. Brings the mind back to the now.
Continuity	Speak an ancestor's name or recall a person who overcame hardship.	Builds resilience by linking you to a lineage of survival and grace.
Gratitude Practice	Before eating or sleeping, name three things that are *true right now*.	Reorients your focus from scarcity (what's missing) to stability (what's constant).

Clinician Insight—Micro-Rituals as Micro-Regulation

Every act of predictability—lighting the same candle, saying the same phrase—conditions the nervous system to anticipate calm. It's not about belief; it's about repetition.

Activity 18.2: Your Daily Ritual Tracker

Purpose
To create gentle accountability for practicing micro-rituals that reinforce nervous-system regulation.

Day	Ritual Practiced	How My Body Felt Before	How My Body Felt After	Noticed Child's Response
Monday	Candle & gratitude breath	Tight chest	Softer shoulders	Calmer bedtime
Tuesday	Music & evening walk	Numb	Grounded	Shared laughter
Wednesday	Prayer or silence	Distracted	Clear	Child smiled

Clinician Insight

Tracking physiological change creates evidence of progress for both clinician and parent. The goal isn't consistency—it's awareness of which rituals restore safety fastest.

Activity 18.3: Your Expanded Ritual Inventory Map

Purpose

To consciously rebuild a rhythm of regulation and connection. Use this table to distinguish between rituals that regulate the *self* and those that strengthen *relationships*.

Practice (Be Specific)	Solo/Shared	Frequency (Daily/Weekly)	Feeling Evoked	Core Value Modeled
Morning Candle	Solo	Daily	Calm, Intention	Self-Respect
Ancestral Music	Shared (car rides)	Weekly	Connection, Memory	Belonging
Prayer Before School	Parent + Child	Daily	Safety, Focus	Vulnerability
Sunset Walk	Solo	Weekly	Release, Awe	Acceptance
New Ritual Idea:				

Reflection Prompts

1. Which ritual—regardless of its origin—feels like oxygen for your body and spirit?

2. Choose one and commit to that practice once daily. Healing is not a performance; it's a rhythm.

"Regulation becomes ritual when repetition turns into reverence."

Intergenerational Healing and Belonging

Every act of presence, every repair, and every boundary you hold (Chapter 7) is a quiet prayer for the generations that came before you—the ones who never found safety in their own lineage.

Healing in this context isn't about rewriting history; it's about refusing to repeat it. Each calm breath, each apology, each moment of regulation becomes an offering of peace that ripples both backward and forward in time.

Intergenerational Healing Practices

Healing generational pain means naming what ended with you and practicing what begins anew.

- **Name the Pattern You're Changing**
  Speak it aloud.
  "They believed silence was safety; I choose to listen."
  Naming breaks survival patterns and makes conscious what trauma made automatic.

- **Let Parenting Be Prayer**
  See the small acts of attuned parenting—the bedtime story, the apology, the steady tone—as sacred.
  Every regulated moment is a restoration of safety that your ancestors may have never known.
  Every repair is sacred.

- **Lineage Blessing**
  Speak this or create your own:
  "May my children know rest and truth.
  May they be free from the chaos we carried."

Clinician Note—Somatic Repair as Lineage Repair:
Regulation doesn't just calm your child; it rewrites inherited stress patterns.
Your nervous system is the bridge between what hurts and what heals.

Your Chosen Family and Cultural Humility

Not all roots grow in the same soil.
For many, safety is found not in biological or religious lineage, but in **chosen family—**
the communities that practice care without condition.

- **Chosen Family Belonging**
  Include your child in rituals with your trusted community—shared meals,
  volunteer work, activism, or support circles.
  Laughter becomes liturgy; presence becomes prayer.

- **Cultural Humility**
  When reclaiming or reinterpreting traditions, speak openly about their origins.
  Teach your child that understanding where something comes from is itself an act
  of reverence.
  Learning the roots is how we honor the bloom.

Clinician Note—Cultural Repair Over Cultural Perfection
You don't have to "get it right." You only need to get it honest.
Curiosity, not certainty, creates belonging.

Including Your Child—Without Pressure

Rituals are invitations, not obligations. Your child's sense of spirit is felt first through
safety—through play, wonder, rhythm, and imagination. When we make spirituality about
control or correctness, the nervous system contracts; when we make it about connection,
it expands.

This section isn't about passing down beliefs—it's about modeling curiosity and trust.

Guidance for Your Gentle Invitation

- **Let Them Observe First**
  "You can just watch me do my breath work."
  Observation builds safety before participation. Presence is permission enough.

- **Make It Sensory**
  Use rhythm, scent, texture, or color—a drumbeat, a candle, the smell of incense, or a soft fabric.
  Predictable repetition regulates the body more than complex explanations regulate the mind.

- **Ask Open Questions**
  "What do you think happens when we talk to the sky?"
  Keep curiosity alive without turning it into a quiz. Children find their own meaning when they feel safe to wonder.

- **Normalize Disagreement**
  "You don't have to believe what I believe. You'll find your own way."
  This communicates that love is not conditional on agreement.

Spiritual Safety Check

Before introducing a new ritual, pause and ask:

1. **Does this feel safe in my body?** *(Trauma filter)*

2. **Does my child feel peace or pressure?** *(Consent)*

3. **Does this increase calm, connection, or control?** *(Alignment)*

If the ritual invites calm and curiosity, it's safe. If it invites tension or fear, slow down.

Clinician Note—Safety Over Symbolism
The most healing rituals aren't necessarily sacred by tradition; they're sacred because they restore regulation and belonging.

Reflection—Belonging Without Performance

1. Where do I still confuse worth with belief or compliance?

2. How do I know when my child feels safe in spiritual spaces?

3. Which rituals (mine or theirs) build connection instead of control?

4. What do I want our family's spiritual story to teach about love and safety?

Therapeutic Rationale

This reflection integrates *agency* and *regulation*. It helps readers distinguish between participation driven by curiosity versus survival.

Closing Thoughts

Healing a lineage doesn't erase its history—it reorients it.
You are not rewriting your ancestors' story; you are giving love a louder one to pass down.

Your child doesn't need a perfect faith story.
They need to see you reaching—again and again—for something true, calm, and kind.

That reaching *is* the ritual.

You've rebuilt the spiritual scaffolding of your family—not through perfection, but through presence. The next chapter, *Looking Ahead—Your Next Turn in the Road*, transforms these internal anchors into forward movement. You'll create a long-term map for sustainable growth, evaluating which practices, boundaries, and rituals will carry your family through the next season of healing

19

Looking Ahead—Your Next Turn in the Road

Introduction—Your Journey Continues

You've carried the heavy weight—through conflict, grief, rebuilding, and growth. You've learned to breathe through rupture, to steady your nervous system, to protect peace, and to keep showing up—again and again—for your child and for yourself.

Now, the work shifts.

This chapter isn't about "happily ever after." It's about what comes *after* survival—the quiet, steady next chapter where healing becomes habit and calm becomes culture. It's where your home stops revolving around recovery and starts orbiting around renewal.

Healing isn't linear, but it *is* alive in you.

Growth doesn't end when the chaos slows—it changes shape.

The Focus of Your Next Season

Use this chapter to pause, recalibrate, and choose where your energy goes next. Healing has given you options again; now you get to decide what to build.

Ask yourself:

- What is shifting in my internal landscape?

- Which stabilizing practices will anchor me in the months ahead?

- What identity am I ready to reclaim—beyond conflict, beyond survival?

> "The future doesn't need perfection. It needs your presence."

Your Progress Inventory—What Your Growth Looks Like Now

Growth rarely looks cinematic. It's often quiet—an unspoken pause, a smaller reaction, or a moment where you choose calm instead of proving your point. Healing doesn't always announce itself with a breakthrough; sometimes, it whispers through restraint.

Don't miss your own progress just because it's quiet.

Activity 19.1: Your Growth Inventory Map—Signs of Quiet, Sustainable Growth

Focus Area	Signs You've Shifted (External)	Signs You've Shifted (Internal)
Boundaries (Chapters 7–8)	You no longer defend or over-explain every decision.	You say *no* without guilt or immediate fear of consequences.
Regulation (Chapters 4–5)	You go longer without rereading old messages or seeking justification.	You recover faster after triggers—minutes instead of hours or days.

Focus Area	Signs You've Shifted (External)	Signs You've Shifted (Internal)
Focus (Chapter 12)	You respond to your child's rhythm, not your co-parent's reactivity.	You can recognize manipulative behavior without making it about your worth.
Energy (Chapter 13)	You invest time and resources in your own life again—joy, hobbies, and rest.	Rest feels safe and deserved, not lazy or indulgent.

Clinician Note—Growth Fatigue

Feeling tired doesn't mean you're backsliding. It means your nervous system is finally relaxing after a long period of hypervigilance. Fatigue is not regression; it's integration.

Reflection—Your Long-Term Parenting Vision (Revisited & Evolved)

Return to the vision you wrote earlier in this workbook. Let it evolve to match your new reality. Growth changes the story you tell about what matters—and how peace looks.

Reflection Prompts *(Take your time; write honestly)*

1. What have I learned about the parent I want to be—even in chaos?

2. How do I want my child to remember the rhythm of our home (Chapter 18)?

3. What goal or fantasy am I ready to release (e.g., "a collaborative co-parenting relationship") to make room for my truth (e.g., "a peaceful parallel parenting rhythm")?

4. What values will guide this next season—joy, autonomy, spaciousness, or something else?

"Parenting vision isn't about perfection—it's about direction."

Planning for Your Transitions: Stay Rooted in Your Response

Parenting will always evolve over custody shifts, developmental changes, new jobs, and new seasons. You can't control every curveball, but you can control your stance. The goal is not to predict the storm, but to stay *rooted in your response* instead of reacting.

Your Grounding Moves for the Unknown

Each transition brings a nervous-system test. When uncertainty hits, use these grounding moves to slow down your body before your mind spirals.

Common Shift	Strategic Grounding Move	The Question to Ask Yourself
Unexpected Change (e.g., custody curveball, job loss)	Pause → Regulate → Review → Respond. *(See Chapter 5.)*	"What does this moment call for—not what does it trigger?"

Common Shift	Strategic Grounding Move	The Question to Ask Yourself
Developmental Shifts (e.g., adolescence, new partners)	Use *If-Then Planning*: "If my teen starts testing rules at the other home, I will restate my boundary clearly and calmly."	"Am I trying to control the outcome or anticipate the response?"
Legal/Logistical Updates	Use visual calendars or transition charts with your child.	"How can I communicate this change clearly without causing fear?"

Inclusive Note

If you're a grandparent, guardian, foster, or chosen family caregiver, your emotional labor is sacred too. Every principle in this book applies to your steadiness and protection. You are the safe place. What matters most is safety, not sameness.

Your Six-Month Steadiness Check-In

Integration doesn't happen once—it needs maintenance. Use this brief reflection every six months to notice where growth holds and where fatigue is creeping in.

Area	Reflection Question	Simple Action to Take Now
Boundaries (Chapters 7–8)	Have any boundaries become blurred or too permeable?	Re-state one boundary clearly (use the Chapter 12 script) without apology.
Regulation (Chapters 4–5)	Which grounding tool (breath, mantra, sensory) am I using least?	Practice it for one minute today—right now.
Connection	Have I laughed with my child (or myself) lately?	Schedule 15 minutes of "no-task" play or rest this week.

Area	Reflection Question	Simple Action to Take Now
Support	Who supports me now? Am I leaning too much on one person?	Reconnect with one secondary ally or schedule a therapy session.
Joy/Energy (Chapter 13)	What still feels heavy—and what can I delegate or simplify?	Add one light, small ritual to the next three days.
Vision (Chapter 6)	Does my direction still feel aligned with who I'm becoming?	Adjust one small goal to match your current season.

"You don't have to be done to be proud. Survival is growth. So is rest."

Reflection—Your Integration Pulse

1. Which area of steadiness has strengthened most since starting this workbook?

2. Where does fatigue show up first—body, mind, or relationships?

3. When peace feels distant, what tool or person helps me remember my capacity?

4. What proof do I already have that healing is holding?

_____

_____

Clinical Framing

This reflection converts abstract "maintenance" into embodied awareness, reducing relapse risk by linking regulation to lived experience.

Reclaiming Your Identity and Healing Path

When the noise finally quiets, a new question emerges: **"Who am I now that I'm not constantly defending or reacting?"** This is not about escaping conflict—it's about expanding life beyond it. You've built stability for your child; now you must rebuild meaning for yourself.

Healing doesn't sound like victory speeches. It sounds like: *"I want to think about something else."*

_____

Stepping Out of Your Co-Parenting Loop

You'll know you're reclaiming your identity when the world starts opening again—when there's space for curiosity, rest, and creation.

Signs You're Ready to Reclaim	New Focus of Your Attention
You stop checking messages compulsively.	**Reclaim Attention:** Invest in a hobby, creative project, or new skill. *(Start a playlist, plant a garden, take a class.)*
You stop rehearsing arguments in your head.	**Practice Silence:** Let the quiet feel unfamiliar. Fill it with peaceful thought, not preparation.
You care more about joy than judgment.	**Plan Connection:** Re-engage with trusted friendships, rituals, and community.

Signs You're Ready to Reclaim	New Focus of Your Attention
You invest energy in your own life again.	**Build Autonomy:** Create something that is intrinsically yours—a goal, practice, or purpose.

"The moment you stop centering the conflict, you start reclaiming yourself."

Your Healing is Your Instruction

Your healing is not indulgence—it's instruction.
Your child learns self-respect, regulation, and resilience by *watching* you live it.

- **Model Self-Respect**
  Cry without shame. Hold boundaries without explaining them.

- **Model Regulation**
  Laugh without guilt. Pause (Chapter 4) before reacting.

- **Model Resilience**
  Try again, even when tired. Repair quickly when reactive—but never at the cost of your boundaries.

"The future you're building for your child begins in how gently you treat yourself."

Activity 19.2: Your Modeling Legacy Worksheet

Purpose
To articulate how your personal regulation practices become intergenerational teaching.

Daily Action	What My Child Sees or Learns	Value Modeled
Apologizing without defensiveness	Accountability is strength	Integrity
Taking breaks before conflict	Calm is a choice, not a gift	Regulation
Keeping financial agreements	Reliability = safety	Trust

Daily Action	What My Child Sees or Learns	Value Modeled
Laughing after tension	Repair is possible	Hope

Clinician Note
Integrates social-learning theory—children internalize not perfection but **patterned repair**.

Your Integration Ritual—Releasing and Carrying Forward

When healing has no finish line, ritual becomes the marker of movement. This is your pause to say,
"This stays. That goes."

You've done the deep repair work—you've rewired your nervous system, redefined your values, and steadied your communication. Now, this ritual helps you integrate those changes, anchoring what will travel with you into the next season of growth.

Ritual Prompt (Write and Reflect)	Focus of the Release/Recommitment
I am keeping…	My clarity, patience, and sense of peace. The routines that ground me—breath before response, reflection before reaction. My worth stays—it is not negotiable.
I am releasing…	The looping thoughts and rehearsed defenses. The need for their understanding or validation. The fear that calm won't last.
I am walking toward…	Spaciousness—more laughter, more energy for creation, more trust in what I've built.
I am already becoming…	A parent whose steadiness is not conditional on chaos. A person whose peace no longer needs permission.

Reflection—The Meaning of this Moment

You are not closing a chapter of conflict—you are crossing into a new rhythm. Healing has taught you how to stay when it's hard, breathe when it's tense, and begin again when it's quiet.

"Healing isn't a finish line—it's a rhythm you live by."

This ritual marks your shift from recovery to mastery. You are ready to hold the tools differently now—not as armor, but as second nature.

Reflection—From Survival to Legacy

1. What am I most proud of sustaining when things got hard?

2. Which tool or mindset became second nature?

3. What lesson do I want my child—or future self—to remember from this season?

4. If healing were a language, how would mine sound today?

_____

_____

_____

Therapeutic Rationale
Anchors the chapter in narrative therapy—turning survival story into authored meaning.

_____

Closing Thoughts

You've completed the internal architecture of healing—awareness, regulation, repair, and reflection.

The next chapter, *Your Master Toolkit—Tools, Trackers and Resources* shifts your focus from introspection to structure. You'll learn how to maintain momentum with reproducible tools—journals, trackers, and planning systems—so steadiness becomes routine, not an effort.

20

Your Master Toolkit—Tools, Trackers and Resources

Introduction—Your Healing in Quiet Patterns

Some healing happens in big, emotional breakthroughs. But most of it happens in quiet, consistent patterns—the dedication you bring to tracking, the commitment to practice, and the self-compassion to return to your regulated self when you stumble.

This chapter is your **reference manual and clinical toolkit** for translating therapeutic insight into sustainable, daily action. It moves beyond intention, offering structure to observe your own nervous system, manage high-conflict interactions, and care for your child's well-being.

Whether you are working solo, deep in individual therapy, or navigating high-conflict co-parenting (HCCP), the tools here are designed to create **psychological safety by introducing predictability.**

This Master Toolkit Will Help You:

- **Observe**
  Track emotional shifts and nervous-system reactions with objective, factual data.

- **Contain**

  Build transition rituals and predictability for your child between homes.

- **Protect**

  Strategically document key communication and boundary violations for legal or therapeutic use.

- **Reflect**

  Convert tracked data into clear, forward-looking direction and reinforce successful behavior.

- **Regulate**

  Master instant tools for self-soothing and conflict avoidance.

Your Master Toolbox Index (24 Tools)

Your tools are organized by the **Rhythm of their Practice:** moving from immediate crisis (Daily) to strategic planning (Quarterly).

Tool No.	Tool Name	Focus/Purpose	Rhythm
DAILY/INSTANT TOOLS			
1	**Neutral Script Bank**	Pre-written, conflict-safe responses.	Daily/As Needed
2	**Four Quick Regulation Cards**	Portable, trauma-informed nervous-system resets.	Daily/Instant
3	**Crisis & Resources Sheet**	Immediate access to safety and support contacts.	Fill Out Once & Secure
4	**Logistics Transfer Checklist**	Ensure critical information (e.g., medications, school) is exchanged predictably.	Per Exchange

Tool No.	Tool Name	Focus/Purpose	Rhythm
WEEKLY PRACTICE TOOLS			
5	**Weekly Co-Parenting Journal**	Self-reflection, wins, and immediate friction points.	Weekly
6	**Weekly Nervous-System Check-In**	Quick awareness check for regulation needs. (Therapeutic Use).	Weekly
7	**Values Mini-Compass**	Anchor weekly decisions to core values.	Weekly
8	**"I Did Not Engage" Log**	Reinforce non-reaction and track behavioral success. (Therapeutic Use).	Weekly
9	**Support System Accountability Log**	Proactively track and use external support resources.	Weekly
AS-NEEDED DOCUMENTATION			
10	**Communication & Emotion Log**	Track triggers, body reactions, and growth. (Therapeutic Use).	As Needed (Post-Trigger)
11	**Court-Safe Documentation Log**	Factual, neutral tracking of interactions. (Legal Use).	As Needed (Post-Violation)
12	**Boundary & Requests Tracker**	Observe co-parent response patterns to your limits. (Legal Use).	As Needed
13	**Co-Parenting Meeting Agenda**	Keep necessary communication short, focused, and objective.	As Needed (Pre-Meeting)

Tool No.	Tool Name	Focus/Purpose	Rhythm
14	**Child Behavior Observation Log**	Targeted tracking of specific behaviors (e.g., meltdowns, withdrawal).	As Needed (Post-Behavior)
15	**Future Focus Worksheet**	Structured problem-solving to avoid rumination.	As Needed (Post-Rumination)
16	**Financial/Expense Tracker**	Court-safe ledger for tracking shared costs, payments, and reimbursement status.	Per Transaction
17	**Safety Ally Check-In Script**	Protocol for structured co-regulation calls with allies, maintaining boundaries during crisis.	As Needed (Red Zone)
18	**HCCP Communication Decryption Key**	Analysis filter for disassembling emotional attacks into factual signals.	As Needed (Post-Trigger)
PLANNING & VISION TOOLS			
19	**Transition Plan**	Create safety and predictability during exchanges (Child-Centered).	Quarterly/Update
20	**Shared Calendar + Weather Key**	Visual tracking of the child's emotional shifts.	Daily/Monthly
21	**Monthly Review Summary**	Turn tracked data into direction and insight for therapy/legal strategy.	Monthly

Tool No.	Tool Name	Focus/Purpose	Rhythm
22	**If-Then Planning Worksheet**	Prepare responses to predictable conflict scenarios.	Quarterly
23	**Progress Reflection Map**	Visualize non-linear growth and small wins over 3-6 months.	Weekly/Quarterly
24	**Child's Voice & Needs Profile**	A one-page, neutral summary of the child's needs for professionals (a court-appointed Guardian ad Litem, Attorney).	Once (Update Annually)

Your Privacy & Data Hygiene—The Mandatory A-S-S-A-D Protocol

Before using any log, you must establish a secure system. Your safety and legal standing depend on this discipline. I recommend the **A-S-S-A-D Protocol—Archive, Separate, Secure, Audit, Delete:**

1. **A—Archive Yearly:** On a set date, move all logs from the past year into a final, dated Archive folder. This mentally resets you and makes discovery easier if required later.
2. **S—Separate Logs:** Use two completely separate systems for logs. **Never mix them:**
   - **Therapeutic (Tools 6, 8, 10):** These are for your internal healing and contain **subjective feelings, emotions, and body sensations.** Keep these on a personal, encrypted device or in a physical journal.
   - **Legal (Tools 11, 12):** These contain **only facts and neutral observations.** Use a dedicated, court-approved app or a locked spreadsheet.
3. **S—Secure Everything:** Use two-factor authentication (2FA) on all communication and storage apps. Keep physical logs in a private, locked location (a safe or locked file cabinet).
4. **A—Audit Discovery Risk:** Review a random log entry once a month and ask: **"If this were read in open court, would it help or hurt my case?"** If it contains attacks, emotion, or speculation, revise your logging habit immediately.

5. **D—Delete What Doesn't Serve:** After a year, or when an issue is resolved, delete logs that no longer serve a legal or therapeutic purpose and only cause re-traumatization. Safety includes letting old data rest.

Your Daily/Instant Tools

Tool 1: Your Neutral Script Bank

(Quick Reference Card—Daily/Instant Use)

Purpose

This tool provides **pre-written, conflict-safe responses** for moments when communication feels triggering, manipulative, or overwhelming.
Each script helps you respond **without defending, over-explaining, or engaging—** while still upholding your boundaries and values.

You can use these scripts verbatim via **text, email, or co-parenting apps**.
They are designed to protect your nervous system from escalation and maintain professionalism even when provoked.

Clinical Rationale (BIFF Communication Method)

This tool draws from the **BIFF Framework** (Brief, Informative, Friendly, Firm), used in trauma-informed communication and high-conflict resolution.

Principle	Definition	Why it Matters
Brief	Limit opportunity for argument by keeping responses short.	Prevents re-engagement or bait escalation.
Informative	Provide only necessary facts, no opinions or emotions.	Reduces ambiguity and misinterpretation.
Friendly	Maintain calm professionalism, even if the tone received isn't.	Builds credibility and models emotional regulation.
Firm	Uphold boundaries without defensiveness.	Reinforces authority and safety in communication.

"Scripts are your nervous system's seatbelt—they keep you secure when the emotional road gets rough."

Action Plan

Print, laminate, or store this list digitally (e.g., in your phone's notes app).
Use as an *instant anchor* before replying to emotionally charged messages.

Time Needed: None—designed for instant use.

Quick Reference Table

Area of Conflict	Neutral Script (Use Verbatim)	When to Use (Trigger)
Enforcing Boundaries	"I will follow the parenting plan."	When asked to deviate from agreed-upon rules or schedule.
Redirecting Communication	"Please send that information via the app/email. Thank you."	When the co-parent tries to discuss sensitive topics via text, call, or in person.
Stalling/Slowing Down	"Noted. I'll review and respond by Friday at 5 PM."	When you need time to regulate before replying or are being pressured for an immediate response.
Handling Abuse/Blame	"I won't respond to messages that include blame or speculation."	To end a hostile conversation without defensiveness. *(The Hard Stop)*
Focusing on Logistics	"We will be at [Location] at [Time] for the exchange."	To keep dialogue strictly logistical and avoid emotional detours.
Protecting Time/Privacy	"I'm not available for discussion right now. Thank you."	During unexpected in-person contact or invasive questioning.
Documentation Signal	"Thank you for the information. This message will be documented."	To flag that the message will be saved without hostility or escalation.

Area of Conflict	Neutral Script (Use Verbatim)	When to Use (Trigger)
The 'Need to Know' Test	"How does this relate to the safety or welfare of the child?"	When a co-parent asks inappropriate or irrelevant questions.
Setting an Immediate Limit	"That's not something I'm willing to discuss at this time."	When a difficult or unexpected topic arises. *(Immediate Boundary)*

How to Use as Homework

1. The Script Automation Drill

Each morning, rehearse **three key scripts** you expect to need most that week. Say them out loud or read them mentally.
This repetition creates **muscle memory** so that calm becomes your default under stress.

Example Focus:

- Redirecting Communication
- Slowing Down
- Handling Blame.

Practice: "Noted. I'll review and respond by Friday."
(Say it until your body relaxes while you say it.)

2. The "Draft and Delete" Rule

When you receive a hostile or baiting message:

- Write your emotional reply **in a private note app or on paper** (never send it).
- **Delete it.**
- Copy-paste the relevant neutral script above and send only that.

This fulfills your body's need for release while maintaining professionalism and legal safety.

3. The Delayed Response Mandate

Pair the "Stalling/Slowing Down" script (see Tool 1) with **Tool 6: Your Weekly Nervous-System Check-In**.
Each time you feel urgency to reply:

- Log your current emotional status (Green/Yellow/Red).
- Use the "Stalling" script.
- Wait two hours, then re-check your zone.

If you've shifted from Yellow → Green, your nervous system just learned that **waiting is safety**—not danger.

Reflection Prompts

Use these monthly to reinforce confidence and neutrality:

- Which script did I use most often? Why?

- Which topic still hooks my emotions?

- How did my body feel after sending a neutral response?

- Which script can I automate next?

Tool 2: Four Quick Regulation Reset Cards

(Printable—Daily/Instant Use)

Purpose

Your *Quick Regulation Cards* are **portable, trauma-informed, nervous-system resets**. They exist for the moments when calm feels unreachable—before an exchange, after a triggering message, or during high-stakes parenting interactions.

Each card delivers a short, body-based exercise to **down-regulate the stress response** and bring you back to safety and choice.

"You don't think your way out of a trigger—you breathe your way through it."

Clinical Rationale (Somatic Regulation)

These cards use evidence-based techniques from **DBT (dialectical behavior therapy), polyvagal theory,** and **somatic psychology** to restore regulation.
When trauma or conflict hijacks the prefrontal cortex, logic and empathy go offline. Only the body—through slow, rhythmic, sensory action—can re-engage the calming parasympathetic system.

Rationale	Focus	Why it Works
Somatic Focus	Targets physical sensations rather than cognitive reasoning.	The body must regulate before the mind can reflect.
Portability	Fits in a pocket, car, or phone photo album.	Makes self-regulation instantly accessible.
Repetition	Builds neural familiarity through use before crises.	Prevents panic by training the body to associate these motions with safety.

Action Plan

Print, cut, and laminate these cards. Keep one set in your car, one near your workspace, and one by your phone.

Use *any time you feel your body shift*—racing pulse, tight chest, shaky hands, or emotional flooding.

Time Needed: 2–3 minutes per reset.

Card A—Your STOP Skill (Mindfulness Reset)

Purpose: Freeze impulsive action and return awareness to the present moment.

S—Stop. Pause immediately. Do not speak, text, or move impulsively.
T—Take One Breath. Long inhale through the nose, longer exhale through the mouth.
O—Observe. Name what's happening inside: "Tight chest. Hot face. Urge to defend."
P—Proceed. Choose the next action that aligns with your *values* (see **Tool 7: Your Values Mini-Compass**).

Mantra—"I move from reactivity to choice."

Card B—Your 4–6 Breathing Anchor (Physiological Reset)

Purpose: Slow your heart rate and activate your calming parasympathetic system.

1. Inhale through the nose for a count of **4**.
2. Exhale through pursed lips for a count of **6**.
3. Repeat **5 times**, focusing only on the count.

Cue
"Longer exhale = slower nervous system."

Body Integration
- *Jaw/Mouth:* Notice if clenching—gently open and close once.
- *Shoulders:* Lift toward ears, squeeze for 3 seconds, then drop.
- *Hands:* Clench fists for 5 seconds, then release.
- *Feet:* Press into the floor; feel the ground.
- *Anchor Phrase:* "I am safe right now."

Card C—Your 5-4-3-2-1 Grounding (Sensory Focus)

Purpose: Reconnect to the here-and-now through the five senses.

5 Name five things you can see.
4 Name four things you can touch (feel chair, clothing, floor).
3 Name three things you can hear.
2 Name two things you can smell.
1 Name one thing you can taste (or imagine a taste).

Clinical Cue
This technique shifts focus from threat to environment, reorienting your brain to safety.

Card D—Your Body Scan & Anchor (Immediate Release)

Purpose: Identify where tension lives in the body and release it consciously.

1. Notice where you feel stress (jaw, shoulders, chest, stomach).
2. Gently squeeze that area for 3 seconds.
3. Exhale while releasing tension, saying: "This energy can move safely."
4. Anchor with a grounding movement—press palms together, touch your chest, or place both feet flat.
5. Repeat the anchor phrase:

"I can stay here. My body knows calm."

How to Use as Homework

1. Your Exchange Drill

Before every exchange or high-stakes interaction, practice **Card B (4–6 Breathing Anchor)** and **Card D (Body Scan & Anchor)** in your car or safe space.
Repeat both **five minutes before** contact to condition your body to associate the event with calm readiness.

Goal: Replace the fight/flight reflex with a self-calming reflex.

2. Your STOP Skill Integration

Use **Card A** together with **Tool 1: Your Neutral Script Bank**.
Before sending any message:

- Perform S–T–O.
- Only proceed if your observation confirms you are in the **Green Zone** (see **Tool 6**).
  If in Yellow or Red, then pause and apply your script—"Noted. I'll review and respond later."

Reminder: "Intervene, don't engage."

3. Your Sensory Audit
At least once per week (ideally when calm), practice **Card C (5-4-3-2-1)** in neutral situations—while driving, walking, or waiting in line.
This ensures the exercise becomes second nature and doesn't register as "emergency-only."

Therapeutic Goal: Teach your body that regulation is routine, not rescue.

Reflection Prompts

Use these during supervision, therapy, or journaling:

- Which card do I reach for most often?

- What triggers seem to demand a physiological reset?

- Do I use the tools preemptively or only in a crisis?

- How does my recovery time change when I regulate first?

Tool 3: Your Crisis & Resources Sheet

(Fill Out Once and Keep Secure)

Purpose

This consolidates all emergency, legal, and therapeutic contacts into one accessible, pre-planned page. Its goal is to protect your **decision-making capacity under stress**—transforming panic into a practiced, grounded protocol.

"When your body forgets what safety feels like, your plan remembers for you."

Clinical Rationale (Reducing Decision Fatigue)

Focus	Explanation	Why it Matters
Decision Fatigue	In a crisis, the prefrontal cortex (decision center) goes offline.	Preloading your crisis plan restores executive control.
Regulation First, Action Second	Emotional flooding creates reactive choices that backfire legally or relationally.	Ensures calm precedes communication.
Safety Script Integration	Pairs emergency contacts with self-regulation tools.	Makes every outreach intentional, not impulsive.

Action Insight

You can't think your way out of panic—but you can follow a plan out of it.

Action Plan

Complete once, update quarterly, and store laminated copies in **three known locations**—
your **wallet, car glove box**, and **home safe or phone notes app**.

Time Needed: 15 minutes (initial setup).

CRISIS & RESOURCES SUMMARY SHEET

Immediate Emergency Contacts (Crisis/Danger)

Contact Role	Name/Agency	Phone Number	My Protocol Action
Emergency Services	Local Police/911	911 (or local equivalent)	If physical threat is present, call immediately and state: "Court order violation in progress."
Safety Ally (Tool 17)	(Primary support for co-regulation)		Use *Safety Ally Check-In Script (Tool 17)* verbatim.
Child's Location Contact	School/Daycare/Activity		Ask for the child's status only. Do *not* engage in parental conflict.
Domestic Violence Hotline	(If applicable/needed)		Follow their directed safety steps immediately.

Legal & Case Information (Documentation/Enforcement)

Information Field	Detail	Location of Evidence/Copy
Case/Matter Number		Stored in legal file & email backup.

Information Field	Detail	Location of Evidence/Copy
Attorney's Name/Direct Line	_____	Email first with *facts only* (Tool 11), then call if urgent.
Nearest Safe Exchange Location	_____	e.g., Police Station Parking Lot.
Protective Order/Restraining Order Status	☐ Active ☐ Pending ☐ N/A	Carry one copy of the active order.

Emotional De-Escalation Protocol (Self-Care/Regulation)

My Protocol Action	Trigger/Need	Supporting Tool
My Anchor Statement	To interrupt panic or spiraling thoughts.	"I am safe, and I am acting on fact—not fear."
My Best Grounding Technique	Immediate physical reset.	4–6 Breathing Anchor (Tool 2)
My Urgent Therapeutic Contact	Therapist/Crisis Line.	Name: _____ • Phone: _____
My Safe Place/Activity	Chosen sensory-safe space or movement.	e.g., "Sit in car, play music, walk two blocks."

How to Use as Homework

1. The Memory Drill

For five consecutive days, mentally rehearse the three most critical numbers on this list—**Emergency**, **Safety Ally**, and **Attorney**—until they're recallable without looking.
The goal is **automatic access under distress**.

"Familiarity is faster than fear."

2. The 'Call the Ally First' Rule

If you enter a **Red Zone (Tool 6)**, contact your *Safety Ally* before reaching out to your co-parent or attorney.
The ally's role (**Tool 17**) is to help you regulate, not react—so that all communication remains factual, not emotional (**Tool 11**).

"Regulate before you communicate."

3. Physical Placement

Keep a copy of this sheet beside your *If-Then Plan* (**Tool 22**).
When your "IF" scenario involves danger, fear, or escalation, this Crisis Sheet defines the "THEN"—
the exact call, number, and action to take.

"Your plan is your lifeline—make it visible."

Tool 4: Your Logistics Transfer Checklist

(Per Exchange—Daily/Instant Use)

Purpose

Your *Logistics Transfer Checklist* transforms chaotic hand-offs into structured, predictable exchanges.
It ensures that vital information—medical updates, school details, and logistics—is exchanged **factually and neutrally**, reducing emotional tension and confusion for both parent and child.

"Predictability is peace—for you, and especially for your child."

This tool replaces verbal check-ins (which invite conflict) with a **professional, written system** that minimizes miscommunication and protects everyone's nervous system during transitions.

Clinical Rationale (Predictability for Your Child)

Focus	Explanation	Why it Matters
Predictable Exchange	Provides structure during emotionally charged moments.	The child's nervous system feels safe when the adults follow a consistent ritual.
Factual, Not Emotional	Limits sharing to objective updates—no opinions or commentary.	Reduces opportunities for baiting or misinterpretation.
Visible Competence	Demonstrates professionalism to the child.	Models steadiness and reliability—key traits for co-regulation.

Actionable Safety

By using a pre-printed form, you automatically apply the BIFF method (Brief, Informative, Friendly, Firm)—without having to think about tone or defense.

Action Plan

Complete this checklist **10 minutes before each exchange**, reviewing only factual items.
Hand it over with the child's belongings—no verbal commentary.
Keep a scanned copy or photo for your own records (see *Tool 11: Court-Safe Documentation Log*).

Time Needed: 3–5 minutes

Logistics Transfer Checklist (Make into a Four-Page Worksheet)

Item	Status (Check Box)	Note/Update (Factual, One Sentence)	Next Parent's Responsibility (Action Required)
Date/Time of Transfer	☐ Box ☐ Shared	e.g., "Exchange completed at 6:00 PM."	—
School/Activity Update	☐ Box ☐ Shared	e.g., "Parent-teacher night is Tuesday. Homework due Friday."	e.g., "Check email for permission slip."
Medication/Health Log	☐ Box ☐ Shared	e.g., "Needs next dose at 8:00 PM."	e.g., "Apply cream to left arm."
Urgent Doctor/Appointment Info	☐ Box ☐ Shared	e.g., "Dentist appointment next Wednesday at 3:00 PM."	e.g., "Follow up for cold."
Unusual Food Intake/Sleep	☐ Box ☐ Shared	e.g., "Refused dinner last night; tried new allergy-safe food."	—
Comfort Object/Device Status	☐ Box ☐ Shared	e.g., "Tablet requires charging; teddy is packed."	e.g., "Ensure device is charged for school use."
Critical Clothing/Specific Items	☐ Box ☐ Shared	e.g., "Uniform needs cleaning; rain boots for field trip."	e.g., "Return by next exchange."
Urgent Request/Question (Limit 1)	☐ Box ☐ Shared	e.g., "Is the health card at your house?" *(must be actionable, not emotional)*	—

Item	Status (Check Box)	Note/Update (Factual, One Sentence)	Next Parent's Responsibility (Action Required)
Required Follow-Up	☐ Box ☐ Shared	e.g., "Please confirm safe arrival via the app."	

Note

All entries must be factual and written in a neutral tone. Do not include assumptions, complaints, or feelings.

How to Use as Homework

1. The Silent Hand-Off

Your job is to maintain silence during exchanges—communication happens *only through the checklist*. If the other parent attempts to discuss the sheet verbally, use your **Redirect Script** (see Tool 1):

"Please send that information via the app/email. Thank you."

Your assignment: complete **three silent hand-offs in a row** without verbal clarification.

2. The "Limit 1" Discipline

The *Urgent Request/Question* section is capped at **one line**—and only for actionable, not emotional, topics.
Ask: "Would this help the child or just ease my anxiety?"
If the answer is the latter, wait 24 hours.

Example: "Is the helmet packed?"
"Why do you always forget?"

Your homework: Complete three exchanges in a row with *no open-ended requests or commentary*.

3. The Documentation Trail

This checklist doubles as evidence for **Tool 11: Court-Safe Documentation Log**.
If a co-parent ignores or refuses critical updates (e.g., medication), scan or photograph your completed form.
Label the file by date (e.g., "Transfer_2025-11-09") and store it in your secure folder.

Reminder: Documentation is not revenge—it's regulation.

Reflection Prompts

- How did the silence feel during the hand-off? (Relief, tension, power?)

- Which item creates the most stress to discuss verbally?

- What part of me wants to explain, and what part wants peace?

- Did my child's body language shift when the exchange was calm?

Your Weekly Practice Tools

These self-awareness and therapeutic tools turn nervous system reactions into actionable data, providing insight for both you and your therapeutic support team.

Tool 5: Your Weekly Co-Parenting Journal

(Print + Digital Hybrid Layout)

Purpose

To create mindful closure for each week, helping you notice emotional patterns, celebrate small wins, and gently correct course without judgment.

Clinical Rationale

High-conflict or post-divorce parenting keeps the body in a constant vigilance loop—searching for threat instead of noticing safety.
This tool retrains your attention toward self-efficacy and consistency.
By documenting small weekly actions, the nervous system begins to *expect steadiness*, lowering baseline cortisol and reinforcing regulation through predictability (polyvagal theory).

When to Use

At the end of each week—ideally Sunday evening or Monday morning—before checking messages or engaging in co-parenting logistics.

Time Needed: 10–15 minutes per entry.

Confidentiality Note

Use this page for emotional reflection, not legal documentation. Keep factual notes separate from private emotional data.

How to Use as Homework

1. *Begin with a deep breath and a short body scan* (*Chapter 4*).

2. *Complete Wins before Friction Points*
   This rewires your nervous system toward competence before problem-solving.

3. *Keep your entries short (2–3 sentences).*
   This is practice, not performance.

Example Entry

Win: Protected my 8 PM phone boundary even when tempted to reply.
Friction Point: Felt frustrated by a last-minute change.
Regulation Need: Tightness in chest—used 4–6 Breathing Anchor and grounded myself.
Forward Fix: Save neutral scripts in the notes app for future use.

Weekly Reflection Log

(Repeatable Page—Fillable or Writable)

Week of: _____   Child(ren):
_____

Section	Reflection Prompt	Why it Matters
Wins (Big or Small)	What small victories or acts of steadiness did I show this week?	Shifts focus from threat to resilience.
Friction Point	What was the hardest interaction or feeling? Keep it factual.	Reduces rumination and emotional reactivity.

Section	Reflection Prompt	Why it Matters
Regulation Need	What did my body do? (e.g., clenched jaw, shallow breath)	Builds nervous-system literacy.
Forward Fix	What one new or repeated action will I take next week?	Translates awareness into change.

Personal Log (Extended Entry)

(Use as many lines as needed. Add new pages as desired.)
1. Wins: _____
2. Friction Point: _____
3. Regulation Need: _____
4. Forward Fix: _____

Integration Notes

Reflect after completing at least three weeks:

- What pattern am I noticing in my Wins?
- How does my body respond differently when I track instead of react?
- What new steadiness is my child beginning to mirror?
-

Tool 6: Your Weekly Nervous-System Check-In

(Therapeutic)

Purpose

To build awareness of your nervous system's rhythms across the week and identify when regulation dips. This tool helps you observe, not judge—turning body cues into data for care instead of self-criticism.

Clinical Rationale (Polyvagal Lens)

The Weekly Nervous-System Check-In uses *polyvagal theory* to track how your body's state affects your behavior and emotional capacity.
Each nervous system "zone"—Green (Safe & Social), Yellow (Mobilized/Anxious), or Red (Defensive/Shutdown)—corresponds to a distinct physiological response. Recognizing these shifts helps you anticipate activation, practice self-intervention early, and retrain your body toward safety.

When you consistently log your **Triggering Events** and **Interventions Used**, you build a factual record of your capacity for repair and regulation. Over time, this log becomes therapeutic data you can share with your clinician to refine treatment or co-parenting strategies.

When to Use

Complete this tool a minimum of **three times per week** (e.g., Monday AM, Wednesday PM, Friday PM).
End with a **Sunday Review** to identify trends and plan regulation support for the coming week.

Time Needed: 2–3 minutes per check-in.

Confidentiality Note

Keep this record in your therapeutic file. If shared for legal purposes, log only objective patterns (date, time, zone, intervention used) and omit subjective feelings.

Weekly Tracker

Day/Time	Regulation Status (Circle One)	Triggering Event (If Yellow/Red—Factual, One Sentence)	Intervention Used (Specific Reset Tool/Action)	Resulting Insight (What Did I Learn About My Pattern?)
Monday AM	Green/Yellow/Red			
Tuesday PM	Green/Yellow/Red			
Wednesday PM	Green/Yellow/Red			
Thursday PM	Green/Yellow/Red			
Friday PM	Green/Yellow/Red			
Saturday AM	Green/Yellow/Red			
Sunday PM	Green/Yellow/Red			
WEEKLY AVERAGE		Goal Met: Yes/No	Total Resets Used: ___	Next Week's Focus: ___

Regulation Status Key

Zone	State	Description
Green Zone	Safe & Social/Ventral Vagal	Regulated, alert, connected, open to patience and communication.

Zone	State	Description
Yellow Zone	Mobilization/Sympathetic	Increased heart rate, distraction, irritability, or racing thoughts. Regulation needed.
Red Zone	Defense/Dorsal Vagal (Freeze)	Emotional collapse, panic, or numbness. Needs grounding and physical reset (see Tool 2).

How to Use as Homework

1. *The Yellow Zone Intervention*

Catch the *Yellow Zone* before it turns Red. Choose one **specific regulation tool** (Tool 2: Regulation Quick Card) and commit to using it every time you notice Yellow symptoms.

Goal: Build a positive conditioning response—"Yellow = Intervene, not Engage."

2. *The Friday Test*

The most common regulation dip happens at the week's end. Set a micro-goal:

"By Friday PM, I will aim to stay Green (or, at worst, manageable Yellow)."
If you fall into Red, use the *Resulting Insight* section to note what regulation support you skipped earlier in the day.

3. *Therapeutic Data Practice*

Share only your "Triggering Event" and "Resulting Insight" with your therapist. This provides measurable data about your self-regulation trends and reduces self-blame.

Integration Notes

Reflect at the end of the month:

- Which days consistently pull me into Yellow or Red?
- What patterns of rest, nutrition, or boundaries support more Green days?
- How is my recovery time shortening?

Tool 7: Your Values Mini-Compass

(Weekly Practice for Alignment and Integrity)

Purpose

The *Values Mini-Compass* helps you anchor weekly decisions in your **core values** instead of external chaos. In high-conflict co-parenting, emotional reactivity often replaces intention. This practice shifts focus from "What are they doing?" to "Who am I choosing to be this week?"

You're not trying to win the moment—you're protecting the kind of parent you want to be.

Clinical Rationale (Values-Based Living)

When the nervous system perceives threat, integrity is often the first casualty. The urge to defend, justify, or retaliate replaces presence and patience.

This tool bridges the gap between what you **believe** and how you **behave** under stress. Each week, it realigns communication and boundary-setting with your *core values* (Peace, Integrity, Presence, Consistency).

By writing, reflecting, and self-correcting through this compass, you strengthen what psychologists call *cognitive congruence*—the alignment between belief, body, and behavior. Over time, that alignment restores **self-trust**, **inner safety**, and **calm authority**.

When to Use

Complete this reflection **every Monday morning** before entering your communication week.
Keep a printed copy of your most recent entry visible near your workspace or parenting app.

Time Needed: 5 minutes

Confidentiality Note

Keep this document for personal reflection or therapeutic use. Avoid using it as communication evidence.
Focus on your **growth**, not their behavior.

Weekly Values Mini-Compass

Section	Reflection Prompt	Why it Matters
Week Of: *(Date)*	My Identity Anchor: [Value 1]	Focus Check
1. Core Value 1—Primary Anchor	What is the most important value I commit to protecting this week? *(e.g., Peace, Integrity, Presence, Consistency)*	**The Shield**—establishes your non-negotiable focus for the next 7 days.
2. Core Value 2—Supporting Principle	What secondary value will help me stay anchored? *(e.g., Patience, Accountability, Respect)*	**The Guide**—supports complex decision-making when stress rises.
3. Action Check—Last Week	Describe one major interaction or decision from last week *(1 factual sentence).*	**Factual Recall**—identifies the best example for reflection.
4. Alignment Check	Did that action move me **TOWARD** or **AWAY** from my Core Value 1? Why?	**Self-Assessment**—builds honest, nonjudgmental awareness of your choices.
5. Self-Correction	If I moved away, what small action can I take today to re-anchor? *(e.g., 3 minutes of silence, a somatic reset, rewriting an email using only facts)*	**Re-Centering**—defines one tangible next step for alignment.

Weekly Entry Space

Week Of:

_____

Core Value 1 (Primary):

_____

Core Value 2 (Secondary):

_____

314

Action Check (Last Week):

_____

Alignment Check:
☐ Toward   ☐ Away   Why?

_____

Self-Correction:

_____

(Repeat for four weeks; allow for quarterly review.)

How to Use as Homework

1. ### The Visibility Rule
   Write your *Core Value 1* (e.g., *Peace*) on a sticky note or notecard and keep it in sight—near your phone, laptop, or planner.

   Before replying, look at your value first.
   This primes your nervous system to anchor in intention before reaction.

2. ### The "Why" Drill
   During your Alignment Check, replace self-criticism with curiosity.
   Instead of *"I moved away because I was weak,"* reframe to:
   "I moved away because I was rushed and prioritized speed over my value of integrity."

   This turns guilt into strategy—shifting the focus from flaw to trigger.

3. ### The Congruence Goal
   For the next four weeks, aim for **three "TOWARD" responses** (times when your actions aligned with your value).
   When you reach that milestone, celebrate with a value-aligned reward—something restorative, not performative.

   Example: If your value is *Presence*, take 30 quiet minutes with no phone, just breathing and being.

Reflection Prompts (End of Month)

- Which value felt easiest to uphold when calm?
- Which value do I lose quickest under stress?
- How did my child's experience shift when I stayed anchored in my value?
- What reminder or mantra will help me re-center faster next time?

Tool 8: Your "I Did Not Engage" Log

(Therapeutic—Weekly Practice for Strengthening Your Emotional Boundaries)

Purpose

This tool is designed to **reinforce non-reaction**—the single most important success metric in high-conflict co-parenting. Each log entry captures the exact moment you chose composure over chaos. Non-engagement isn't passivity; it's precision. You are teaching your nervous system that calm is safety—and that safety is power.

Clinical Rationale (Positive Reinforcement)

In trauma-informed work, progress isn't only measured by what you fix—it's measured by what you resist. Every time you *don't engage*, you rewire your nervous system toward stability. This tool links each pause to a positive outcome. By documenting successful restraint, your brain learns:

"Every time I choose calm, I gain energy, peace, and control."

This replaces the old cycle of *fight/justify/explain* with the body-based reward of relief.

When to Use

Log each time you successfully pause, redirect, or refuse to engage with bait—in writing, text, or conversation. You can also review weekly for reflection and progress tracking.

Time Needed: 2–5 minutes per entry.

Confidentiality Note

This is a **therapeutic and accountability log**—not documentation for your co-parent. Keep all entries factual, private, and focused on your own response.

Non-Engagement Log Template

Section	Reflection Prompt	Why it Matters (Rationale)
Date/Time	Record the exact time or moment the bait occurred.	**Factual Data:** Helps you identify patterns.
The Bait/Trigger	Describe the co-parent's statement or behavior (1 factual sentence).	**De-Personalizing:** Keeps focus on facts, not motives.
Intended/Impulsive Reaction	What did your body want to do? *(Rage, defend, cry, explain, withdraw)*	**Awareness:** Validates the difficulty of pausing without acting.
The Pause/Intervention Used	Which regulation or communication tool did you use? *(e.g., 4–6 Breathing Anchor, "Noted" Script, Foot Anchor)*	**Competence:** Reinforces mastery of specific coping tools.
The Resulting Feeling/Shift	What was the emotional outcome? *(Relief, steadiness, energy retained, pride)*	**Reward:** Associates non-reaction with emotional payoff.

Weekly Tracker Table

Use one line per instance of non-engagement. At week's end, review your patterns and total number of recorded pauses.

Date/Time	The Bait/Trigger (Factual, One Sentence)	Intended/Impulsive Reaction	The Pause/Intervention Used	The Resulting Feeling/Shift

Date/Time	The Bait/Trigger (Factual, One Sentence)	Intended/Impulsive Reaction	The Pause/Intervention Used	The Resulting Feeling/Shift

Date/Time	The Bait/Trigger (Factual, One Sentence)	Intended/Impulsive Reaction	The Pause/Intervention Used	The Resulting Feeling/Shift

(Repeat across four pages for multiple weeks.)

How to Use as Homework

1. The Weekly Goal

Set one measurable target:

"I will log a minimum of four non-engagements this week."

The goal isn't about the other parent's behavior—it's about the number of times **you protected your peace**.
Use your Value Mini-Compass (Tool 7) alongside this log to note which value guided your restraint (e.g., "Integrity over impulse").

2. The Reward Loop

When you meet your weekly goal, **celebrate** with a restorative, non-food-based reward.
Examples:

- 30 minutes of uninterrupted silence
- Listening to your favorite playlist
- Buying yourself fresh flowers or a candle
- Writing yourself a note of acknowledgment

This isn't self-soothing. It's *self-recognition.*
You are reinforcing emotional regulation with positive pleasure.

3. Pattern Analysis

After one month, review your **Bait/Trigger** column.
Circle or highlight recurring themes (e.g., money, timing, child performance).
Then, use **Tool 22: If-Then Planning Worksheet** to design a proactive strategy for those triggers.

Example:

- If the co-parent sends texts about money after 8 p.m., *then* I will delay replies until morning using a "Noted" Script.
- If I feel the urge to defend myself, *then* I will take 3 breaths before opening the app.

Reflection Prompts (End of Month)

- What type of bait triggers me most easily?

- Which intervention tool worked most consistently?

- How does my body feel after restraint versus reaction?

- How can I remind myself that disengagement is protection, not avoidance?

Tool 9: Your Support System Accountability Log

(Weekly Practice for Preventing Isolation and Burnout)

Purpose

The *Support System Accountability Log* functions as your **maintenance map for emotional sustainability**. It ensures you're not managing conflict in isolation—but using your network (therapeutic, legal, and personal) to co-regulate, strategize, and stay steady.

When the nervous system is in long-term survival mode, it's easy to over-rely on professionals, underuse supportive friends, or stop reaching out entirely. This log keeps your connection ecosystem healthy and balanced.

Clinical Rationale (Preventing Isolation & Burnout)

Chronic high-conflict parenting depletes resources quickly. When every interaction feels like crisis management, burnout and emotional collapse become predictable outcomes.

This log ensures:

- **Proactive Regulation**—You reach out before the breakdown.
- **Balanced Support**—You distribute your needs across diverse allies.
- **Actionable Closure**—You follow through on every insight or resource shared.

By using this consistently, you shift from crisis calls to *co-regulation calls*—staying connected to strategy and calm, not chaos.

"Connection is a skill, not just a comfort."

When to Use

Use this worksheet once per week, ideally at the end of your week (Friday or Sunday). Each entry takes about **5 minutes**.

Keep it private, short, and factual—this is for *tracking, not venting*.

323

Support Accountability Log Template

Section	Reflection Prompt	Why it Matters (Rationale)
Date	Record the date of contact.	**Data Check:** Tracks frequency and consistency of outreach.
Resource Contacted	Use initials and type (e.g., S.A./Therapist, J.L./Lawyer, M.F./Friend).	**Categorization:** Keeps your network balanced across emotional, professional, and legal supports.
Focus of Conversation	Write 1–3 words summarizing the topic (e.g., "Boundary Check," "Calm Reset," "Legal Update").	**Efficiency:** Keeps the interaction outcome-focused, not reactive.
Outcome/Insight Gained	Note what tangible or emotional benefit you received (e.g., "Gained clarity," "Received 1 actionable legal step," "Felt validated").	**Measured Value:** Ensures time spent with others is purposeful and replenishing.
Follow-Up Action	Record your next small, concrete step (e.g., "Email lawyer by Tuesday," "Text friend gratitude," "Book therapist check-in").	**Accountability:** Converts advice and empathy into motion.

Weekly Support Tracker Table

Use this page to log key connections and insights throughout your week.

Date	Resource Contacted (Initials/Type)	Focus of Conversation (1–3 Words)	Outcome/Insight Gained	Follow-Up Action

Date	Resource Contacted (Initials/Type)	Focus of Conversation (1–3 Words)	Outcome/Insight Gained	Follow-Up Action

(Repeat on four pages for monthly tracking.)

How to Use as Homework

1. The Non-Legal/Non-Therapy Rule

Each week, you must include **at least one connection** with a non-professional ally (friend, mentor, spiritual guide, or peer).
This prevents emotional outsourcing to professionals and rebuilds your **belonging muscle**—reminding you that human connection is still safe.

Example Script:

"I just need 10 minutes of calm conversation—not about the conflict. Can we talk about the new recipe you tried or share one thing that made you laugh this week?"

This shifts emotional energy from *analysis* to *nourishment*.

2. Pre-Scripting Ally Calls

Before reaching out, set your intention clearly:

- "I need to feel grounded, not get advice."
- "Can you help me reframe this through compassion?"
- "I want to end this call feeling more centered than I started."

Pro Tip: State your focus at the beginning of each call. It invites containment and safety for both people.

3. The Lawyer/Therapist Integration

For professional contacts, use the **Outcome/Insight** column to record one clear takeaway.
Immediately move the **Follow-Up Action** to your planner or task list.
This prevents valuable guidance from getting lost in overwhelm.

Example:

"Therapist: Practice one grounding exercise before opening co-parenting app."
Follow-Up: Add 3-minute breath reset to evening routine.

Reflection Prompts (End of Month)

- Who do I reach out to most when I'm calm vs. when I'm distressed?

- Which type of support (emotional, logistical, professional) feels underused?

- How did my body feel after each contact—grounded, drained, or neutral?

- Did I follow through on advice or let it fade?

_____

_____

_____

Use these prompts to evaluate whether your connections are helping you *regulate*, not just *relate*.

Your As-Needed Documentation Tools

Tool 10: Your Communication & Emotion Log

(Therapeutic Use Only)

Purpose

The *Communication & Emotion Log* is a trauma-informed journaling tool designed to help you track **what triggers your body**, **how your emotions respond**, and **how well you regulate afterward**.
It transforms moments of reactivity into measurable progress toward emotional mastery.

"You can't heal what you can't see—but you can chart what you feel."

Clinical Rationale (Internal Awareness)

Focus	Explanation	Why it Matters
Somatic Awareness	Connects emotions to body sensations (e.g., jaw tension, racing pulse).	Builds interoception—your ability to notice activation early.
Emotional Clarity	Names emotions as data, not danger.	Reduces shame and confusion around triggers.
Measurable Repair	Records how calm returns after regulation.	Turns healing into observable, trackable progress.

Actionable Growth

By documenting each reaction and your *After Effect (Calm Score)*, you create data that can be reviewed in therapy or coaching—evidence of change, not chaos.

Action Plan

Use this immediately after any interaction (text, call, exchange) that triggers dysregulation—especially when you notice Yellow or Red Zone activation (see Tool 6). This is for **therapeutic tracking**, not for documentation or evidence.

Time Needed: 5–10 minutes per entry

Communication & Emotion Log (Make into a Four-Page Worksheet)

Section	Reflection Prompt	Rationale
Date/Time	Record when the event occurred.	*Factual Anchor:* Grounds the experience in time, not emotion.
Event/Trigger	Write a one-sentence, neutral description of what happened. (e.g., "Co-parent sent a text demanding payment.")	*De-escalation:* Keeps the focus on the event, not the story.
My Reaction (Before Tool Use)	Identify the emotion + body sensation. (e.g., Rage + clenched jaw; Shame + stomach drop.)	*Somatic Tracking:* Creates separation between stimulus and response.
Tool Used (Specific Action)	What regulation technique did you use? (e.g., 4–6 Breathing Anchor—Tool 2; STOP Skill—Tool 2; Safety Ally—Tool 17.)	*Competence:* Captures intentional self-regulation, even if imperfect.
After Effect (1–10 Calm Score)	Rate your current level of calm (1 = Crisis, 10 = Total Peace).	*Measurable Repair:* Quantifies your healing process.
Note for Therapy (Insight/Pattern)	What insight did this reveal? (e.g., "I need validation when accused of money issues.")	*Perspective:* Turns triggers into therapeutic direction.

Therapeutic Tracker (Make into Four Pages for Ongoing Use)

Date/Time	Event/Trigger (Factual, One Sentence)	My Reaction (Emotion + Body Sensation)	Tool Used (Specific Action)	After Effect (1–10 Calm Score)	Note for Therapy (Insight/Pattern)

How to Use as Homework

1. The 7+ Calm Score Challenge

Aim for an *After Effect Calm Score* of **7 or higher** on at least 75% of entries.
If your average falls below 5, it's a signal to repeat your regulation practice (e.g., 4–6 Breathing Anchor for 10 cycles) before journaling.

Goal: Build measurable evidence that regulation is becoming automatic.

2. Somatic Focus Assignment

For one week, track only one body reaction (e.g., chest tightening, jaw clenching). Log each time that sensation appears—even when there's no external conflict.

This teaches you to recognize early stress cues before escalation.

3. Therapy Preparation Exercise

Before your next session, review your "Note for Therapy" column. Highlight the **three most common emotional patterns** and bring those to therapy as your focus.

Keeps therapy strategic—based on insight, not narrative venting.

Tool 11: Your Court-Safe Documentation Log

(Legal Use Only)

Purpose

The *Court-Safe Documentation Log* is your factual, structured record of all co-parenting interactions that violate court orders, parenting agreements, or threaten a child's well-being.
It transforms emotional chaos into clean, admissible data.

"This is not for venting. It's for verification."

The goal is to protect your credibility by recording **only verifiable facts**—never feelings, opinions, or assumptions.

Clinical + Legal Rationale (The Five Ws)

Each log entry must answer:

Who, What, Where, When, and Witnesses.

Focus	Explanation	Why it Matters
Factual Clarity	Centers only on the observable event—no emotion, no adjectives.	Meets the legal standard of admissibility.
Pattern Tracking	Highlights repeat violations, not isolated incidents.	Courts prioritize consistency over single events.
Child-Centered Impact	Includes observed reactions or disruptions to the child.	Reinforces your focus on welfare, not revenge.
Legal Linkage	Quotes the specific clause violated (e.g., "Section 4.B. Exchange Time must be 6:00 PM").	Creates a direct trail to your parenting order or agreement.

Actionable Protection

Each entry is a *shield*, not a weapon—neutral evidence that strengthens your case and preserves your credibility.

Action Plan

Use this log **immediately after** any factual violation, unsafe event, or non-compliance. Keep it separate from emotional notes (see *Tool 10: Communication & Emotion Log*).

Time Needed: 3–5 minutes per entry

Court-Safe Documentation Log (Make into a Four-Page Worksheet)

Section	Prompt for Entry	Rationale
Date/Time	Record the exact time the incident occurred.	*Verifiable Record:* Builds the legal timeline.
Interaction Type & Channel	e.g., *In-Person Exchange, App Message, Text, Call.*	*Context:* Establishes how the exchange occurred.
Factual Summary/Verbatim Quote	Write only objective facts or direct quotes. *(e.g., "Co-parent arrived 45 minutes late for exchange.")*	*Neutrality:* Keeps the entry emotion-free.
Non-Compliance/Violation	Quote the specific order or clause violated. *(e.g., "Order Section 4.B: Exchange Time 6:00 PM.")*	*Legal Linkage:* Connects the event directly to court terms.
Child Impact (Observed Behavior)	Factual observation only. *(e.g., "Child began crying," "Child refused to exit car.")*	*Harm/Welfare:* Documents behavioral impact without speculation.
Attachment Location (File Name)	Where evidence is stored. *(e.g., "Email 2025-05-15.pdf," "Video Clip 004," "Transfer Checklist 05-15-25.")*	*Evidence Trail:* Directs your attorney to the proof.

Legal Documentation Tracker (Make into Four Pages for Ongoing Use)

Date/ Time	Interaction Type & Channel	Factual Summary/ Verbatim Quote	Non-Compliance/ Violation (Clause)	Child Impact (Observed Behavior)	Attachment Location (File Name)

Date/ Time	Interaction Type & Channel	Factual Summary/ Verbatim Quote	Non-Compliance/ Violation (Clause)	Child Impact (Observed Behavior)	Attachment Location (File Name)

How to Use as Homework

1. The "No Emotion" Filter

Before submitting or saving any entry, **read it aloud** and remove every emotional word (e.g., *angry, threatening, chaotic*).
Replace them with factual descriptors (e.g., *used all caps, sent 10 messages in one hour, arrived 40 minutes late*).

Ask: *"If a judge read this, would they see fact or feeling?"*

2. The Pattern Focus

With your legal counsel, identify **one type of violation** to track for 30 days (e.g., refusal to share medical information).
Your goal: document **eight separate instances** before presenting it legally.

This establishes a *pattern of conduct*, which courts weigh far more heavily than isolated events.

3. Cross-Referencing Rule

If the same event caused strong emotional activation, make **two entries**:
- One here (factual, legal), and
- One in Tool 10 (emotional/therapeutic).

Keeping them separate maintains integrity between **your legal evidence** and **your personal healing.**

Tool 12: Your Boundary & Requests Tracker

(Legal Use)

Purpose

The *Boundary & Requests Tracker* helps you identify the co-parent's predictable reactions to your healthy limits.
It shifts your focus from emotional frustration to **behavioral data**—patterns that show whether boundaries are respected, ignored, or weaponized.

"You're not documenting drama—you're tracking patterns."

Each log entry captures how your boundaries are tested, which in turn reveals **where your energy is wasted** and **where your strategy must shift**.

Clinical Rationale (Identifying Predictable Testing)

Focus	Explanation	Why it Matters
Behavioral Pattern Recognition	Conflict isn't random—it's often repetitive testing.	When you know the pattern, you stop personalizing the behavior.
Response Mapping	Tracks the co-parent's consistent reaction type: *Comply, Deny, Attack, or Stonewall.*	Predictability reduces reactivity.
Strategic Adjustment	Shows when to stop communicating and start documenting (Tool 11).	Saves energy and creates objective proof.

Actionable Insight

By using this log, you replace emotional confusion with observable trends, moving from "Why do they do this?" to "Here's what they always do."

Action Plan

Use this immediately after setting a factual boundary or making a clear, child-related request.
Focus on **what** happened, not **how** it felt.

Time Needed: 3–5 minutes per entry

Boundary & Requests Tracker (Make into a Four-Page Worksheet)

Section	Prompt for Entry	Rationale
Date/Time	Record when the boundary or request was sent.	*Timeline Anchor:* Supports legal or therapeutic review.
Boundary Set/Factual Request	State the request clearly. *(e.g., "I will not respond to texts after 8 P.M." "Please send the report card by Tuesday.")*	*Clarity Check:* Keeps the focus on factual language.
Communication Channel	*e.g., Co-Parenting App, Email, In-Person.*	*Context:* Identifies where communication patterns occur.
Co-Parent Response (Factual Summary)	Record *only* what they did or said. *(e.g., "They replied at 8:15 P.M.; sent a photo of a dog instead of the report card.")*	*Neutrality:* Focuses on behavior, not tone.
Response Pattern (Circle One)	Compliance/Deny/Attack/Stonewall	*Pattern Identification:* Core data for strategic shifts.
My Next Action (Tool Used)	Document your next regulated response. *(e.g., Sent Tool 1 Neutral Script 4; Logged in Tool 11.)*	*Competence:* Logs deliberate follow-up rather than reaction.

Response Pattern Key

- **Compliance:** Boundary respected; request granted.
- **Deny:** Request refused with or without minimal justification.
- **Attack:** Personal insults, blame, or deflection (JADE).
- **Stonewall:** No response, long delay, or irrelevant reply.

Tracker Template (Four Pages for Ongoing Use)

Date / Time	Boundary Set or Factual Request Made	Communication Channel	Co-Parent Response (Factual Summary)	Response Pattern (Circle One)	My Next Action (Tool Used)
				Compliance/Deny/Attack/Stonewall	
				Compliance/Deny/Attack/Stonewall	
				Compliance/Deny/Attack/Stonewall	

(Repeat across four pages for cumulative trend tracking.)

How to Use as Homework

1. The "Three-Strike Rule" Assignment

Choose your most frequently tested boundary (e.g., response time, financial communication).
Track it for three consecutive instances.
If the pattern is **Deny**, **Attack**, or **Stonewall** three times in a row—shift your next step from communication to documentation (*Tool 11*).

You're not escalating; you're conserving energy.

2. Values Check (Tool 7 Integration)

Every time your boundary holds, connect the success to your core value (e.g., Peace, Presence, Dignity).

339

Example: "The boundary held—I protected my value of Peace."
This rewires your nervous system to associate boundaries with self-respect, not punishment.

3. The Factual Summary Discipline

If emotion creeps into your notes, rewrite the "Co-Parent Response" using *only observable data.*

Instead of: "They rudely refused."
Write: "The co-parent stated they would not comply."

This single practice increases the credibility and clarity of your entire log.

Tool 13: Your Co-Parenting Meeting Agenda

Purpose

The *Co-Parenting Meeting Agenda* is your containment structure for high-stakes or required communication (e.g., medical updates, school coordination, legal mediations).
It prevents conversations from being hijacked by emotion, blame, or baiting—ensuring all contact stays **factual, time-limited, and predictable.**

"Structure is safety. Predictability is peace."

This form replaces reactive talk with pre-planned logistics.
You will decide *what to discuss*, *how long to discuss it*, and *exactly how to end it*.

Clinical Rationale (Containment & Predictability)

Focus	Explanation	Why it Matters
Containment	Time limits and factual scope reduce spontaneous chaos.	Keeps power balanced and emotional hijacking low.
Predictability	The agenda defines order, not emotion.	Reinforces your authority to stay in control of structure, not tone.
Actionable Closure	A clear termination statement ends the meeting safely.	Ensures regulated endings even if the co-parent escalates.

Action Insight

When you control *structure*, you control *exposure*.

341

Action Plan

Complete this agenda **before** any scheduled meeting or joint discussion. Refer to it in real-time to redirect the focus to neutral, factual items only.

Time Needed: 15–20 minutes (prep)

Co-Parenting Meeting Agenda (Make into a Four-Page Worksheet)

Section	Topic (Must Be Factual & Future-Focused)	Time Limit (Strictly Enforced)	Goal (Desired Factual Outcome)	Prepared Neutral Script (Tool 1)	Notes/Action Items
I. Logistics/Safety	*(e.g., Upcoming schedule change, medical insurance, school forms)*	5 min	Clarity on logistics or documents	"Let's confirm this update is reflected in the app."	
II. Review/Transition	*(e.g., Review of last week's exchange or expense)*	5 min	Close the loop on prior issues without rehashing.	"Thank you—I'll note that in the parenting app."	
III. Future Planning	*(e.g., Summer schedule, holiday travel, long-term school choice)*	5 min	Confirm next concrete step.	"I'll email the written summary by Friday."	
IV. Termination (Mandatory Closing)	Factual statement confirming	2 min	Neutral, calm ending	"Thank you for the factual discussion.	

Section	Topic (Must Be Factual & Future-Focused)	Time Limit (Strictly Enforced)	Goal (Desired Factual Outcome)	Prepared Neutral Script (Tool 1)	Notes/Action Items
	next steps or contact.		regardless of tone.	I'll document agreements and communicate next steps via the app."	

Meeting Date	Meeting Type	Total Time	Section	Topic	Time Limit	Goal (Outcome)	Prepared Script	Notes / Actions
			I. Logistics/Safety					
			II. Review/Transition					
			III. Future Planning					
			IV. Termination			"Thank you for the factual discussion..."		

How to Use as Homework

1. The Time-Keeper Role

Your job is to enforce the time limits. If the co-parent veers off topic or exceeds five minutes, calmly use your redirect script:

"That's important, but we only have 3 minutes left for this item. Let's return to discussing it."

This resets control without escalation.

2. The Termination Mandate

Always end meetings with the Termination Script, no matter the tone or state of the conversation.

"Thank you for the factual discussion. I'll document our agreements and communicate next steps via the app."

This simple act protects your nervous system, sets boundaries, and avoids emotional re-entry loops.

3. Pre-Meeting Regulation

Before attending the meeting, use:
- *STOP Skill (Tool 2)*—pause and breathe.
- *4–6 Breathing Anchor (Tool 2)*—calm your vagus nerve.

You can't hold structure externally unless your body is regulated internally.

Mantra—"My calm sets the clock. My script ends the story."

Tool 14: Your Child Behavior Observation Log

Purpose

The *Child Behavior Observation Log* is a targeted documentation tool used to record factual, observable patterns in your child's behavior—particularly following high-conflict exposure, transitions, or distressing exchanges.
It is a **behavioral record**, not an emotional journal.

"You don't document feelings—you document what you can see."

Your goal is to produce clear, neutral data that supports your child's therapeutic team and builds a bridge between your parenting insight and professional intervention.

Clinical & Legal Rationale (The A-B-C Model)

Focus	Explanation	Why it Matters
Antecedent (Trigger/Context)	What happened *immediately before* the child's reaction.	Identifies external patterns such as transitions or calls from the other parent.
Behavior (Observable Action)	The measurable or visible behavior itself—what was seen or heard.	Creates objective data that can be verified.
Consequence (Parent Response)	How you responded to regulate, soothe, or document.	Demonstrates appropriate, regulated intervention.
Legal Relevance	You cannot testify to feelings, only to behavior.	This ensures your entries are credible, admissible, and clinically useful.

Clinical Note

This log aligns with trauma-informed A-B-C tracking used in behavioral therapy, making it ideal for coordination with child clinicians or court-appointed evaluators.

Action Plan

Use this log *immediately* after noticing concerning behaviors or when a pattern emerges over time.

Time Needed: 3–5 minutes per entry

Child Behavior Observation Log (Make into a Four-Page Worksheet)

Section	Prompt for Entry	Rationale
Date/Time	Record the exact time the behavior started.	*Timeline Anchor:* Keeps data accurate and sequential.
Context (Antecedent)	What happened right before? *(e.g., 5 min after exchange; during call with co-parent).*	*Trigger Identification:* Reveals patterns that precede distress.
Specific Observable Behavior	Describe the behavior neutrally. *(e.g., "Cried for 15 min," "Refused dinner," "Scratched arm.")*	*Factual Integrity:* Must be measurable, not interpretive.
Duration/Intensity	How long it lasted and how severe it appeared. *(e.g., 10 min, intensity 4/5).*	*Data Quality:* Quantifies scope of distress.
Child's Words/Scripting	Record verbatim if relevant. *(e.g., "Daddy said you don't care about me.")*	*Evidence of Enmeshment:* Tracks potential emotional scripting.

Section	Prompt for Entry	Rationale
Parent Action (What You Did)	Note your specific, regulated intervention. *(e.g., "Used 4–6 Breathing Anchor," "Maintained calm silence.")*	*Consequence/Competence:* Shows containment and appropriate regulation.

Child Behavior Tracker (Make into Four Pages for Continued Use)

Date / Time	Context (Antecedent)	Specific Observable Behavior (Factual)	Duration/Intensity	Child's Words/Scripting (Quote Verbatim)	Parent Action (What You Did to Regulate/Contain)

Date / Time	Context (Antecedent)	Specific Observable Behavior (Factual)	Duration/Intensity	Child's Words/Scripting (Quote Verbatim)	Parent Action (What You Did to Regulate/Contain)

(Repeat across four pages to identify cumulative patterns.)

How to Use as Homework

1. The Single-Focus Rule

Choose **one behavior** to track for 14 days—e.g., meltdowns, scripting, or sleep refusal.

Your aim is to gather at least **six clean entries** on that same behavior, allowing professionals to identify consistent triggers and measurable improvement.

348

Broad tracking shows chaos. Focused tracking shows progress.

2. Immediate Documentation Mandate

Begin your entry **as soon as the behavior starts**, even if you can't fully intervene yet.
At minimum, log the first three fields: *Date/Time*, *Context*, *Behavior*.
This real-time entry prevents memory distortion and creates reliable data for both therapeutic and legal purposes.

3. Cross-Referencing with Legal Logs

If the **Context** overlaps with a documented custody or exchange issue, link your entry to *Tool 11 (Court-Safe Documentation Log)*.

Example: "Exchange was 45 minutes late—logged in Tool 11."
This connection builds a direct, factual line between the co-parent's behavior and the child's distress, strengthening both your legal and therapeutic narratives.

Mantra

"I can't control the behavior, but I can control the clarity of the record."

Tool 15: Your Future Focus Worksheet

Purpose

The *Future Focus Worksheet* is your structured antidote to rumination—a step-by-step process that transforms "what if" anxiety into a single, clear, factual action.
It's designed for moments when high-conflict co-parenting triggers the *Worry Loop*: catastrophizing, replaying worst-case scenarios, or scanning for threats.

"Fear is imagination with no plan. Planning is how we take imagination back."

This tool trains the brain to exit the *fight-flight freeze* of emotional reasoning and return to the rational, problem-solving prefrontal cortex.

Clinical Rationale (Converting Rumination to Tasking)

Focus	Explanation	Why it Matters
Externalizing the Fear	Turning the abstract fear into a written, concrete scenario.	Writing down the fear stops emotional looping and gives it form.
Reality Testing	Checking the fear against verifiable facts and probabilities.	Reduces catastrophizing and grounds you in evidence, not emotion.
Tasking Over Thinking	Identifying the *only next warranted action* rather than solving everything.	Prevents overwhelm by restoring focus to the next single step.
Somatic Release	Ending the loop with a regulation tool.	Ensures closure in the body, not just the mind.

Action Plan

Use this worksheet anytime a worry occupies your mind for longer than 15 minutes or resurfaces repeatedly.

Time Needed: 10 minutes

Future Focus Worksheet

Section	Reflection Prompt	Rationale
Date/Time	Record when the worry began.	*Factual Anchor:* Grounds the start of the thought loop in time.
1. The Worry Loop (Identify)	Write the full worst-case scenario. *(e.g., "They'll move out of state and I'll never see the child again.")*	*Externalizing the Fear:* Moves it from imagination into form.
2. Factual Warrant (Check the Plan)	List two immediate, verifiable facts that contradict or weaken the fear. *(e.g., "Passport is secured," "Court order prevents relocation.")*	*Reality Testing:* Separates fact from fear.
3. Risk Assessment (Scale 1–10)	On a scale of 1–10 (1 = Impossible, 10 = Certain), how likely is this to occur in the next 30 days?	*Prioritization:* Helps decide if this is an emergency or anxiety.
4. Warranted Action (The Only Next Step)	If the risk is 6 or higher, what single action is warranted? *(e.g., "Email lawyer re: travel clause.")*	*Tasking:* Turns anxiety into motion.
5. Self-Regulation (Release)	What regulation tool will you use to release residual tension? *(e.g., "5-4-3-2-1 grounding," "4–6 Breathing Anchor," "15 minutes of quiet reading.")*	*Closure:* Ends the loop with calm, not analysis.

Continuation Pages (Make into a Four-Page Worry-to-Action Converter)

Date/Time	The Worry Loop (Identify)	Factual Warrant (Check the Plan)	Risk Assessment (1–10)	Warranted Action (The Only Next Step)	Self-Regulation (Release)

Date/Time	The Worry Loop (Identify)	Factual Warrant (Check the Plan)	Risk Assessment (1–10)	Warranted Action (The Only Next Step)	Self-Regulation (Release)

(Use up to four pages per month or per recurring anxiety theme.)

How to Use as Homework

1. The Stop-and-Switch

Your assignment is *not* to solve the fear—it's to interrupt it.
You complete the worksheet when you reach **Section 5** and implement a regulation tool.

The goal is to move from mental looping to physical calm.

2. The Task Transfer

If the **Risk Assessment** is **6 or higher**, transfer your **Warranted Action** to your daily task list (or communicate it to your legal or therapeutic professional).
Then close the worksheet.

Once it becomes a task, it no longer belongs in your worry cycle.

3. The Low-Risk Release

If the **Risk Assessment** is **5 or lower**, skip Section 4 entirely.
Go straight to **Self-Regulation (Section 5)** and complete a calming action.
This teaches your brain that low-probability fears require *soothing*, not *solving*.

"Not every fear deserves a plan. Some just need a pause."

Tool 16: Your Financial/Expense Tracker

Purpose

The *Financial/Expense Tracker* transforms reactive, emotionally charged financial exchanges into a clean, factual ledger.
It provides verifiable documentation of payments, reimbursements, and shared expenses—turning potential power struggles into transparent accountability.

"You can't argue with numbers—only with noise."

This is not just about money; it's about **mental clarity and legal credibility.**

Clinical + Legal Rationale

Focus	Explanation	Why it Matters
Clear Accounting (Legal)	Tracks each transaction by date, category, and supporting documentation.	Ensures your records are admissible and unambiguous.
Reducing Anxiety (Clinical)	Creates a single, trusted location for all financial records.	Eliminates repetitive checking or rehashing about money.
Minimizing Manipulation	Removes emotional context from financial communication.	Prevents baiting, guilt-tripping, or power imbalance.

Action Insight

Your calm ledger is stronger evidence than any emotional argument.

Action Plan

Log every transaction (payment, reimbursement, or request) **immediately** after completion or communication.
Attach all supporting receipts or proof of payment digitally.

Time Needed: 2–3 minutes per entry

Financial/Expense Tracker

Section	Prompt for Entry	Rationale
Date of Transaction	When was the expense paid or requested?	*Timeline Anchor:* Creates chronological accuracy.
Description of Expense	Be specific. *(e.g., Q3 tuition, pediatric dental visit, school uniform.)*	*Clarity/Verification:* Categorizes purpose of expense.
Total Cost	Enter the full verified amount from the receipt.	*Factual Data:* Removes ambiguity.
My Payment/Co-Parent's Share	Record your payment and the portion the co-parent owes.	*Allocation Transparency:* Documents proportional responsibility.
Authority/Agreement Reference	Cite the legal or court clause mandating this expense. *(e.g., "Order Sec. 7.C—Uncovered Medical 50/50")*	*Legal Linkage:* Ties payment to binding authority.
Status (Circle One)	Paid/Requested/Reimbursed/Overdue	*Actionable Status:* Summarizes where the item stands.

Section	Prompt for Entry	Rationale
Attachment Location (File Name)	Where is the proof stored? *(e.g., "Receipt_Pediatric_11.2025.pdf")*	*Evidence Trail:* Links physical or digital proof to record.

Continuation Tables (Make into a Four-Page Worksheet)

Date of Transaction	Description of Expense	Total Cost	My Payment / Co-parent Share	Authority/Agreement (Specific Clause)	Status (Circle One)	Attachment Location (File Name)

Date of Transaction	Description of Expense	Total Cost	My Payment / Co-parent Share	Authority/Agreement (Specific Clause)	Status (Circle One)	Attachment Location (File Name)

(Use multiple pages per quarter or per major financial category.)

How to Use as Homework

1. The "No Discussion" Rule

Never discuss money verbally or outside the approved communication app/email. All documentation and reimbursements belong *here* and in your digital record—nowhere else.

If baited or guilted into a financial argument, respond only with:

"Please refer to the receipt and record logged on [Date]."

If the co-parent continues, use your neutral BIFF script (Tool 1):

"This is documented in the financial tracker for clarity."

2. The Overdue Trigger

Set a firm policy for overdue reimbursement.
If **30 days** pass after the *Date of Transaction*, automatically mark the entry as **Overdue** and document your next step:

- Send a single, BIFF-compliant reminder via the approved app.
- Do not argue or justify.

"Per our order, reimbursement for [Expense] dated [Date] is now overdue. Please remit payment per Section [Clause]."

Then update this tool's **Status** field and close the entry.

3. The Legal Summary Protocol

When preparing documentation for your attorney or case, export or summarize the following three data points only:

- Total Cost
- Co-Parent Share/Outstanding Balance
- Overdue Entries

Do *not* include emotional commentary.
Your lawyer (and the court) needs a **factual pattern**, not a narrative.

Tool 17: Your Safety Ally Check-In Script

Purpose

The *Safety Ally Check-In Script* formalizes how to reach out to your trusted support person (ally) during moments of crisis, emotional flooding, or dysregulation.
It ensures you get **co-regulation**, not emotional chaos—protecting both you and your ally from overwhelm or miscommunication.

"Connection is healing—but only when it's contained."

This tool gives your nervous system structure during distress, providing calm, clarity, and closure.

Clinical Rationale (Co-Regulation and Boundary Protection)

Focus	Explanation	Why it Matters
Co-Regulation	Accesses safe, human connection to downshift from a Yellow/Red nervous-system state.	The body calms faster through relational safety than isolation.
Boundary Protection	Creates a pre-defined script to prevent venting or retraumatization.	Protects the ally's bandwidth and ensures the call restores—not drains—safety.
Containment & Role Clarity	Sets specific limits on time, topic, and need.	Allies know exactly how to help, and you stay self-directed.

Action Insight

Clear roles protect relationships. You can be vulnerable without becoming volatile.

Action Plan

Complete this brief script **before** calling or texting your ally.
You'll identify:

- your **current regulation state** (see Tool 6),
- how long you need,
- and what kind of support you're asking for.

Time Needed: 1 minute of prep + 10–15 minutes of co-regulation

Safety Ally Check-In Script (Quick Reference Card)

Section	Preparation (My Work Before Calling)	Script (What I Say to My Ally)	Rationale/Goal
1. Regulation Status	My current state (Tool 6): *Yellow/Red*	"Hi [Ally's Name], I'm checking in because my nervous system is in the [Yellow/Red] zone."	*Immediate Honesty:* Establishes urgency and skips small talk.
2. Time Boundary	Set a time cap. *(Max 15 minutes)*	"I only need [Time] minutes of your time to get regulated."	*Respecting Limits:* Protects your ally's energy and keeps you concise.
3. Defined Role	Identify the type of support you need: *Validation/Grounding/Distraction.*	"I need you to primarily function as my [Role] right now."	*Clarity of Purpose:* Prevents advice-giving or emotional spirals.
4. The Stop Limit	Define your off-limits topic. *(e.g., "The co-parent's behavior.")*	"Please interrupt me if I start talking about [Topic] or	*Containment:* Reinforces the boundary when stress rises.

361

Section	Preparation (My Work Before Calling)	Script (What I Say to My Ally)	Rationale/Goal
		blaming the co-parent."	
5. Exit Protocol	Plan your next regulation step. *(e.g., 4–6 Breathing Anchor, walk, shower, or other grounding ritual.)*	"Thank you. I have enough calm now to execute [Tool Name]. I'll talk to you later."	*Self-Efficacy:* Ends the call with agency and playfulness.

Safety Ally Check-In Script (Printable Script Card—Fill Before Dialing)

Step	My State/Preparation	Script to Say
1. Status	[Yellow/Red]	"Hi, my nervous system is in the [Yellow/Red] zone, and I need a quick check-in."
2. Time	[Set time]	"I only need [Time] minutes of your time to get regulated."
3. Role	[Validation/Distraction/Grounding]	"I need you to primarily function as my [Role] right now."
4. Limit	[Off-limits topic]	"Please interrupt me if I start talking about [Topic] or blaming the co-parent."
5. Exit	[Next Tool or Action]	"Thank you. I have enough calm now to execute [Next Action]. I'll talk to you later."

How to Use as Homework

1. The Ally Pre-Brief

362

Before crisis moments arise, share this script with your primary allies during a calm state.
Tell them this is your new *safety structure*—and that their role is to help you regulate, not problem-solve.

"If I call, it's not for advice—it's for calm."

This pre-brief ensures everyone knows the limits and purpose before the emotion hits.

2. The Immediate Regulation Rule

Before calling your ally, execute **4–6 Breathing Anchor (Tool 2)** for one full minute.
Then fill out this script and *call from control, not collapse.*
This is the difference between venting and self-led co-regulation.

3. The "Distraction Mandate"

Choose **Distraction** as your ally's role for at least 50% of calls.

Ask them to talk about neutral, life-affirming topics—a movie, music, weekend plans, or something funny.

This practice rewires your brain to associate safety with *everyday connection*, not just crisis recovery.

"Joy is regulation, too."

Tool 18: Your HCCP Communication Decryption Key

(Analysis Worksheet—Emotional → Factual Conversion)

Purpose

The *Communication Decryption Key* is a structured, trauma-informed worksheet that transforms emotional triggers into neutral, strategic responses.
It systematically breaks down hostile or manipulative communication into three parts:
The Tactic, The Trigger, and The Factual Signal.

> "You don't have to match their chaos—you can decode it."

Clinical Rationale (Decoupling Emotion and Action)

Focus	Explanation	Why it Matters
Trauma-Informed Delay	Introduces a pause between activation and action.	Prevents reaction from hijacking your nervous system.
Cognitive Deconstruction	Turns a manipulative message into neutral data points.	Restores your prefrontal cortex—logic over panic.
BIFF Communication Model	Ensures every response is Brief, Informative, Friendly, and Firm.	Protects credibility in both legal and parenting contexts.

Action Insight

The goal is not to win the argument—it's to win back regulation.

Action Plan

Use this immediately after receiving a triggering message.
Do *not* reply until this worksheet is complete.

Time Needed: 5–10 minutes.

HCCP Communication Decryption Key (Make into a Four-Page Worksheet)

Input: Factual Capture

Section	Prompt for Analysis	Rationale for Inclusion
1. Date/Time & Channel	Record when and how the message was received. *(e.g., "Tuesday, 10:30 AM, Co-Parenting App.")*	**Legal Anchor:** Creates a verifiable record of evidence.
2. Verbatim Quote/Theme	Write the exact text or summarize the theme. *(e.g., "You never follow the plan; you're always irresponsible.")*	**Objectivity:** Captures data without interpretation.

Deconstruction: Therapeutic Filter

Section	Prompt for Analysis	Rationale for Inclusion
3. My Somatic/Emotional Trigger	Name the first emotion and physical reaction. *(e.g., "Rage + Tight jaw" or "Shame + Stomach drop.")*	**Regulation Check (Tool 2):** Identifies the body's entry point for self-soothing.
4. HCCP Tactic Detected (Check One)	☐ Projection ☐ Gaslighting ☐ Victim Stance ☐ Trivial Demand ☐ Hostile Label	**Depersonalization:** Naming the tactic removes its power.

365

Section	Prompt for Analysis	Rationale for Inclusion
5. My Vulnerable "Why"	What fear does this exploit? *(e.g., "Fear of being judged as a bad parent.")*	**Therapeutic Insight (Tool 10):** Reveals the root emotional wound for self-work.

Output: Strategic Reframing

Section	Prompt for Analysis	Rationale for Inclusion
6. Factual Re-Statement	Rewrite the content neutrally, removing judgment, emotion, or accusation. *(e.g., "The parenting app message referenced a schedule change.")*	**BIFF Principle:** Keeps the response legally and emotionally clean.
7. The Actual Request/Issue	Identify the logistical or legal item underneath the insult. *(e.g., "They're requesting a pickup time change.")*	**Signal vs. Noise:** Pinpoints the actionable fact.
8. The Strategic Decision (Check One)	☐ Respond ☐ Document (Tool 11) ☐ Ignore	**Intentional:** Ensures your next move is deliberate, not reactive.
9. The BIFF Script (Actionable Reply)	Write one factual, one-sentence response. *(e.g., "Please confirm the exchange time is 5 PM.")*	**Final Product:** Safe, firm, and minimal communication.

Worksheet Example (Simplified Layout)

Step	Input/Reflection
1. Date/Time	Tuesday, 10:30 AM, Co-Parenting App
2. Verbatim Quote	"You're ruining our child's life."
3. My Trigger	Shame + Chest Tightness

Step	Input/Reflection
4. Tactic	Gaslighting
5. Vulnerable "Why"	Fear of being seen as unfit
6. Factual Re-Statement	Message referenced child's school issue.
7. Actual Request	Clarification of homework submission.
8. Strategic Decision	Respond
9. BIFF Script	"Please confirm if homework was turned in by Tuesday."

How to Use as Homework

1. Somatic Interruption

When the trigger hits, stop immediately and perform **4–6 Breathing Anchor (Tool 2)** until your physical distress level drops below 5/10.
Only then begin analyzing the message.
This separates *emotion* from *execution*.

"Regulated responding is always the higher ground."

2. The Double-Log Mandate

If Section 8 = *Document*, transfer your *Factual Re-Statement* (Section 6) into **Tool 11: Court-Safe Documentation Log**.
Do not copy the emotional content—only the factual event.

"Record what happened, not how it felt."

3. Goal Alignment (Values Check)

Before sending your BIFF reply, ask:
"Does this response protect my core value of Peace, Dignity, or Integrity?"
If yes, you are responding from alignment—not defense.

"A response from your values will always outlast their reaction."

Your Planning & Vision Tools

Tool 19: Your Transition Plan

Purpose

The *Transition Plan* is your protocol for ensuring every child exchange happens with calm, clarity, and complete predictability.
It replaces last-minute chaos and verbal negotiation with a structured, repeatable system that prioritizes your child's safety and your own emotional regulation.

"Structure isn't rigidity—it's what keeps love steady when emotions rise."

This plan is both a **safety map** and a **regulation ritual**, guiding you through the highest-stakes moments with precision and peace.

Clinical Rationale (Predictability & Co-Regulation)

Focus	Explanation	Why it Matters
Predictability	Children thrive when they know what to expect—who, where, and when.	Reduces transition anxiety and builds trust in routines.
Co-Regulation	Structure helps both parent and child stay emotionally grounded.	Prevents escalation and keeps the nervous system in "safety mode."
Containment	Limits unnecessary dialogue or improvisation with the co-parent.	Converts chaotic interactions into calm, factual exchanges.

Action Insight

The more predictable the system, the less power conflict has.

Action Plan

Complete this plan once, review it weekly, and reference it before each transition. Keep one printed copy in your car and one saved in your co-parenting app.

Time Needed: 20 minutes (initial setup), 2 minutes (per exchange review)

Transition Plan

Section	Protocol Details (Specific & Factual)	My Role (Action)	Co-Parent's Role (Action)
Time & Location	Specific location *(e.g., Central Library parking lot, north entrance)*	Arrival Time: _____	Departure Time: _____
Exchange Protocol (Arrival)	Arrival procedure *(e.g., Wait in vehicle, headlights on)*	Child is ready and buckled; I execute 4–6 Breathing Anchor.	Approaches passenger side only; no contact.
Communication Limit (The Hand-Off)	Communication limited to checklist-only exchange; no verbal discussion.	Smile at child, hand over Checklist (Tool 4).	Checks seatbelt; drives away immediately.
Post-Exchange Decompression (Child-Centered)	Immediate decompression activity *(e.g., Quiet music, reading, 30-minute calm time)*	Execute your reconnection ritual (see Chapter 14). Avoid questions about other home.	N/A

Section	Protocol Details (Specific & Factual)	My Role (Action)	Co-Parent's Role (Action)
Mandatory Transition Items	Required items *(e.g., Medication, charger, uniform, comfort object)*	Ensure each item is packed and noted on Checklist (Tool 4).	Confirmed upon receipt.

Continuation Pages (Make into a Four-Page Protocol Worksheet for Multiple Exchange Locations or Schedules)

Time & Location	Arrival/Departure	Exchange Protocol	Child-Centered Activity	Required Items

Time & Location	Arrival/Departure	Exchange Protocol	Child-Centered Activity	Required Items

(Use for each location or day-specific variation, e.g., weekday vs. weekend exchanges.)

How to Use as Homework

1. The Time Discipline

Your assignment is to arrive *exactly* at the listed location and time, regardless of the co-parent's actions.

If they are late, document it in **Tool 11: Court-Safe Documentation Log**, but do not engage, negotiate, or extend beyond any legally defined grace period.

"Consistency is your authority."

2. The Decompression Mandate

The first 30 minutes after each transition are non-negotiable decompression time. This is when your child's nervous system resets and your presence becomes their anchor.

Choose one consistent ritual (quiet drive, music, reading, or grounding activity) and repeat it after every exchange.

3. Cross-Reference Drill

Before every exchange:

- Review this **Transition Plan** and your **Logistics Transfer Checklist** (Tool 4) together.
- Verify all mandatory items are present and logged.
- End every exchange with your post-transition ritual—not with a conversation.

"The exchange ends when the door closes, not when the argument does."

Tool 20: Your Shared Calendar + Weather Key

Purpose

The *Shared Calendar + Weather Key* bridges logistics and emotional awareness. It integrates your child's **daily schedule** (objective data) with their **observable emotional climate** (subjective data translated into simple symbols).

This dual-entry system helps you and professionals (therapists, Guardians ad Litem, evaluators) identify predictable stress cycles—like spikes in anxiety before exchanges or emotional crashes after transitions.

"Patterns are the language of safety—when you track them, you reclaim calm."

Clinical Rationale (Pattern Recognition & Predictability)

Focus	Explanation	Why it Matters
Pattern Recognition	Tracks your child's regulation using simple "weather" icons	Turns emotional chaos into measurable trends.
Data Integrity	Focuses on observation, not interpretation—"what you see," not "why it happened."	Keeps entries legally and clinically admissible.
Anticipatory Regulation	Allows you to identify high-stress triggers (e.g., exchanges, calls, school transitions).	Supports proactive use of other tools (Tools 2, 14, 19).

Action Insight

Observation replaces overwhelm. Seeing it clearly is safer than feeling it constantly.

Action Plan

Update this tracker **daily**, ideally in the evening.
Each entry should take no more than **2 minutes**—one symbol and one factual note.

Shared Calendar + Weather Key (Make into a Four-Page Monthly Worksheet)

Section 1: Weather Key—Emotional Regulation Scale

Symbol	Weather Key (Child's Observable Mood)	Intervention Required?
Sunny	Calm, regulated, happy. No visible distress.	None. Maintain routine.
Cloudy	Withdrawn, lethargic, quiet. Low energy or mild avoidance.	Use gentle comfort; avoid demands.
Rainy	Irritable, easily frustrated, visibly tense.	Use 4–6 Breathing Anchor (Tool 2); keep engagement low-demand.
Storm	Meltdown, panic, or extreme defiance. High distress.	Use Grounding (Tool 2); note event in Child Behavior Observation Log (Tool 14).

Section 2: Monthly Calendar Tracker (Page 1 of 4)

			Weather Key: ○ (Calm) • (Withdrawn) • ... (Irritable) • 🌧 (Crisis)	

Month: _____			**Weather Key:** ○ (Calm) • (Withdrawn) • ... (Irritable) • 🌧 (Crisis)	

Day	Date	Key Logistics/Appointments	Child's Mood (Circle or Draw Symbol)	Notes (Factual, 1-Sentence Observation)
Monday		School & pickup by co-parent	○	"Played music in car; laughed."
Tuesday		Exchange at 6 PM	...	"Fidgety, complained of stomachache before hand-off."
Wednesday		Call with co-parent at 7:30 PM	○	"Quiet after phone call, asked to go to bed early."
Thursday		Homework review	○	"Focused well, smiled."
Friday		Exchange at 10 AM	🌧	"Cried before leaving, refused jacket."
(Continue across four pages for the full month.)				

How to Use as Homework

1. The Predictive Check

At the start of each week, review upcoming exchange or call dates.
Mark potential stress days (e.g., "Exchange" or "Co-parent Contact") with a small pencil mark.
This visual pre-warning helps you prepare, not panic.

"Anticipation is power—fear loses leverage when you plan for it."

2. The Observation Discipline

When logging moods:

- Focus only on what is seen or heard, not what's believed.

  Don't write: "Child was sad because Dad was mean."

  Do write: "Child sat silently for 30 minutes and avoided eye contact."

- Avoid emotional language or speculation.
- Keep each note to one sentence—data over drama.

This objectivity protects both your credibility and your child's emotional privacy.

3. The Pattern Analysis

At the end of each month:

- Count total **(Rainy)** and **(Storm)** days.
- If there are **5 or more** in a 30-day period, flag the pattern in:

  - **Tool 14: Your Child Behavior Observation Log** (for context or escalation).
  - **Tool 21: Your Monthly Review Summary** (for your therapist or Guardian ad Litem).

This transforms anecdotal worry into evidence-based reporting.

"Patterns are proof—and proof builds protection."

Tool 21: Your Monthly Review Summary

Purpose

The *Monthly Review Summary* transforms a month's worth of emotional and behavioral data into meaningful direction.
It shifts your narrative from *"I'm constantly managing chaos"* to *"Here's what improved, what still triggers me, and what I'll do next."*

"Patterns tell the truth that panic forgets."

This document becomes your **anchor between months**—equally useful for self-assessment, therapy progress tracking, and professional communication (Guardian ad Litem, attorney, parenting coordinator).

Clinical Rationale (Identifying Growth & Pain Points)

Focus	Explanation	Why it Matters
Quantifiable Growth	Turns repeated experiences into data you can measure and improve.	Shifts your brain from survival ("I'm drowning") to structure ("Here's the pattern").
Pattern Visibility	Makes hidden emotional, behavioral, or co-parent patterns obvious.	Allows targeted interventions rather than reactive cycles.
Objective Documentation	Replaces narrative storytelling with verifiable metrics.	Creates legal and therapeutic clarity without emotional bias.

Action Insight

What you can measure, you can manage—and heal.

Action Plan

Complete this worksheet **on the first day of each month**, summarizing the previous 30 days using data from your logs.
Keep one version for yourself and one for your professional team.

Time Needed: 15–20 minutes

Monthly Review Summary (Make into a Four-Page Worksheet)

Section	Data Point (Quantification)	Source Tool	Summary/Interpretation (1–2 Sentences)
I. Conflict & Regulation Metrics			
A. Total Attempts to Engage (HCCP)	Count of co-parent-initiated conflict (emails, texts, calls).	Tools 1/10	
B. Successful Non-Engagements	Count of times you used BIFF/ignored/paused successfully.	Tool 8	
C. Red/Storm Status Days	Number of days you or your child hit "crisis" regulation levels.	Tools 6/20	
D. Boundaries Tested (Deny/Attack/Stonewall)	Total boundary attempts met with resistance.	Tool 12	
II. Child Well-Being Metrics			

Section	Data Point (Quantification)	Source Tool	Summary/Interpretation (1–2 Sentences)
E. Observed Child Crises (Storms)	Number of meltdowns or panic events.	Tools 14/20	
F. Transition-Related Crises	Count of child distress events within 2 hours of exchange.	Tools 14/19	
G. Most Frequent Trigger	Antecedent (context) appearing most often in behavior logs.	Tool 14	
III. Strategic Direction & Goal-Setting			
H. Key Pattern Insight (Therapy)	The emotion or belief you struggled with most this month. *(e.g., "Guilt when accused of neglect.")*	Tool 10	
I. Key Pattern Insight (Legal)	The most repeated, documentable co-parent violation. *(e.g., "Exchange 30+ minutes late.")*	Tools 11/16	
J. Goal for Next Month (Actionable)	One new measurable habit or boundary to reinforce. *(e.g., "Use Tool 2 before every check-in.")*	Tools 6/7	

Page Template for Ongoing Months

(Repeat this table across all four pages for consistent multi-month comparison.)

| Month: _____ | Summary Period: _____ → _____ |
| Primary Focus for Next Month: _____ |
| Therapist/Legal Notes: _____ |

How to Use as Homework

1. The Attorney's Memo

On the first of every month, draft a short, factual paragraph summarizing metrics from **Section I (A–D)** and **Section II (E–G)**.
This becomes your professional update for your attorney or co-parenting coordinator.

Example:
"This month, there were 9 co-parent engagement attempts, 7 successful non-engagements, and 3 boundary violations (late exchanges). The child experienced 1 meltdown, coinciding with the exchange day."

This shows pattern and stability—not reactivity or blame.

2. Therapy Focus

Bring **Section III (H–J)** to your therapist or support group.
Focus sessions on *pattern insight* rather than storytelling.
You're no longer reliving the event; you're studying the data.

> "Therapy becomes calibration, not confession."

3. The Growth Metric

Track your **Successful Non-Engagements (Section I–B)** as your emotional success score.
Your progress isn't about the co-parent changing—it's about *how little power their chaos has left over your system.*
If that number rises and your Storm Days (I–C) drop, that's genuine healing.

Tool 22: Your If-Then Planning Worksheet

Purpose

The *If-Then Planning Worksheet* rewires impulsive reaction into regulated response.
It leverages **implementation intention**—a cognitive technique that links a predictable trigger ("If ...") to a pre-decided, calm action ("Then ...").
This creates an **automatic safety script** that protects your nervous system and your credibility.

"Peace isn't luck—it's preparation."

Clinical Rationale (Interrupting the Stress Cycle)

Focus	Explanation	Why it Matters
Predictable Triggers	High-conflict co-parents repeat the same tests.	Predicting them converts surprise into strategy.
Emotional Urges as Data	By naming your reactive impulse, you defuse shame.	Awareness creates a pause before the reaction.
Pre-Scripted Regulation	Having the "Then" action ready bypasses the fight/flight loop.	You act from logic, not emotion.

Action Insight

The more specific your *Then*, the faster your body trusts you to stay safe.

Action Plan

Complete this once per month, updating your top 3–5 recurring conflict scenarios from your Monthly Review Summary (Tool 21).
Keep a copy near your phone or co-parenting app for quick reference.

Time Needed: 10–15 minutes per month

If-Then Planning Worksheet (Make into a Four-Page Template)

Section	Prompt for Entry	Rationale
1. **The IF (Predictable Trigger)**	Factual behavior that consistently sets off stress. *(e.g., IF co-parent sends accusatory texts after 8 PM.)*	**Factual Anchor:** Defines objective triggers, not feelings.
2. **My Emotional Trap (Reactive Urge)**	What my body/mind usually does. *(e.g., My urge is to defend or argue.)*	**Self-Awareness:** Names the pattern to disarm it.
3. **The THEN (Regulated Response)**	My planned, neutral action. *(e.g., THEN I log it in Tool 11 and silence notifications until morning.)*	**New Command:** Replaces impulse with intentional safety.
4. **Required Tool/Script**	Which tool supports this action? *(e.g., Tool 1 Neutral Script Bank, Tool 2 Breathing Anchor technique.)*	**Resource Connection:** Links calm to competence.

Scenario-Tracking Table

(Pages 2–4 for continuation—use monthly rotation.)

Scenario #	1. The IF (Predictable Trigger)	2. My Emotional Trap (Urge)	3. The THEN (Regulated Response)	4. Required Tool/Script
1	IF ____	My urge is to ____	THEN I will ____	Tool ____

Scenario #	1. The IF (Predictable Trigger)	2. My Emotional Trap (Urge)	3. The THEN (Regulated Response)	4. Required Tool/Script
2	IF ____	My urge is to ____	THEN I will ____	Tool ____
3	IF ____	My urge is to ____	THEN I will ____	Tool ____
4	IF ____	My urge is to ____	THEN I will ____	Tool ____
5	IF ____	My urge is to ____	THEN I will ____	Tool ____

(Continue through scenarios for multi-month tracking.)

How to Use as Homework

1. The Immediate Check

When a conflict starts, ask yourself:

"Is this on my If-Then plan?"
If yes, execute the exact response from Column 3 (**The THEN**) *without debate or delay.*
No analysis. No scrolling. No re-reading the message.
Just implement the plan.

2. The Success Metric

Each time you successfully follow an If-Then plan, log it in your "I Did Not Engage" Log (Tool 8).
Over time, you'll see a clear ratio: **fewer reactions = greater regulation.**

"Your consistency becomes your shield."

3. The Drill Practice

Choose your #1 most common trigger and mentally rehearse your If-Then response three times a day for a week.
Visualization strengthens neurological pathways—so when the real trigger arrives, your body obeys the plan before panic can speak.

"Repetition turns strategy into instinct."

Purpose

The *Progress Reflection Map* is a non-linear growth tracker. It helps you visualize progress through small, measurable wins, shifts in self-talk, and moments of learning.

It is **not a productivity chart**—it's a **healing timeline**, showing that even when recovery isn't straight, it's still moving forward.

"The path may curve, but every step counts."

Clinical Rationale (Visualizing Non-Linear Growth)

Focus	Explanation	Why it Matters
Externalizing Progress	Healing in high-conflict dynamics is rarely immediate or obvious.	By mapping weekly data, you *see* growth instead of forgetting it.
Reframing Setbacks	Turning "I failed" into "I noticed sooner" builds resilience.	Trains your brain to view mistakes as skill-building, not regression.
Tracking Competence	Small factual wins are evidence of stability under pressure.	Reestablishes agency—the belief that you are capable and steady.

Action Insight

Hope is data you can see.

Action Plan

Update this tool **once per week** (ideally alongside Tool 5 and Tool 6).
Review the map every **three months** to visualize your overall trajectory.

Time Needed: 5 minutes per entry.

Progress Reflection Map (Make into a Four-Page Worksheet)

Section	Reflection Prompt	Rationale
Date	Record today's date.	**Timeline Anchor:** Establishes progress over time.
Small Win/Shift	Note one factual success or change in behavior. *(e.g., "I waited 8 hours before responding to a hostile message.")*	**Competence:** Focuses on agency and effort, not outcome.
Self-Talk Change	Describe one way your internal voice shifted. *(e.g., "I stopped calling myself a bad parent and replaced it with, 'I'm doing my best under pressure.'")*	**Internal Growth:** Reinforces new cognitive patterns.
Setback/Learning Moment	Identify any mistake or challenge and what you learned. *(e.g., "I reacted defensively for 2 minutes, then paused.")*	**Acceptance:** Converts setbacks into learning data.
Next Focus (Goal from Tool 21)	Write one actionable focus for the next 7 days. *(e.g., "Hold my 8 PM boundary without rechecking messages.")*	**Direction:** Ensures reflection transitions into forward motion.

Weekly Tracker Template (Page Example)

Week	Small Win/Shift (Factual)	Self-Talk Change (Core Belief)	Setback/Learning Moment	Next Focus (From Tool 21)
Week 1				

Week	Small Win/Shift (Factual)	Self-Talk Change (Core Belief)	Setback/Learning Moment	Next Focus (From Tool 21)
Week 2				
Week 3				
Week 4				

(Continue this structure through 16 weeks for a quarterly visual map.)

How to Use as Homework

1. The Evidence Review

After 12 weeks, sit down and highlight all your *Small Wins/Shifts*.
Your goal is to overwhelm your brain with visual proof of your resilience.
If you're tempted to retell the story of conflict, **show the data instead.**

"You're not stuck—you're just mid-climb."

2. Setback Reframing

Whenever you record a *Setback/Learning Moment*, identify which tool you could've used instead (e.g., Tool 22—If-Then Plan, Tool 2—Regulation Cards).
Label it as *"missed execution,"* not failure.
This reframes the setback as an opportunity to re-practice the skill next time.

"I didn't fail—I forgot my tool."

3. Values Integration (Tool 7)

When you log a *Small Win/Shift*, name which **core value (Tool 7)** it protected.
(e.g., "I used a Neutral Script—I protected my value of Dignity.")
This links external behavior to internal alignment, proving that your growth isn't random—it's rooted in meaning.

"Every boundary held is a belief protected."

Tool 24: Your Child's Voice & Needs Profile

(Summary for Professionals—Therapeutic & Legal Neutral Format)

Purpose

This profile is a one-page factual summary of the child's **emotional, therapeutic, and educational stability**.
It's designed to center *the child's needs*—not the parents' opinions—when interacting with professionals such as therapists, attorneys, Guardians ad Litem, or coordinators.

"In high conflict, adults speak the loudest. This profile makes sure the child's truth isn't lost in the noise."

Clinical Rationale (Removing Conflict from the Narrative)

Focus	Explanation	Why it Matters
Factual Neutrality	Uses verifiable, non-emotional data points.	Prevents escalation, bias, and hearsay in professional reports.
Child-Centered Summary	Highlights the child's medical, therapeutic, and educational needs directly.	Ensures the professional sees *needs*, not narratives.
Continuity of Care	Consolidates medical, academic, and therapeutic info in one location.	Simplifies coordination across providers and legal systems.

Action Insight

Data replaces drama.

Action Plan

Complete once and update whenever a medical, educational, or therapeutic change occurs.
Keep one copy with your **Transition Plan (Tool 19)** and another for professional use.

Time Needed: 15–20 minutes (update review).

Child's Voice & Needs Profile—Template

General Child Profile & Contact Information

Field	Details
Child's Full Name	
Date of Birth/Age	
Primary School/Grade	
Current Teacher/Contact	
Primary Care Physician	
Phone Number/Clinic	
Date of Last Physical Exam	

Therapeutic & Mental Health Needs

Field	Analysis Notes
Mental Health Therapist	☐ Current ☐ Prior (Date_____) ☐ None—Contact Info: _____
Current Medications	Name: _____ Dosage: _____ Frequency: _____
Formal Diagnosis (if applicable)	e.g., Anxiety Disorder, ADHD, PTSD—*Date of Diagnosis:* _____
Therapeutic Recommendation (1–2 lines)	e.g., "Needs predictable routines, positive reinforcement, and weekly parent check-ins."
Therapeutic Release Status	☐ Signed by Both ☐ Signed by One ☐ None—Note: Confirm legal accessibility.

Educational & Developmental Needs

Field	Details/Data Point
Individual Education/504 Plan	☐ Yes ☐ No—*Date of Last Review:* _____
Learning/Sensory Needs	e.g., "Auditory processing issues; benefits from sensory breaks."
Current Extracurriculars	e.g., "Art Club; Soccer (2x/week)"
Best Method for School Communication	☐ Email ☐ School App ☐ Shared Calendar
Transition Support	e.g., "Needs 30-min decompression after exchanges; comfort item required."
Dietary/Allergy Information	e.g., "Peanut allergy; carries EpiPen."
Sleep Routine	e.g., "Lights out by 8:30 PM; uses white noise machine."

Specific Co-Parenting Needs (Critical Stability Factors)

Field	Details/Examples
Observed Behavioral Triggers (Tool 14)	e.g., "High anxiety after missed calls or delayed exchanges."
Observed Positive Anchors	e.g., "Reading before bed; park walks; building with LEGOs."

How to Use as Homework

1. The "Third Party Only" Rule

Never share this profile directly with the co-parent.
It is intended solely for neutral professionals—doing so prevents it from being weaponized or distorted.

"This profile protects your child's truth from becoming a talking point."

2. Annual Review Mandate

Update the document on the child's **birthday** or **annual physical date**.
This ensures all medical, educational, and therapeutic information remains current and legally reliable.

"Consistency is care."

3. Integrating Log Data

Each point in the Specific Co-parenting Needs section should directly connect to previous logs:

- **Tool 14:** Child Behavior Observation Log
- **Tool 19:** Transition Plan.

When summarizing, cite the tool number or date range as the data source to show measurable evidence rather than assumption.

"You're not guessing the pattern—you're documenting it."

Navigating Your Master Toolkit to Practice Calm

Your Emotional Regulation Flow Map

If You Are Feeling...	Primary Goal	Go To Tools	Why it Works
Triggered/Flooded (Red Zone)	Deactivate fight-flight-freeze.	Tool 2: Regulation Quick Cards Tool 17: Safety Ally Check-In Tool 18: HCCP Communication Decryption Key	Stops physiological escalation before action; builds separation between trigger and response.
Anxious/Overthinking (Yellow Zone)	Ground + clarify facts.	Tool 6: Weekly Nervous-System Check-In Tool 15: Future Focus Worksheet Tool 23: Progress Reflection Map	Shifts rumination to structure; transforms fear into factual problem-solving.
Calm but Overwhelmed (Green Zone Fatigue)	Simplify and restore clarity.	Tool 7: Values Mini-Compass Tool 9: Support System Accountability Log Tool 21: Monthly Review Summary	Converts emotional noise into measurable data, highlighting progress and stability.
Depleted/Burned Out	Reconnect to community and structure.	Tool 5: Weekly Co-Parenting Journal Tool 9: Support System Accountability Log Tool 17: Safety Ally Script	Rebalances isolation by linking emotional data to human support and boundary recovery.

How to Move Through the Toolkit by Rhythm

Rhythm	Purpose	Tools	Mantra
Daily/Instant Tools	Stop escalation before it starts.	1, 2, 3, 4	"Regulation first, reaction never."
Weekly Tools	Build consistent nervous-system awareness.	5, 6, 7, 8, 9	"Patterns are progress—even quiet ones."
As-Needed Documentation Tools	Capture data that protects you and the child.	10, 11, 12, 13, 14, 15, 16, 17, 18	"Facts are safer than feelings."
Planning & Vision Tools	Chart stability and long-term direction.	19, 20, 21, 22, 23, 24	"Calm becomes culture through structure."

The Regulation Sequence (Use Order When in a Crisis)

1. **Tool 2** → Regulate the body.
2. **Tool 18** → Decode the message.
3. **Tool 11** → Document the facts.
4. **Tool 1** → Craft a BIFF response.
5. **Tool 7** → Anchor to your values before sending.

Hint: Practice this five-step sequence once a week until it becomes automatic.

Cross-System Anchors

Life Area	Primary Tool	Support Tools	Core Skill Built
Parent-Child Regulation	Tool 19 (Transition Plan)	Tool 14, Tool 20	Co-regulation & safety rhythm.

Life Area	Primary Tool	Support Tools	Core Skill Built
Legal/Documentation	Tool 11 (Court-Safe Documentation Log)	Tool 12, Tool 16, Tool 24	Evidence integrity + neutral tone.
Therapeutic Processing	Tool 10 (Communication & Emotion Log)	Tool 22, Tool 23	Internal clarity + integration.
Boundary Holding	Tool 1 (Neutral Script)	Tool 6, Tool 8, Tool 18	Emotional detachment + self-command.
Recovery & Support	Tool 9 (Support System Accountability Log)	Tool 17, Tool 21	Sustainable self-regulation & allyship.

Monthly Reset Reflection Prompt

At the end of each month, ask:

1. *What tool am I avoiding because it feels tedious or confronting?*
2. *What nervous-system state has become my default? (Green, Yellow, or Red)*
3. *What rhythm feels easiest to maintain—and which needs reinforcement?*
4. *Where did calm save me more energy than control would have?*

"Avoidance often hides the tool that will free you most."

Building Your Practice Loop

Daily Regulation → Weekly Reflection → As-Needed Documentation → Monthly Planning → Calm Integration

Repeat.
Each cycle builds a stronger nervous system, a cleaner record, and a more peaceful home environment.

Closing Mantra

"This isn't about perfection. It's about predictable calm. Calm is not passive—it's practiced protection."

21

Your Master Toolkit System in Action

Introduction—Integration and Execution

The **Master Toolkit** is not a stack of separate documents; it's a synchronized ecosystem—a living system designed to move your life out of chaos and into *predictable safety.*

By now, you've spent weeks mastering the individual tools: how to track your emotions with **Tool 10**, communicate factually with **Tool 1**, and identify crisis patterns with **Tool 6**. Each tool taught you a vital skill. Now, it's time to integrate them—to run the entire engine.

This chapter is your **operational manual**—the bridge between insight and execution. Here, you'll learn to stop reacting to external drama and start leading from internal precision. Your success will no longer be measured by what the co-parent does, but by the *coherence of your data* and the *predictability of your responses.*

From this point forward, every ounce of your energy belongs to two commitments:

- **Regulation over reaction.**
- **System over story.**

Your Toolkit Philosophy—Fact Over Feeling

The strategy for navigating high-conflict co-parenting (**HCCP**) is not emotional endurance—it's *energy conservation.* In the old model, 90% of your energy was spent defending, arguing, ruminating, and recovering. The Toolkit reverses that economy.

Energy Budgeting

Every time the co-parent attempts to initiate conflict, they're essentially sending you a bill—for your time, your nervous system, and your dignity. The only way to win this game is simple: **reject the bill.**

Old Energy System	New Energy System (The Toolkit)
Response: Emotional, defensive, immediate.	**Response:** Measured, factual, delayed.
Focus: The co-parent's opinion or fault.	**Focus:** My own **Tool 6** status and protocol.
Outcome: Exhaustion, scattered documentation.	**Outcome:** Regulation, undeniable data trail.

The tools demand a trade—the exhausting release of reaction for the sustainable discipline of *response.* You learn to stop performing emotional labor for the conflict and start investing in precision, boundaries, and peace.

This is the clinical shift from **survival to strategy.** Instead of running on adrenaline, you begin operating on **principle**—the principles defined in **Tool 7: The Values Mini-Compass.** Every choice you make from this point forward aligns with a measurable value, grounding your identity in clarity rather than chaos.

Your energy becomes data. Your calm becomes evidence. And your consistency becomes the new definition of control.

Your Core Workflow—The Four-Phase Loop

All 24 tools operate within a continuous, four-phase strategic loop. This loop is the **engine of the system**—a repeatable roadmap for navigating any communication, conflict, or crisis. Your task is to identify which phase you're in and apply the corresponding protocol.

This model integrates **neuroscience, behavioral sequencing, and trauma-informed response** into a single, executable rhythm. When practiced consistently, it transforms reactivity into regulation and documentation into data-driven protection.

Phase 1: Your Instant Intercept (Stopping the Bleeding)

Objective—To create *immediate space* between the trigger and your response. These steps must be completed in minutes—often seconds.

Action Step	Protocol & Tools Used	Clinical Function
1. Stop the Somatic Bleeding	**Tool 6** (Nervous-System Check-In) + **Tool 2** (Regulation Quick Cards). Identify if you are **Yellow or Red**, then execute 60 seconds of the **4–6 Breathing Anchor.**	Interrupts the panic or hyperarousal response, returning the body to a regulated baseline.
2. Identify the Trap	Reference **Tool 22** (If-Then Planning Worksheet). Ask: *"Did I prepare a response for this exact scenario?"*	Bypasses emotional debate by activating a pre-scripted, regulated response.
3. Execute Non-Engagement	Use **Tool 1** (Neutral Script Bank) or initiate the **Silent Treatment Protocol** (no emotional communication).	Deprives the co-parent of emotional reinforcement, stabilizing the nervous system and neutralizing escalation.
4. Log the Success	If you maintained non-engagement, record it immediately in **Tool 8** ("I Did Not Engage" Log).	Reinforces the new behavior through measurable, factual self-accountability.

Phase 2: Your Data Capture (Factualizing the Event)

Objective—To filter out emotion and record objective facts. This is the process of converting *noise* into *signal*.

Action Step	Protocol & Tools Used	Therapeutic/Legal Function
1. Decrypt the Attack	Use **Tool 18** (HCCP Communication Decryption Key). Identify the **HCCP** tactic (Gaslighting, Projection, Victim Stance, etc.) and produce the **Factual Re-Statement.**	Depersonalization: separates manipulation from meaning, ensuring emotional neutrality and factual accuracy.
2. Log the Legal Evidence	Transfer the **Factual Re-Statement** (Tool 18, Section 6) into **Tool 11** (Court-Safe Documentation Log).	Creates the **Evidence Trail**—a verifiable legal record devoid of speculation or affect.

Action Step	Protocol & Tools Used	Therapeutic/Legal Function
3. Log the Emotional Cost	Record the trigger and somatic reaction in **Tool 10** (Communication & Emotion Log).	Creates the **Healing Trail**—integrates body-based data for therapeutic reflection and progress tracking.
4. Conduct a Boundary or Financial Review (if relevant)	Update **Tool 16** (Financial/Expense Tracker) or **Tool 12** (Boundary & Requests Tracker).	Ensures **categorical compliance**—no data gap in fiscal or boundary integrity.

Phase 3: Your Child-Centered Shield (Proactive Stability)

Objective—To ensure the child's environment remains *safe, predictable, and regulated*, regardless of external instability.

Action Step	Protocol & Tools Used	Child Safety Outcome
1. Automate the Exchange	Review **Tool 19** (Transition Plan) and **Tool 4** (Logistics Transfer Checklist).	Removes verbal and emotional negotiation, reducing child's anticipatory anxiety.
2. Track Their Stability	Log all behavioral or emotional shifts (withdrawal, anger, regression) in **Tool 14** (Child Behavior Observation Log).	Produces clinical data using the **Antecedent-Behavior-Consequence** chain, supporting therapeutic accuracy.
3. Visualize the Pattern	Update **Tool 20** (Shared Calendar + Weather Key).	Reveals emotional rhythm across exchanges, identifying correlations between conflict and child regulation.
4. Summarize Needs	Prepare **Tool 24** (Child's Voice & Needs Profile) for therapists, Guardians ad Litem, or school teams.	Centers factual needs, not parental narrative, ensuring the child's care plan is driven by data.

Phase 4: Your Strategic Review (Pattern Analysis)

Objective—To step out of reaction mode, assess the long-term trajectory, and reorient to your core values.

Action Step	Protocol & Tools Used	Strategic Outcome
1. Weekly Self-Assessment	Review **Tool 5** (Weekly Co-Parenting Journal) and align with **Tool 7** (Values Mini-Compass).	Ensures consistency with your "Why," preventing emotional drift.
2. Monthly Quantification	Complete **Tool 21** (Monthly Review Summary). Pull numerical data: total conflicts, successful non-engagements, Red Zone days.	Data Presentation: transforms emotion into quantifiable progress for legal or therapeutic use.
3. Proactive Defense Update	Review top triggers from **Tool 21** and update **Tool 22** (If-Then Planning Worksheet) with new scripted defenses.	Shifts focus from *defending the past* to *engineering the future*.
4. Visualize Growth	Use **Tool 23** (Progress Reflection Map) to log weekly wins and self-talk evolution.	Counteracts stagnation; creates visual proof of non-linear recovery and long-term integration.

Clinical Integration Summary

The Four-Phase Loop transforms chaotic reaction into clinical rhythm.
Each pass through the loop strengthens **neural regulation, legal protection**, and **emotional coherence.**

The system is not punitive—it's preventative.
By the time you reach Phase 4, your nervous system no longer reacts to the conflict; it organizes it.
This is what operational safety looks like: predictability without paralysis, regulation without retreat.

Your Integration Drills—Practice Makes Permanent

The system only works when it's *embodied*—when the brain and body develop the muscle memory required to execute the tools automatically, even under duress. These drills train your nervous system to operate the Four-Phase Workflow as reflex, not recall.

Each exercise pairs procedural repetition with regulation. They are designed to close the gap between knowledge and instinct—so that when crisis hits, you no longer *think* your way through the storm; you *flow* through it.

Drill 1: Your Crisis Chain Protocol

Purpose
To ensure that, when crisis strikes, you rely on your regulation system—not your reactive self.

Scenario
You receive a hostile or inflammatory message that immediately triggers a **Red Zone (Tool 6)** response. You feel the surge—the urge to defend, explain, or vent.

The Chain

1. **Stop.** Drop the phone and execute **Tool 2 (4–6 Breathing Anchor)** to halt the somatic escalation.
2. **Locate.** Grab your pre-printed **Tool 3 (Crisis & Resources Sheet)** for immediate structure and containment.
3. **Call.** Dial your **Safety Ally** and execute **Tool 17 (Safety Ally Check-In Script)** verbatim. Focus only on your **Status**, **Time Limit**, and **Role**. Do not narrate or justify.
4. **Result:** You engaged three tools in sequence to achieve immediate *regulation and containment*—without sending a single reactive communication.

Clinical Rationale
This drill rewires the panic-to-communication reflex by pairing physiological reset (Tool 2) with structured interpersonal containment (Tool 17). The nervous system experiences rapid safety restoration, reducing impulsive behaviors by building a procedural safety net.

Drill 2: Decryption to Legal Evidence

Purpose
To solidify Phase 2 of the workflow—converting conflict language into factual, court-safe data.

Scenario
The co-parent sends an email combining both a **hostile label** and a **legitimate logistical question.**
(Example: "You're a terrible parent, but are you picking up the field trip form on Tuesday?")

The Chain

1. **Analyze:** Fill out the HCCP Communication Decryption Key **(Tool 18).** Identify the **Tactic** ("Hostile Label") and the **Actual Issue** ("Pickup form Tuesday").
2. **Act (Tool 1):** Use the "Actual Issue" (Section 7) to craft a **BIFF response**.
   o Example: "I will pick up the field trip form on Tuesday."
3. **Document (Tool 11):** Log the incident in the **Court-Safe Documentation Log.**
   o Entry: "Co-parent used hostile label on [Date]. Factual action taken: Form pickup confirmed."
   o **Do not** log the hostile label verbatim.
4. **Result:** You responded factually and neutrally to the required issue while successfully isolating and documenting the manipulative behavior for record integrity.

Clinical Rationale

This drill strengthens the **executive function bridge** between emotional activation and legal neutrality. The act of identifying both the "attack" and the "ask" retrains cognitive processing toward evidence-based responses and away from emotional storytelling.

Drill 3: Your Annual Strategic Audit

Purpose

To ensure your planning and reflection remain rooted in objective metrics, not emotional bias. This is your quarterly systems check—where your data becomes your mirror.

Scenario

It's the first day of the quarter. Time for your **strategic reset.**

The Chain

1. **Review Performance:** Pull your last three **Monthly Review Summaries (Tool 21).** Identify the top two recurring violations or themes (e.g., late exchanges, financial withholding).
2. **Defend Proactively:** Update **Tool 22 (If-Then Planning Worksheet)** with pre-scripted defenses targeting those recurring patterns.
3. **Check Stability:** Update **Tool 19 (Transition Plan)** and **Tool 24 (Child's Voice & Needs Profile)** to confirm that safety, decompression, and school protocols remain current.
4. **Result:** You're no longer operating from memory or emotion—you're operating from *data integrity*. Each quarter, you shift from reacting to the past to designing your next season.

Clinical Rationale

This audit integrates trauma-informed practice with cognitive-behavioral strategy. It anchors reflection in measurable progress, reducing subjective distortion ("I'm failing again") and reinforcing the factual evidence of stability, agency, and growth.

Clinical Integration Summary

These drills move the system from *theoretical learning* to *neural automation*. Through repetition, each step strengthens procedural safety—replacing emotional reactivity with conditioned regulation.

By practicing these sequences under calm conditions, you train your nervous system to default to regulation during real-world stress.
This is how healing becomes muscle memory.

Strategic Application—Working with Professionals

Your documentation system is not busywork—it's a **force multiplier** for your professional team. Each log, summary, and worksheet converts chaos into usable signals, allowing your legal and therapeutic allies to bypass the noise of conflict and move directly into targeted strategy.

Maximizing Your Attorney Time

Attorneys bill by the hour. Never pay for them to emotionally decode your inbox. Your job is to deliver *clarity, not commentary.*

The Rule of the Clean File

Never forward full chains of emotional emails. When your attorney requests documentation, provide only three essential documents:

1. **Monthly Review Summary (Tool 21):** Shows the *pattern*—the frequency and consistency of incidents.
2. **Court-Safe Documentation Log (Tool 11):** Shows the *evidence*—the factual entries that substantiate the pattern.
3. **Financial/Expense Tracker (Tool 16):** Include if the issue involves reimbursement, support, or fiscal withholding.

Testimony Protocol

Your **Tool 11** training prepares you to testify from data, not emotion.

In court or deposition, your language must reflect observation and documentation:

- Say: *"I observed…"/ "I documented…"/ "This entry is from [Date/Time]…"*
- Never say: *"I felt…"/ "I believe…"/ "I think they were trying to…"*

Clinical Rationale

Fact-based language reinforces cognitive regulation under stress and strengthens legal credibility. Emotional phrasing introduces bias; factual phrasing communicates reliability.

Maximizing Your Therapeutic Time

Your therapist's role is not to referee the conflict but to strengthen your *internal architecture*. The goal of therapy is to process vulnerability, not to retell volatility.

Therapy as Insight

Bring your **Tool 10 (Communication & Emotion Log)** and the *Vulnerable Why* section from **Tool 18 (HCCP Communication Decryption Key).** These tools identify the emotional and physiological vulnerabilities that the co-parent's tactics exploit.

By presenting these logs, you transform your therapy session from narrative reactivity ("This happened again…") into clinical analysis ("Here's the pattern of activation and the regulation gap we're closing.").

Working with Child-Focused Professionals

When meeting with a **Guardian ad Litem**, **Co-Parenting Coordinator (CPC)**, or therapist supporting your child, begin with **Tool 24 (Child's Voice & Needs Profile).** This single sheet instantly positions you as the regulated parent—the one focused on the child's factual stability, not the interpersonal drama.

Clinical Rationale

Documentation reframes your identity in professional spaces. Rather than appearing emotionally reactive, you are perceived as *data-informed, child-centered, and therapeutically aligned*. It's not about proving who's right; it's about demonstrating who's regulated.

Integrated Reflection

When your documentation becomes fluent, it's not just a toolset—it's a treatment protocol.

Your attorneys see strategy.

Your therapist sees insight.
Your child sees safety.

And you—you see proof that regulation is not weakness; it's leadership.

Conclusion—Your Sustained Mastery and Legacy

The moment you commit to this system, you stop participating in the conflict and start managing it.
You are no longer a reactor in chaos—you are the **strategic manager** of a high-conflict dynamic. This is the line between surviving and thriving.

Measuring Success Beyond the Law

You will know the system is working when the following shifts occur:

- The number of **Red Zone days (Tool 6)** drops to zero—not because conflict disappears, but because your nervous system no longer joins it.
- The number of successful entries in **Tool 8 (I Did Not Engage)** surpasses the number of conflict attempts logged in **Tool 21 (Monthly Review Summary)**.
- The emotional tone in your **Tool 10 (Communication & Emotion Log)** transforms into objective, neutral observation—proof that your body and language have learned regulation.

Your Ultimate Goal

Mastery is not the absence of conflict; it is the presence of coherence.
The aim is to build a life where the co-parent's attempts at disruption become **background noise**, irrelevant to the stability you maintain.

When you review your **Progress Reflection Map (Tool 23)** after six months, you won't just see fewer crises—you'll see *nonlinear recovery*.
You'll see growth plotted in real data points: proof that safety can become your default state.

The Legacy You Leave

Your greatest defense is not force—it's regulation.
Your greatest power is not control—it's documentation.
And your greatest legacy is not perfection—it's predictability.

Every time you respond with calm precision, you model safety to your child.
Every log you complete is a record of resilience.
Every boundary you hold is a quiet revolution.

You have built not just a toolkit—but a system of truth.
A system that restores dignity, protects the nervous system, and replaces chaos with structure.

This is the legacy of stability you offer your child—the living proof that even in conflict, **safety is possible, and healing is sustainable.**

The system is complete. The power is now yours.
Not the power to control others—but the power to stay anchored, deliberate, and free.

The Practice of Steady

You've made it to the end—not of the conflict, but of your old way of surviving it.
What you hold in these pages is not a rulebook. It's a rhythm.
A way of living that trades the adrenaline of reaction for the architecture of peace.

This system will never ask you to be perfect.
It only asks you to stay present—to keep returning to your tools, your breath, your truth.
That is what healing looks like now: **not absence of pain, but presence of practice.**

You will forget. You will flare. You will pick up the phone and almost send the message.
But then—you will remember.
You will exhale.
You will reach for the structure you built and realize: the storm no longer gets to decide who you are.

Every log you complete is a record of that remembering.
Every boundary you keep is a love letter to your future self.
Every regulated response is a generational repair.

You are not just managing conflict—you are interrupting inheritance.
You are teaching your child, your nervous system, and your lineage what safety sounds like.

When the noise rises again—and it will—don't aim to win.
Aim to stay.
Because staying steady *is* the win.

You are now the system.
And the system is peace in motion.

References & Further Reading

Amato, P. R., & Afifi, T. D. (2018). Parent-child relationships in divorced and separated families. *Journal of Family Theory & Review, 10*(2), 206–226.

Beck, J. S. (2021). *Cognitive behavior therapy: Basics and beyond* (3rd ed.). Guilford Publications.

Bowlby, J. (1988). *A secure base: Parent-child attachment and healthy human development.* Basic Books.

Brown, B. (2018). *Dare to lead: Brave work. Tough conversations. Whole hearts.* Random House.

Carter, L. (2012). *The worry book: Twelve steps to breaking the worry habit.* Thomas Nelson.

Cloud, H., & Townsend, J. (2017). *Boundaries: When to say yes, how to say no to take control of your life* (Updated ed.). Zondervan.

Courtois, C. A., & Ford, J. D. (2013). *Treatment of complex trauma: A sequenced, relationship-based approach.* Guilford Press.

Dana, D. (2020). *Polyvagal exercises for safety and connection: 50 client-centered practices.* Norton.

Eddy, B. (2020). *BIFF: Quick responses to high-conflict people, their hostility, their demands, and their crazy ideas.* HCI Press.

Eddy, B. (2018). *Splitting: Protecting yourself while divorcing someone with borderline or narcissistic personality disorder.* HCI Press.

Eger, E. (2017). *The choice: Embrace the possible.* Scribner.

Emery, R. E. (2016). *Two homes, one childhood: A parenting plan to last a lifetime*. Avery.

Feldman, D. B., & Krasner, M. S. (2020). *The healing power of hope*. Oxford University Press.

Fine, C. (2017). *Therapy with high-conflict parents and their children: A pragmatic guide*. Routledge.

Fisher, J. (2017). *Healing the fragmented selves of trauma survivors: Overcoming internal self-alienation*. Routledge.

Fisher, R., Ury, W., & Patton, B. (2011). *Getting to yes: Negotiating agreement without giving in* (3rd ed.). Penguin.

Germer, C. K. (2009). *The mindful path to self-compassion: Freeing yourself from destructive thoughts and emotions*. Guilford Press.

Hayes, S. C., Strosahl, K. D., & Wilson, K. G. (2012). *Acceptance and commitment therapy: The process and practice of mindful change*. Guilford Press.

Herman, J. L. (2015). *Trauma and recovery: The aftermath of violence—from domestic abuse to political terror* (Rev. ed.). Basic Books.

Hüther, G., & Bonney, H. (2010). *Neuroscience for therapy and the healing arts*. Routledge.

Johnston, J. R., Roseby, V., & Kuehnle, K. (2009). *In the name of the child: A developmental approach to understanding and helping children of conflict and violent divorce* (2nd ed.). Springer.

Kabat-Zinn, J. (2013). *Full catastrophe living: Using the wisdom of your body and mind to face stress, pain, and illness* (Rev. ed.). Bantam.

Kelly, J. B., & Emery, R. E. (2003). Children's adjustment following divorce: Risk and resilience perspectives. *Family Relations, 52*(4), 352–362.

Levine, P. A. (2010). *In an unspoken voice: How the body releases trauma and restores goodness*. North Atlantic Books.

Lowenstein, L. F. (2015). Parental alienation: Research review and recommendations for practice. *Journal of Family Therapy, 37*(3), 284–296.

Markman, H. J., Stanley, S. M., & Blumberg, S. L. (2010). *Fighting for your marriage: Positive steps for preventing divorce and preserving love* (3rd ed.). Jossey-Bass.

McGonigal, K. (2015). *The upside of stress: Why stress is good for you, and how to get good at it.* Avery.

Menakem, R. (2017). *My grandmother's hands: Racialized trauma and the pathway to mending our hearts and bodies.* Central Recovery Press.

Moran, P. M., McCall, M., & Sullivan, S. (2021). *The coparenting handbook: Resources for professionals & parents in difficult divorces.* Overcoming Barriers.

Neff, K. D. (2011). *Self-compassion: The proven power of being kind to yourself.* William Morrow.

Neff, K. D., & Germer, C. K. (2018). Self-compassion and mindfulness: The science of kindness. In C. Feldman & W. Kuyken (Eds.), *Mindfulness: Classical foundations and contemporary applications* (pp. 321–343). Guilford Press.

Neff, K. D., & Germer, C. K. (2019). *The mindful self-compassion workbook: A proven way to accept yourself, build inner strength, and thrive.* Guilford Press.

Neuman, M. G. (2018). *Helping your kids cope with divorce the sandcastles way.* Random House.

Ogden, P., & Fisher, J. (2015). *Sensorimotor psychotherapy: Interventions for trauma and attachment.* Norton.

Perry, B. D., & Winfrey, O. (2021). *What happened to you? Conversations on trauma, resilience, and healing.* Flatiron Books.

Porges, S. W. (2011). *The polyvagal theory: Neurophysiological foundations of emotions, attachment, communication, and self-regulation.* W. W. Norton & Company.

Saini, M., & Birnbaum, R. (2017). *Parenting plans for children after separation or divorce: A developmental approach.* Oxford University Press.

Schnarch, D. M. (2018). *Intimacy & desire: Awaken the passion in your relationship.* Beaufort Books.

Schore, A. N. (2012). *The science of the art of psychotherapy.* Norton.

Siegel, D. J. (2012). *The developing mind: How relationships and the brain interact to shape who we are* (2nd ed.). Guilford Press.

Siegel, D. J., & Bryson, T. P. (2018). *The yes brain: How to cultivate courage, curiosity, and resilience in your child.* Bantam.

Stevens, J., & Syedullah, J. (2016). *Radical dharma: Talking race, love, and liberation*. North Atlantic Books.

Substance Abuse and Mental Health Services Administration (SAMHSA). (2014). *Trauma-informed care in behavioral health services*. Treatment Improvement Protocol (TIP) Series 57.

Tannen, D. (2020). *You're the only one I can tell: Inside the language of women's friendships*. Ballantine Books.

Tutu, D., & Tutu, M. (2015). *The book of forgiving: The fourfold path for healing ourselves and our world*. HarperOne.

Van der Kolk, B. A. (2014). *The body keeps the score: Brain, mind, and body in the healing of trauma*. Viking.

Warshak, R. A. (2014). Social science and parenting plans for young children: A consensus report. *Psychology, Public Policy, and Law, 20*(1), 46–67.

About the Author
Nahomie Julien, LCSW, CADC II, CAMS II, CDVS II

Nahomie Julien is a trauma-informed therapist, author, and creative strategist who bridges rigorous clinical practice with deep cultural and human awareness. For more than two decades, she has specialized in guiding individuals and families through the complex intersections of trauma, addiction recovery, and high-conflict resolution.

Her approach is grounded in neuroscience and evidence-based practice, helping clients move from survival to steadiness and from silence to authentic voice. As a clinical leader, she has founded therapeutic and healing spaces dedicated to making emotional wellness accessible and culturally responsive.

Through her writing, Nahomie develops practical tools and creative resources that translate clinical insight into strategies people can use in their daily lives. Her work explores how people rebuild their lives after rupture, reclaim their voice, and establish clear, consistent boundaries—the same principles woven throughout this workbook and her broader body of work.

Readers and clients often describe her presence as "equal parts mirror and balm," recognizing both the warmth and the clarity she brings to difficult conversations. Her mission is to make healing feel real, reachable, and relevant—ensuring that growth, no matter how hard-won, is always rooted in self-compassion.

Permissions & Licensing

www.ingramcontent.com/pod-product-compliance
Lightning Source LLC
Chambersburg PA
CBHW041532120626
46551CB00019B/2667